AF622399

# Buddhism in Medieval Sri Lanka

*Bibliotheca Indo-Buddhica Series*

Sunil Gupta, Editor

*Bibliotheca Indo-Buddhica Series No. - 77*

# Buddhism in Medieval Sri Lanka

**H.B.M. Ilangasinha**
B.A., M.A. (Vidyalankara),
Ph.D. (London).

**Sri Satguru Publications**
*A Division of*
INDIAN BOOKS CENTRE
DELHI – INDIA

*Published by :*

SRI SATGURU PUBLICATIONS
Indological and Oriental Publishers
A Division of
Indian Books Centre
40/5, Shakti Nagar,
Delhi-110007
(INDIA)

ISBN - 81-7030-245-5

First Edition : Delhi 1992

No part of this book may be used or reproduced in any manner whatsoever without written permission except in the case of brief quotations embodied in critical articles and reviews.

*Typeset at :*
Sita Composers Pvt. Ltd.
H-135 Ashok Vihar, Phase-I,
Delhi-110 052. Tel. 723-1789

*Printed at :*
D.K. Fine Arts Press

PRINTED IN INDIA

*Dedicated to the loving memory of my grand-mother, Loku Kumarihamy of Inamaluva Ihala Walavva, a faithful exponent of the Sinhala Buddhist Culture of ancient Sri Lanka.*

# Contents

# Preface

Buddhism in Sri Lanka has increasingly become a subject of major importance in Sri Lankan studies in recent times. However, despite the existence of several scholarly publications on the history of Buddhism during the Anuradhapura period, so far no study concerning the history of the religion after the twelfth century A.D. has been published. Hence the publication of this monograph in which an attempt has been made to deal with Buddhism during the medieval period with special emphasis on the fifteenth and sixteenth centuries would, I believe, help to supply the need for such a work.

The present work has evolved out of thesis submitted by me to the University of London for the degree of Doctor of Philosophy (1973). However I have made certain revisions in order to bring it up to date.

The research connected with this study was carried out under the supervision of Prof. J.G. de Casparis, then Reader in History of South and Southeast Asia in the School of Oriental and African studies of the University of London. I have benefitted a great deal from Professor Casparis' incisive comments and criticisms which have immensely helped me to improve the quality of this study. It has indeed been a pleasant and profitable experience to work under a scholar of Professor Casparis' academic attainments and eminence.

I also owe a debt of gratitude to Professor N.A. Jayawickrama and Dr. Wendy D'O' Flaherty for the guidance they gave me during the initial stages of my work.

My thanks are due to the staff of the libraries of the Senate House of the University of London, School of Oriental and African Studies and the British Museum for their very helpful and courteous services.

My sincere thanks are also due to Professor Y. Karunadasa, Director, Postgraduate Institute of Pali and Buddhist Studies, who always encouraged me to publish this work and even wrote a foreword for it.

I wish to mention that the interest shown by Mr. Sunil Gupta, Indian Books Centre has been a source of encouragement in prompting me to publish this work at this stage. I take this opportunity to express my sincere gratitude to Mr. Gupta and his staff for undertaking the publication of the work.

Finally, I would like to thank my youngest daughter, Risini Vasana, who helped me much in arranging the indexes of the publication.

Professor H.B.M. Ilangasinha

Head of the Department of History
University of Kelaniya
Sri Lanka
25. 08. 1991.

# Foreword

The work here presented provides a critical and comprehensive account of the state of Buddhism in Sri Lanka during the 15th and 16th centuries. This was the period that witnessed, for the last time, the political unification of the entire Island under the suzerainty of the Sinhala monarchy and also its subsequent collapse resulting in the emergence of three regional kingdoms. It was also during this period that the first-ever arrival of a Western Colonial Power and its gradual consolidation in the Maritime Provinces of the Island took place. Hence a systematic inquiry into the state of Buddhism during this period should show the changes it underwent, and also the changes it brought about in other spheres, in response to the changing political scenario of the Island. Among the historical sources pertaining to this period are the local and foreign chronicles, epigraphical data mainly in the form of royal *sannasas* (charters), official documents, foreign records, semi-historical writings and literary works, all written in a variety of languages. Hence a scholar who addresses himself to the task of reconstructing the history of Buddhism during this period should be equipped not only with the critical appartments of historical interpretation, but also with a sound knowledge of the languages in which these historical sources are recorded. That the author of this monograph is eminently qualified for such a task is amply demonstrated by his skilful exploitation of the relevant sources to yield a comprehensive and highly authoritative exposition on the subject under review. The author's main contribution to our knowledge of the state of Buddhism during this period is sought to be presented through a series of historical disquisitions on the Buddhist monastic order and its institutional framework, the relations between the Sangha and the State, Sri Lanka's relations with the Buddhist countries of South East Asia, and finally the cults, rituals and ceremonies that came into vogue during this period.

It is to the credit of the author that in dealing with these diverse aspects he has also identified their antecedent historical trends so as to bring the whole subject within a wider historical perspective.

Professor Mangala Ilangasinha, the author of this work, is the Head of the Department of History at the University of Kelaniya, from where he graduated in 1963, obtaining an Honours Degree in History. The present work is an unabridged version of his doctoral thesis for which he was awarded the degree of Doctor of Philosophy of the University of London in 1973.

The author and his publishers deserve our grateful thanks for making available this thoroughly -researched and well documented monograph to a wider reading public.

Professor Y. Karunadasa
Director, Postgraduate
Institute of Pali and
Buddhist Studies,
University of Kelaniya

27th February 1991.

# Abbreviations

| | |
|---|---|
| AAGP. | The Art and Architecture of the Gampola Period. |
| ADK. | Alutnuvara Dēvālē Karavīma. |
| ASCAR. | Archaeological Survey of Ceylon, Annual Report. |
| ASCM. | Memoirs of the Archaeological Survey of Ceylon. |
| Bdgnl. | Buduguṇālaṃkāraya. |
| BEFEO. | Bulletin de I'Ecole Francaise d'Extreme-Orient. |
| Br. Mus.Ms. | British Museum Manuscript. |
| CALR. | Ceylon Antiquary and Literary Register. |
| CCMT. | Culture of Ceylon in Medieval Times. |
| CHJ. | Ceylon Historical Journal. |
| CJSc.G. | Ceylon Journal of Science, Section G. |
| CPE. | Ceylon: the Portuguese Era. |
| Cv. | Cūlavaṃsa. |
| Dls. | Daḷadāsirita. |
| EC. | The Epochs of the Conqueror, (Jinakālamālī tr. N.A. Jayawickrama). |
| Ep. Birm. | Epigraphia Birmanica. |
| EZ. | Epigraphia Zeylanica. |
| GAP. | The God of Adam's Peak. |
| GCPC. | The Gazeteer of the Central Province of Ceylon. |
| Grs. | Girā-sandeśaya. |
| Gtlk. | Guttila-*kāvyaya*. |
| HBC. | History of Buddhism in Ceylon. |
| Hms. | Haṃsa-sandeśaya. |
| IA. | Indian Antiquary. |
| ISSA. | The Indianized States in Southeast Asia. |
| JCBRAS. | Journal of the Ceylon Branch of the Royal Asiatic Society. |
| Jkm. | Jinakālamālī. |

| | |
|---|---|
| Kks. | Kokila-sandeśaya. |
| Kts. | Katikāvat Sañgarā. |
| Kvsk. | Kāvyasekharaya. |
| Mv. | Mahāvaṃsa. |
| Myrs. | Mayūra-sandeśaya. |
| Nks. | Nikāya-saṅgrahaya. |
| NS. | New Series. |
| Pdst. | Padasādhana-tīkā. |
| Pjv. | Pūjāvaliya. |
| PLC. | Pali Literature of Ceylon. |
| Prs. | Parevi-sandeśaya. |
| PS. | Pāli Sāhityaya. |
| PTS. | Pali Text Society, London. |
| PTSD. | PTS, Dictionary. |
| PTSJ. | PTS, Journal. |
| Rjrt. | Rājaratnākaraya. |
| Rjv. | Rājāvaliya. |
| RKD, | The Report on the Kegalle Distirct. |
| Sdhrlk. | Saddharmālaṃkāraya. |
| Sdhrt. | Saddharmaratnākarāya. |
| SHC. | A Short History of Ceylon. |
| Sls. | Sälalihiṇi-sandeśaya. |
| Smp. | Samantapāsādikā. |
| SPL. | Saparagamuvē Pāraṇi Liyavili. |
| SRS. | Śrī Rāhula Saṅgharāja-tumā. |
| SSL. | Siṅhala Sāhitya Lipi. |
| SSS. | Siṅhala Sandeśa Sāhityaya. |
| ŚSŚk. | Śrī Sumaṅgala Śabda Koṣaya. |
| Ssv. | Sāsanavaṃsa. |
| Ssvp. | Sāsanavaṃsa-pradīpaya. |
| SUD. | The Shrine of Upulvan at Devundara. |
| Svls. | Sävul-sandeśaya. |
| TB. | Theravādī Bauddhācāryayo. |
| Tss. | Tisara-sandeśaya. |
| UCHC. | University of Ceylon History of Ceylon. |

| | |
|---|---|
| UCR. | University of Ceylon Review. |
| Vmkts. | Vimuktisaṅgrahaya. |
| Vss. | Vuttamālā-sandesa-sataka. |

## Chapter One

# Introduction and Sources

In this study an attempt will be made to reconstruct the history of Buddhism in Sri Lanka in the fifteenth and sixteenth centuries. The first scholar who composed a systematic history of Buddhism in Sri Lanka was E.W. Adikaram, whose doctoral thesis on the *Early History of Buddhism in Ceylon* was published in 1946. He was followed by W. Rahula, who dealt with the period from the third to the tenth century A.D. in his thesis: *History of Buddhism in Ceylon*, published in 1956. The third contribution to this field of study was made by R.A.L.H. Gunawardhana, whose thesis, *History of the Buddhist Sangha in Ceylon from the time of Sena I to the Invasion of Māgha* (800-1215 A.D.), was published in 1982 under the title *Robe and Plough*. The subject has been continued by Y. Dhammavisuddhi, whose work, *The Buddhist Sangha in Ceylon* (circa 1200-1400 A.D.), deals with the period immediately preceding that of this study.

Hence, it is hardly necessary to stress that the present study in which we have sought to examine the history of Buddhism in Sri Lanka in the fifteenth and sixteenth centuries (circa 1400-1600) could well be a continuation of, and a complementary monograph to the works cited above.

It may be seen that this study covers the period of two centuries during which the main seat of political power of the Island was Jayavardhana-pura, i.e. Kōṭṭē, a south- western stronghold of the Sinhaḷese culture.

In fact, apart from the fact that the preceding centuries have already been dealt with, there is hardly any reason to consider these two centuries a unique period as far as the religious history of the country is concerned. For, as will be seen in the course of this monograph, these two centuries may also be looked upon as a continuation of the religious developments that took place after the unification of the Sangha in the reign of Parākramabāhahu I in the twelfth century. These developments went side by side with those in the political, social and economic fields which arose as a result of the abandonment of Polonnaruva as the centre of Sinhalese culture. The unification of the Sangha brought under a common leadership the clerical community which had remain divided into several independent factions for more than a millennium; this seems to have contributed to the development of two fraternities, Gāmavāsa and Vanavāsa. Buddhism, during this whole period, inspired no great monuments, apart from the Laṅkātilaka and the Gaḍalādeniya temples at Gampola in the fourteenth century. The Sinhalese kings during this period of insecurity paid great attention to the Tooth Relic, the sysmbol of the legitimacy of their power. One outstanding feature of this period of instability were the attempts at reforming the Sangha, none of which produced lasting results.

We have taken 1600 A.D. as the termination point of this study for more than one reason. First, the last decade of the sixteenth century marks the end of Kōṭṭē as the centre of Sinhalese power and the beginning of a new dynasty in Kandy under Vimaladharmasūriya I. This was followed by the introduction of the Portuguese rule in the most of the southern and south-western provinces of Sri Lanka which were formerly under the hegemony of the Kōṭṭē and Sītāvaka rulers. These decisive events paved the way for a new phase of the history of Sri Lanka. Second, by this time the higher ordination, reinstituted in the reign of Vijayabāhu I in the eleventh century A.D., disappeared from Sri Lanka, which resulted in the need of calling on monks from Rakkhaṅga for the reestablishment of this all-important religious function at the beginning of the seventeenth century. The introduction of this new form of higher ordination into Sri Lanka and its consequences have been discussed by a previous writer.[1] Third, the history of Buddhism of the period beginning from the seventeenth century have already been discussed by two writers in their doctoral theses. Of these, K. Wachissara, in his thesis, *Välivița Saranankara and the Revival of Buddhism in Ceylon*[2], examines the conditions of Buddhism in Sri Lanka before and after the Saṅgharāja Välivița Saranaṅkara. The other writer, A.H. Mirando, makes a study of Buddhism in Sri Lanka in the seventeenth and eighteenth centuries in his thesis, *Buddhism in Ceylon in the Seventeenth and Eighteenth Centuries with Special Reference to Sinhalese Literary Sources.*[3] Thus, the present monograph bridges a gap in the religious history of the country.

So far no comprehensive study of the history of religion in our period has appeared, but the subject has received the attention of a few writers. In a chapter devoted to the civilization of the period after the downfall of Polonnaruva,[4] Paranavitana presents an outline of the main developments in the history of Buddhism up to the sixteenth century. Vincent Pandita also gives a brief sketch of religion in the fifteenth century in his contribution entitled *'Kōṭṭē yugaye bauddha tatvaya'* to the *Sāhityaya,*[5] the official organ of the Department of Cultural Affairs, Sri Lanka. Besides these contributions directly dealing with the field of study, there are a small number of works containing discussions more or less related to it. Of these, Pali Literature by C. E. Godakumbura, Culture of Ceylon in Medieval Times, a posthumous publication of W. Geiger edited by H. Bechert, *Pali Sāhityaya* and *Theravāadī Bauddhācāryayo* by A.P. Buddhadatta, *Kōṭṭe Sāhityaya* by K. D. P. Wickramasinha, *Sinhala Sandeśa Sāhityaya* and *Sinhala Sāhitya Vaṃsaya* by P. B. Sannasgala, *Political History of the Kingdom of Kōṭṭē* by G. P. V. Somaratna[6] and *The Evolution and History of the Buddhist Monastic Order with Special Reference to the Sangha in Ceylon* by G. Panabokke[7] deserve special mention.

## Sources

The investigation of the condition of Buddhism in Sri Lanka during this period is greatly assisted by the many chronicles, inscriptions, and official documents which have been preserved. Many of these sources utilised in this study are well known to students of history of Sri Lanka and have been discussed by different scholars. It should, however, be mentioned here that these discussions were primarily based on the political history of the period. Although the political aspect is not overlooked in our study we intend to assess these sources in so far as they depict religious conditions of the country during the period under review.

Apart from the sources mentioned above, there are semi-historical writings and literary works of the period containing useful information and accounts of foreign writers such as those of Burma, Pali chronicles from Chieng Mai, as well as Chinese and Portuguese accounts which can be used after careful examination.

Naturally, as in almost any study of medieval Sri Lanka, the continuation of the *Mahāvaṃsa*, generally known as the *Cūlavaṃsa*, forms one of the important sources of our information. This was written in three different parts by different scholars belonging to different periods.[8] In his edition of the text Geiger has discussed the trustworthiness of this work, at the same time drawing attention to some of its deficiencies.[9] The first part of the *Cūlavaṃsa* deals with the history of the country to the end of the reign of Parākramabāhu I '(1153-1186); the second section continues to the reign of Parākramabāhu IV (1302-1326) of Kurunägala.

The third part of the chronicle, which deals for the most part with our period, was composed in the eighteenth century in the reign of Kīrti Śrī Rājasiṅha (1747- 1782) of Kandy. According to the information given in its colophon this was written at the request of this monarch.[10] Geiger, who made a critical study of the Pali chronicles of Sri Lanka, concludes that this part of the *Cūlavaṃsa* was composed by a monk called Tibboṭuvāvē Buddharakkhita of the Malvatu Vihāraya in Seṅkhanḍaselapura (Kandy).

This part of the *Cūlavaṃsa* is intended to deal with the history of the Island from the reign of Bhuvanekabāhu III (1326-1335) to that of Kīrti Śrī Rājasiṅha (1747- 1782). This entire part of the chronicle contains ten chapters.[11] A careful examination of the work reveals that the object of the author was not to record the history of the country but to eulogise the religious activities of his patron Kīrti Śrī Rājasiṅha. This is quite clear from the fact that more than half of the work is taken up by the last two chapters which deal with the reign of this monarch.[12] Even in these chapters no attempt seems to have been made to record the significant political events of the day. To provide a historical background to Kīrti Śrī Rājasiṅha's reign it appears that the author has made a deliberate attempt to narrate the history of the Kandyan kingdom. For this purpose a long narrative of the religious works and endowments of the rulers of this kingdom has been given. The four chapters preceding the last two are devoted to the reign of these rulers.[13]

It is striking that in the third part of the *Cūlavaṃsa* only three chapters comprising eighty-four verses pertain to our period which covers two centuries.[14] In these chapters the author seems to have lost the significance of many of the political events of the time and history seems to have been relegated to the background. The Chinese incursion in the first decade of the fifteenth century, in which the ruler of the time was taken captive to China, an event which has not only political but also religious significance, is altogether ignored. It seems that this important episode in the history of Sri Lanka, the knowledge of which we owe above all to Chinese sources,[15] was unknown to the chronicler. The author of this part of the *Cūlavaṃsa* gives no information about the events that preceded the reign of Parākramabāhu VI (1415-1467) of Kōttē- apart from mentioning that his mother's name was Sunettā.[16] Furthermore, he has not recorded the significant political events that took place during the reign of this monarch. There is no mention of the manner in which he gained sovereignty over the Sinhalese kingdom. The *Cūlavaṃsa* does not stand alone in this omission, for even the authors who lived during his long reign and eulogised him elaborately, do not appear to have seen the significance of the political events of the day. However, they referred to his victory over the Tamil kingdom of Jaffna and some South Indian raiders.[17] The date of the accession of Parākramabāhu VI given in the *Cūlavaṃsa* (1953 B.E. 1410/11 A.D.) is also found in the *Saddharmaratnākaraya*.[18] But even this date is not free from ambiguity.[19]

However, ın spite of these shortcomings, the *Cūlavaṃsa* description of the religious conditions of the country during the reign of Parākramabāhu VI should not undervalue for it gives a long narrative of the king's religious activities. It should be borne in mind that this record is entirely confined to the benefactions of Parākramabāhu VI towards the Tooth Relic and the Order. Contemporary sources give more credible accounts of the religious activities of this king. It is noteworthy that the author of the *Cūlavaṃa* gives hardly any detail about the monastic educational institutions which earned great fame during the major part of the fifteenth century. In the description of the benefactions of Parākramabāhu VI towards the Order the author writes:- '(This ruler) in memory of his mother, had erected in the Papphaṭa Grove (Päpiliyāna) in her name the Sunetta- *pariveṇa* and a monastery for the community and granted to it many villages and fields.[20] Apart from this brief account the author seems to have lost the significance of this monastic educational establishment and other institutions of the period, but he describes the restoration and construction of religious buildings undertaken by Parākramabāhu VI in various parts of the country.[21] This information, in spite of its deficiencies, has considerable value for our study.

After the reign of Parākramabāhu VI the reigns of seven rulers in the Kōṭṭē kingdom are mentioned in five verses of chapter XCII. On the other hand, Parākramabāhu IX, who reigned in the Kōṭṭē kingdom on the eve of the arrival of the Portuguese in Sri Lanka in 1505, is not even mentioned in the chronicle. After merely naming those seven kings the author seems to have taken great pains to narrate the religious activities of Vikramabāhu (Vīravikrama) who ruled in the kingdom of Kandy at the last phase of the fifteenth century.

It is characterisitic of the attitude of the author of this part of the *Cūlavaṃsa* and his indifference to the significant events that took place in the country that he does not mention the Portuguese until the reign of Senarat (1604- 1635), when he records the name *paraṅgi* more than a century after their arrival.[22] The author is perhaps reluctantly compelled to mention the Portuguese on this occasion as it was the time in which Senarat had to abandon his kingdom temporarily as a result of General Azavedo's invasion of Kandy.[23] Until that time, although there were sporadic incursions such as those leading to the burning of the border villages of the Kandyan kingdom, they may not have been regarded as a threat to the nation, at least by the chronicler and his contemporaries, for the chronicle does not mention any of these invasions before the reign of Senarat. This invasion, however, was taken as a serious threat by the chronicler:

"At the time merchants in the seaport of Kolamba who had sojourned there a long time had become puffed up with pride. They were, all of them, the so-called *paraṅgi,* heretical evil-doors, cruel and brutal. They spread themselves over several fair provinces, laid waste fields and gardens, burned down houses and villages, destroyed the noble families and in this way brought ruin on Sīhaḷa.[24]

This was the period of the Portuguese official rulership of the Maritime Provinces of Sri Lanka. Until then the coastal areas of the country had belonged either to the kingdom of Kōṭṭē or to the kingdom of Sītāvaka up to the demise of Dharmapāla (1551-15967). Perhaps, this situation may have caused the author of the chronicle to underrate the activities of the Portuguese in the country.

But this is no excuse for the attitude of the author of *Cūlavaṃsa* in relegating to the background the significant political events that took place in the country, for Dharmapāla, the figurhead ruler of Kōṭṭē residing with the Portuguese in Colombo, who adopted Christianity as his religion, is not even mentioned in the *Cūlavaṃsa*. Moreover, Māyādunne, a man of importance, who championed the cause of Buddhism during the time of the Portuguese influence over the Kōṭṭē kingdom, is dismissed by the author with the mere mention of his name.[25]

An analysis of the *Cūlavaṃsa* shows that it is heavily dependent on the *Rājaratnākaraya* for the political history of the Island up to the end of the fifteenth century. The shortcomings and errors that are to be found in **the latter work** have crept into the *Cūlavaṃsa* as well. But in spite of that, the information given on the religious activities of some of the rulers of this period is valuable. This information may have been taken from some independent source, probably from a *puññapotthaka,*[26] a book in which the meritorious deeds of kings are recorded. This may be proved by the fact that the *Cūlavaṃsa* gives more details of the almsgivings and other religious activities of Vīravikrama than are found in the *Rājaratnākaraya.*[27] There is evidence to show that this kind of record of meritorious deeds was popular in the eighteenth and nineteenth centuries. They were called *pinvaṭṭōruvas* or *dinapotas.*[28] It may be conjectured that these records were used by the chronicler. However, there is comparatively little information to gather from these narratives given in the chronicle as far as a comprehensive study of the religious history of the country is concerned. It is, therefore, justified to conclude that in spite of its being the continuation of the Great Chronicle of the Island, the third part of the *Cūlavaṃsa* possesses very little value in connection with the period under review.

Among the contemporary chronicles of our period which contain valuable information is the *Rājaratnākaraya,* a Sinhalese work, the date of composition of which is not known for certain. Godakumbura assumes that it was written in the latter part of the fifteenth century or the first part of the sixteenth century, taking into account the long narrative of the work pertaining to the reign of Sēnāsammata Vikramabāhu of Kandy.[29]

The colophon of some of the manuscripts of the work gives the name of its author as the *mahāthera* of Valgampāya. It appears that the object of the author was mainly to justify the claims of Vikramabāhu to rule the country. He seems, therefore, to have devoted great efforts to tracing the lineage of this king. The information given in this work concering the period before the beginning of the Kōṭṭē kingdom has evidently been borrowed from earlier works such as the *Nikāyasaṅgrahaya* and the second part of the *Cūlavaṃsa*. The name of Dharma Parākramabāhu (1503-1520) is omitted from the list of kings after the reign of Parākramabāhu VI (1415-1467). Events of political importance are not recorded in it and only the religious activities of Parākramabāhu VI and later kings are mentioned. This narrative of the religious activities of these rulers is quite similar to that given in the third part of the *Cūlavaṃsa* is heavily dependent on the *Rājaratnākaraya* for his information.

The *Rājaratnākaraya* has considerable value as a contemporary work with regard to the religious policy adopted by Senāsammata Vikramabāhu of Kandy. The gradual development of this kingdom into a centre of Sinhalese Buddhists during the period of political insecurity in the *Kōṭṭē* kingdom can be traced from this work. It gives a long narrative of the benefactions of Vikramabhāhu towards the Order.[30] The most important reference in this respect is the purification of the Sangha carried out under the patronage of this king.[31] In spite of its deficiencies and repetitions the *Rājaratnākaraya* can be taken as a valuable source for our study.

Among the later Sinhalese chronicles mention may be made of the *Rājāvaliya,* which literally means 'line of kings.' It has been observed by Godakumbura, who gives a detailed account of the nature of the work, that when one refers to the *Rājāvaliya* as a text, it should be clearly understood that there is no single work by that name, but there are various recensions and versions of the work.[32] He divides these into seven groups.[33] According to this scholar, the *Rājāvaliyas,* which were originally histories of provinces or districts, developed into histories of the whole Island, and such compositions were known as *Mahārājāvaliyas,* which were again abridged into *Rājāvaliya.* There are several published versions and translations of the main *Rājāvaliya,* which differs among themselves over details. One version of the text has been edited and translated by Gunasekara[34] while Vatuvatte Pemananda utilises another version of the work in his edition.[35] There is another published version of the text entitled *Alakeśvarayuddhaya.*[36] Apart from these, the most valuable foreign editions of this chronicle are presented by the Protuguese historian Diego do Couto and the eighteenth century Dutch historian Valentijn.[37] The *Rājāvaliya* version translated by Upham bears a great resemblance to that eidted by Gunasekara.[38] All these published versions of the work end with the reign of Vimaladharmasūriya II of Kandy, thus falling into one category. The others, such as *Vanni Rājāvaliya, Vijitavällē Rājāvaliya* taking narrative down to early British times, fall into another category.[39]

Even in the case of the published versions of the *Rājāvaliya* we do not know who the writer of this chronicle was. It has been suggested that the work was continued by various hands.[40] This suggestion is based on the composition of the work, which displays different styles of language and idiom. Dates are recorded in the Buddhist Era, the Śaka Era and even in the Christian Era.[41] Some passages of the *Rājāvaliya* show a Christian hand at work, for example that which relates the first arrival of the Portuguese in Sri Lanka: 'At that time, in the year 1552 of our Lord Jesus Christ, there came a ship to the harbour of Colombo from the Portuguese settlement in Jambudvīpa. having, by the power of God, escaped the perils of the deep.'[42] Godakumbura is of the opinion that these discrepancies are probably due to the material being drawn from different sources, and not to different writers taking a share in the composition of the chronicle.[43]

The object of the *Rājāvaliya* was to deal with the reigns of the kings of Sri Lanka from the very begining of its known history. Before dealing with this main object, it gives a descripton of the universe, and goes on to deal with the origin of kingship, which is supposed to have begun with the election of King Mahāsammata by the people. From this account up to the reign of Parākramabāhu II (1236- 1270) the *Rājāvaliya* agrees in main with the other Sinhalese chronicles such as the *Pūjāvaliya* and the *Nikāyasaṅgrahaya*. Moreover, in this earlier part of the work, although it has its own method of arranging the material, the *Rājāvaliya* follows the *Pūjāvaliya*, sometimes even to the point of word for word.

The *Rājāvaliya* is more useful for the political history of the Kōṭṭē kingdom, for which the *Cūlavaṃsa* is of little value. It is significant that the author of the *Rājāvaliya* seems to have lost the importance of the Kurunegala period, for, there is not a single reference made to this period in the work. Furthermore, he seems to have been unaware of the rulers of the Gampola kingdom, and this kingdom is dealt with only after the rise of Alakeśvara.[44] Somaratna has drawn attention to the disagreement of the various versions of the work regarding the Chinese expedition, which took place at the beginning of the fifteenth century.[45] It should be borne in mind that even in information given about the Kōṭṭē period there are numerous errors in the *Rājāvaliya*. Thus, this work refers to Parākramabāhu VI's father as a king called Vijayabāhu.[46] Giving much credit to this reference some modern writers tried to prove that the father of this moarch was a ruling king known as Vijayabāhu, who, according to them, was the sixth of that name.[47] The *Vrttaratnākara-pañjikā*, a contemporary Sanskrit work, which refers to the father of this monarch as *mahīpati*, seems to have been accepted by these scholars as an additional argument.[48] Besides, they are of the opinion that the king who was taken captive to China by Cheng-ho was this ruler. But the *Saddharmaratnākaraya*, a contemporary Sinhalese work, mentions the name of the ruler who was taken captive to China as Vīra Alakeśvara, not Vijayabāhu.[49] On the other hand, we are told by the contemporary literary works that the name of Parākramabāhu's father was Jayamahalāna and his mother was Sunetrā.[50] Simon de Silva has substantiated his argument that there was no king by the name of Vijayabāhu before the accession of Parākramabāhu VI and after the death of Bhuvanekabāhu V (1372-1408).[51]

As its name denotes, the *Rājāvaliya* is an attempt to write a continuous account of the kings of Sri Lanka from the earliest times. It deals mainly with political events and seems to have neglected the history of the Sāsana. However, it has some scattered remarks on religion, which have considerable value for our survey. For instance, the narration of the childhood of Parākramabāhu VI, which has not been given in any other indigenous source, has implications for the state of the Sangha in this period.[52] Vīdāgama *mahāsāmi*, under whose care the prince Parākrama grew up, seems to have held considerable political power during the early decades of the fifteenth century. According to do Couto, Alakeśvara, the usurper of the time, having died without heir, the political authority in the Island devolved on a religioux,[53] obviously, Vīdāgama *mahāsāmi*, referred to in the *Rājāvaliya*. According to both sources, this Elder installed the prince Parākrama on the throne.

Apart from that it makes some remarks about the reign of Bhuvanekabāhu VII (1521-1551), who ruled most of the ancient Koṭṭē kingdom with the help of the Portuguese. This account is of some significance for the evaluation of the religious and administrative policy adopted by this king. In one of the remarks the author of the *Rājāvaliya* criticises him thus:-

"This king, Bhuvanekabāhu, after having reigned for twenty years, brought ruin on the country by giving it into the hands of strangers and likewise poured contempt upon the religion".[54]

This remark suggests the feelings of later generations about the reign of Bhuvanekabāhu VII. Apart from this scattered information the *Rājāvaliya* has very little value in connexion with the religious life of the period under review.

Among other works which have a direct bearing on the period under review is the *Saddharmaratnākaraya*, a Sinhalese prose work composed in the reign of Parākramabāhu VI, which gives very useful information.[55] The author of the work was a monk named Dhammadinna Vimalakīrti belonging to the famous school of Dharmakīrti of Palābatagla.[56]

In composing the work the intention of the author was to give an exposition of the Dhamma in a manner that could be easily understood by the laymen. It was composed at the invitation of a fellow monk named Vikkamabāhu, who requested the author to compose a work on the Dhamma in the Sinhalese language, and also in response to a similar request by a lay devotee by the name of Vīrasundara Kumāra.[57] Because of this special purpose the book was intended to serve, the *Saddharmaratnākaraya* has but a restricted historical value.

The work is divided into 36 chapters each different according to the nature of the topics dealt with.[58] The twelfth chapter of the *Saddharmaratnākaraya* is called Dharmādbhuta-saṅgraha-kathā, and deals with the wonderful powers of the Dhamma. The first section here is the story of the first Council which was held under Mahā Kāśyapa, immediately after the Nirvāṇa. After the account of the first Council there is a brief history of the Sangha. In giving this acount it seems that the object of the author was to record the attempts of the ancient Sinhalese rulers to uphold the Theravāda School of Buddhism by suppressing rival sects and heretical beliefs. The author appears to have based his account on the *Nikāyasaṅgrahaya.*[59]

The *Saddharmaratnākaraya* has been used by modern scholars to clarify doubts regarding some political events in the first decade of the fifteenth century. For instance, its list of the members of the Alakeśvara family who held political power in the country before Parākramabāhu VI (1415-1467) has been accepted.[60] As has been mentioned above it is from the account given in the *Saddharamaratnākarya* that we have identified the ruler who was taken captive to China by Cheng-ho in 1410-1411.[61]

The most useful section of the work comes towards the end of the twelfth chapter which is devoted to an account of the religious works of Parākramabāhu VI. This long narration is of a special significance because it is contemporaneous with the events which it describes. According to information given in it the author was invited to compose the *Saddharmaratnākaraya* in the seventh regnal year (1422 A.D) of Parākramabāhu VI.[62] But the description of the religious works of this ruler, given in this chapter, may have been written at a later time. This assumption may be substantiated by the fact that he mentions the Päpiliyāna monastery which this king caused to be built; it was dedicated to the memory of his mother and named after her.[63] According to the Päpiliyāna document No. I the construction of the monastery took place in the seventh regnal year of the king.[64] Further developments of this establishment are recorded in the Päpiliyāna document No.II, issued in the 45th regnal year (1460) of the king.[65] Even though the account of the *Saddharmaratnākaraya* is a brief one, it mentions every part of the establishment given in the documents. It is, therefore, correct to asume that if the composition of the book was completed in the seventh year or immediately after that of the king this account could not have been included. This may lead us to suppose that at least the final portion of twelfth chapter of the *Saddharmaratnākaraya* was written in a later year. However, this account cannot be considered as a complete and accurate one regarding the religious policy adopted by Parākramabāhu VI, for his religious works described in the Maha Saman Dēvālaya Sannasa[66] and Munnēśvaram Dēvālaya inscription[67] are not included in this section.

The colophon of the *Saddharmaratnākaraya* gives a detailed account of the lineage of Dharmakirti of Palābatgala[68] to which the author himself belonged. This includes the literary works carried out by these monks and their various other services towards the promotion of religion. This description is more useful in tracing the history of the high dignitaries of the Sangha in the thirteenth and fourteenth centuries.

It is noteworthy that although the *Saddharmaratnākarya* refers to the Päpiliyāna Pirivena established by Parākramabāhu VI no mention is made of the monastic or educational life in that institution or other institution of the day. Owing to this shortcoming of the work we have to depend on other sources for data on the affairs of the Sangha and educational life in this period.

Another important work that deals with the religious affairs of this period is the *Alutnuvara dēvālē Karavīma* which gives the history of the Upulvan shrine at Alutnuvara near Māvanälla in the Sabaragamuva Province.[69] Neither the author nor the period to which the work belongs is known with certainty. But a close examination of its contents suggests that it may have been written in a period not earlier than the sixteenth century. What is most important in this work is the information it supplies regarding the religious activities of the kings from the Dambadeṇiya dynasty to Vimaladharmasūriya I (1592-1604) of Kandy.

A part of this work was published by Jayatilaka in his *Siṅhala Sāhitya Lipi.*[70] As far as we know, no other manuscripts of this document are available apart from that which is preserved in the British Musuem.[71] The published portion of the work which deals with the Äsaḷa festival at Devinuvara does not mention the date of this work. As Jayatilaka published it with his article concerning the reign of Parākramabāhu II (1236-1270), it may create the impression that the work was written in the reign of that king. But this can be easily ruled out because the last king mentioned in this work is Vimaladharmasūriya I whose reign dates from 1592 to 1604.[72] This would substantiate the fact that the composition of the work could not have taken place before the end of the sixteenth century.

The *Alutnuvara Dēvālē Karavīma* gives us useful information pertaining to the reign of Parākramabāhu II, such as his date of accession in the year 1779 of the Buddhist Era. It has been observed that this date agrees with that given in other sources, notably the Devinuvara inscription of this ruler.[73] This would suggest that the author of the document used some reliable sources in compiling his work.

After its account of Parākramabāhu II the work goes on to deal with the edifices built by Bhuvanekabāhu in (1274- 1284). It then gives an account of the grants of lands and other endowments to the *dēvālaya* by successive Sinhalese rulers, making brief allusions at times to political events that took place in their respective reigns. In this part of the document, which has not been published so far, Parākramabāhu VI of Kōṭṭe, Māyādunne and Rājasiṇha I of Sītāvaka are mentioned. These references give their dates of accession according to Śaka era. It is noteworthy that the author of the *Alutnuvara Dēvālē Karavīma* mentions even some provincial rulers such as Sakala-kalā Vallabha of Udugampola who ruled that province at the beginning of the sixteenth century.[74] In this connection the information given in the work is quite similar to that of the *Rājāvaliya*.[75]

The information given in this work about the Alutnuvara and Devinuvara shrines of Upulvan is very useful in tracing the history of these important places of worship. Furthermore, it depicts the popularity of Upulvan in medieval Sri Lanka. Apart from that there are valuable references to the affairs of the Sangha from the Daṁbadeṇi period to the end of the sixteenth century. For instance, it mentions the Galaturumula institution of monks, who were the incumbents of the Buddhist monastery adjacent to the shrine of Upulvan at Alutnuvara. Besides, it describes their duties and the endowments made to them by the Sinhalese rulers in various times.[76] This information helps us to trace the administration of the Buddhist monastic establishments in medieval Sri Lanka.

The best known and the most important of the histories of the Sāsana is the Sinhalese chronicle, the *Nikāyasaṅgrahya*,[77] also called the *Sāsanāvatāra*, which was written by Jayabāhu Devarakṣita of Gaḍalādeniya. The author began his work to record the history of the Sāsana from the Nirvāṇa to the fifteenth year of Bhuvanekabāhu V. that is 1375 A.D. He drew his material from variety of sources such as the *Aṭṭhakathās* and the *Vaṃsa* literature for the early part of his work. For the later sections of the *Nikāyasaṅgrahaya* the author made use of the *Cūlavaṃsa*, the *Katikāvatas* and the *Pūjāvaliya*. It has been observed that Jayabahu used, other sources too besides these which are now lost.[78]

Although the author began his work with the intention of bringing the history of the Sāsana up to the fifteenth year of Bhuvanekabāhu V, he later continued it for a further period until after Vīrabāhu had held an enquiry into the conduct of monks and purified the Sangha in 1939 B.E. (1396 A.D).[79] At the time of composition of this portion of the work Jayabāhu had become the Head of the Order after his teacher, Dharmakīrti II, and assumed the title Dharmakīrti after him.[80]

The purpose of the author in recording the history of the Sāsana seems to have been mainly to emphasise the part played by the Mahāvihāra fratenity in the history of Sri Lanka, and to reconstruct the history of the heretical movements and the attempts made to eradicate them. He has taken much pains to relate the purifications of the Sangha and the explusion of evil monks from the very earliest times to the end of the fourteenth century. The last purification of the Sangha mentioned in this text is dated B.E. 1941 (1396 A.D).[81] There is no doubt that the author witnessed both purifications of the Sangha, which took place in the latter part of the fourteenth century: the first in 1369 A.D. and the second in 1396 A.D. Yet it is striking that he contents himself with condemning the monks who were expelled from the Sangha as 'evil doers' *(duśśīla)* or 'shameles people' *(alajjīn)*;[82] he does not take pains to elucidate the reasons which led to their expulsion from the Order. In spite of this reticence of the *Nikāyasaṅgrahaya,* it helps us to understand the state of the Sangha especially in the thirteenth and fourteenth centuries.

Because of the shortcomings and unusual brevity of the chronicles with regard to this period we have to collect important data from other literature including poetical works of the time. It should be pointed out here that the most outstanding feature of Sinhalese literature in the fifteenth century is its emphasis on poetry. This trend in literature is noticeable to a pronounced degree to the fifteenth century and to a lesser degree throughout the greater part of the sixteenth century. We are fortunate to have a large number of poems which give useful information in varying degrees pertaining to the religious life of the period.

Our attention should be mainly focussed here on the *sandeśa* poems, otherwise called *dūta-kāvyas,* which were the most popular and significant literary genre in Sinhalese at this time. Although the *sandeśas* are old as a literary style, and a work called *Miyuru-asna* (Peacock Message) is said to have existed earlier,[83] it was only during the Gampola period that the *sandeśas* proper began to appear.[84] They gradually gained in popularity, and became a regular feature of the writings of the Kōṭṭē period. The secular outlook of the *sandeśas,* in contrast with the exclusively religious character of the earlier literary works, allowed more freedom of expression for the Sinhalese poets. Thus the poets began to describe contemporary life and what they saw around them, the beauties of nature, the forms of worship, seats of learning, men of eminence, etc., to an extent never done before. These *sandeśas* were intended as messages to various gods and distinguished personalities in the county; and they differ in their subjects. They have considerable historical value for their authors seem to have taken great pains to depict a faithful picture of the society of the time. Therefore a careful study of these works of the Sinhalese literature will help us to some extent to reconstruct the religious life of the country in the fifteenth and sixteenth centuries.

Among these poems the *Haṃsa- sandeśaya* may be reckoned as the earliest of the *sandeśa* poems in the fifteenth century.[85] The author's purpose is to send a message through a swan to the Elder Vanaratana of Kāragala to recite the Ratana-sutta a hundred thousand times and invoke the blessings of the gods on Parākramabāhu VI of Kōṭṭē, the ruler of the country.[86] As the Elder Vanaratana held the rank of *saṅgharāja* quite early in the reign of this king,[87] this poem too appears to have been composed at an early period of his reign. The colophon of the poem says that it was composed by Vīdāgama Maitreya of Mahanetpāmula at Rayigama.[88]

The *Haṃsa-sandeśaya* gives a most interesting account of the court of Parākramabāhu VI, which is valuable for the study of political institutions of the time. Besides, the description of the Padmāvati Pirivena at Kāragala, given in this poem, provides a true picture of a seat of learning devoted to religious studies in the fifteenth century.[89] Furthermore, the *Haṃsa- sandeśaya* helps us to form some idea of the views of the Vanavāsi fraternity of the Buddhist monks which appears to have tried to defend pure Theravāda from the Mahāyānic and Hindu influence.

The *Parevi-sandeśaya* is another "message poem" composed by the most famous scholar of the time, Śrī Rāhula of Toṭagamuva, during the early stages of his literary career.[90] The object of this poem was to request Upulvan at Devinuvara to give a suitable husband to Princess Candrāvati, a daughter of Parākramabāhu VI, and also a son who would have the good fortune to rule the country after the demise of the king.[91]

However it is not confined to this purpose. The god is also besought to protect the Elder designated as Anumuni (but not named), the king, his retinue and the ministers and the army.[91] The manifold purposes of the *Parevi-sandeśaya* enable us to infer the interest of the Gāmavāsi fraternity, to which Śrī Rāhula himself belonged, in the political affairs of the country.

A significant feature of the poem is the belief of the author in auspicious times and auspicious signs which are looked down upon in Buddhism. This shows the influence of popular beliefs on the Sangha of this period. The *Parevi-sandeśaya* is still more useful for the topographical information it contains, for Śrī Rāhula covered the ground from Kōṭṭē to Devinuvara. In this long journey his information about the religious places is useful; his account of the geography of Devinuvara even helps the archaeologist of the present day to understand what the city of Upulvan was like in the fifteenth century.[92] Besides, his eulogy of Upulvan has a peculiar feature which helps us to trace the influence of Hindu and Mahāyānic mythology on the religious life of the day.[93]

The *Sälalihiṇi-sandeśaya,* the last of the three Sinhalese poems of Śrī Rāhula, was composed in the 35th year of the reign of Parākramabāhu VI.[94] The message of this poem, somewhat similar to that of the *Parevi-sandeśaya,* is a request to Vibīṣaṇa of Kelaṇiya to confer a worthy son on Ulakuḍaya-devi, another daughter of the king, and it is sent by her husband Nannūrutunayyān, a minister of the king's court.[95] This poem gives a vivid picture of the Kelaṇiya Temple in the fifteenth century, a century before the destruction of this sacred place by the Portuguese.[96]

Next in order of the *Sandeśa* poems is the *Girā-sandeśaya,* a message sent through a parrot by an unknown author from Jayavardhana-pura (Kōṭṭē).[97] Its object was to request Śrī Rāhula, the principal of the Vijayabāhu Pirivena at Toṭagamuva, to invoke the blessings of Nātha to protect Parākramabāhu VI and his retinue as well as Buddhism in Sri Lanka.[98]

Although the name of the author of this work is not given in it, some scholars are of the opinion that he was a great admirer of Śrī Rāhula.[99] In spite of the explicitly stated object of this poem, it appears to have been an excuse to write a *sandeśa* poem, for there was hardly any necessity to seek protection for the king by invoking blessings from any god, as he was not faced with any trouble at this time; indeed according to information given in this poem itself and other sources, he was ruling supreme in the Island in all his glory.[100]

The *Ambalamē-saṁvādaya* (the discussion in the rest house), a section in the *Girā-sandeśaya*, has great historical value since it gives an account of the political career of Parākramabābu VI which is not found in any other contemporary source.[101] In the description of the monastery at Päpiliyāna the author correctly states that it was built by Parākramabāhu VI.[102] He failed, however, to describe the Sunetrādevi Pirivena situated there. This may be due to the fact that the Pirivena here was not of such a standard and status as the Vijayabāhu Pirivena at Toṭagamuva, which he describes in detail.[103]

We have in the *Girā-sandeśaya* an account of the Vijayabāhu Pirivena at Toṭagamuva which had the fame of a University, where many secular subjects were taught.[104] Among the students of this institution there were even *brahmin* youths from India. According to this account the curriculum of the Vijayabāhu Pirivena, over which Śrī Rāhula presided, included a greater range of subjects than that of the contemporary college at Kāragala.

The last and the longest *sandeśa* poem of the fifteenth century is the *Kokila-sandeśaya*.[105] The author of the poem as mentioned in its colophon was the principal of the Tilaka Pirivena (otherwise called Irugalkula Tilaka Pirivena) at Devinuvara.[106] The author's knowledge of Tamil in addition to traditional monastic studies, and his familiarity with the geography of the country, from the southern-most point up to Jaffna, as revealed by the poem, were exceptional for a Buddhist monk in the fifteenth century.

The message of the poem was intended to be submitted to Prince Sapumal who ruled Jaffna as a viceroy of Parākramabāhu VI.[107] The author did not neglect to mention every place of religious significance along his route from Devinuvara to Jaffna. Although he was a Buddhist monk he never failed to recognize other faiths and temples. He asked his messenger to see the Nāga Kōvila after Vällēmadama,[108] the Gaṇeśa Kōvila close to Potupiṭiya,[109] the Pattini *dēvāle* near Kōṭṭē,[110] the Munneśvaram Kōvila, near Chilaw (Halāvata)[111] and the temple of Ayyanār (Sinh. Ayyanāyaka) at Māvatupaṭṭanam (ancient Mahātittha).[112] In this respect the *Kokila-sandeśaya* as a historical source is higher than the others because it extends from the southern-most point of the country to the extreme north.

The last Sinhalese *sandeśa* poem which concerns us is the *Sävul-sandeśaya* composed in the reign of Rājasiṁha I of Sītāvaka.[113] The author of this work is Alagiyavanna Mukavetti who contributed several poems to the Sinhalese literature.[114] This *sandeśaya* was a message from Sītāvaka to be carried by a cock to the god Saman (Sumana) of Saparapura, modern Ratnapura. It prays for the protection of Rājasiṁha I and his army. This prayer was perhaps necessiated by the king's constant wars with the Portuguese. By this time the shrines of Upulvan at Devinuvara and Vibhīṣaṇa at Kelaṇiya were destroyed by the Portuguese and the poet had to resort to a god who was in a safe region.

The author of this poem mentions several Buddhist temples and distinguished Buddhist monks in the realm of Rājasiṁha I,[115] who was alleged to have done great damage to Buddhism and persecuted Buddhist monks. This allegation made against him by the author of the third part of the *Cūlavaṃsa* and its motives and validity will be discussed later in this study.[116]

Concering the historical value of the description in the *sandeśa* poems of the religious life of the country, one has to take not of the *Vuttamālā-sandesa-sataka*, a Pali poem, written by a monk called Gatārā Pirivena Upatapassi.[117] In the colophon of the work the author calls himself the nephew of Sarasigāmamūla Mahāsāmi, the Primate at the time and the chief incumbent of the Raja Mahāvihāraya at Dädigama (Pali. Jātigāma).[118] Malalasekara and some other scholars attribute the date of composition of this work to the reign of Parākramabāhu VI (1415-1467), on the grounds that it purported to convey a message to Vibhīṣaṇa at Kelaṇiya asking him to protect a king called Parakkama and his mother, who were residing at Dädigama, from their enemies.[119] This opinion is difficult to substantiate, because none of the contemporary sources mentions that Parākramabāhu VI ever made Dädigama his capital, whereas we learn from the *Tisara-sandeśaya* that there was a king named Pärakum (Parākrama) who ruled the country while residing at Dädigama.[120] The *Tisara- sandeśaya* is the oldest of existing Sinhalese *sandeśa* poems, and is attributed to the reign of Parākramabāhu V (1344- 1359) of Dädigama.[121] The purpose of the *Tisara- sandeśaya* was to convey a message through a swan from Devinuvara to the King (Parākramabāhu) at Dädigama to inform him that a monk residing at Devinuvara was engaged in prayers to Upulvan, that he might be pleased to protect the king and made him victorious over his enemies, and also to bless his royal mother, Sumitrā, and to keep watch over his ministers of state.[122] This information reveals that the name of the mother of the king who ruled at Dädigama was Sumitrā, contrary to all the contemporary sources who are unanimous that the name of Parākrmabahu VI's mother was Sunetrā.[123] Hence it follows that the king mentioned in the *Vuttamālā-sandesa-sataka* was Parākrmabāhu V.

The *Vuttamālā-sandesa-sataka* is valuable for us to collect some information about the organization of the Sangha during the fourteenth century. After his description of Dädigama the author extols Parakkama and his mother. This is followed by an account of the Raja Mahāvihāraya at Dädigama, probably the administrative centre of the Sangha at the time.[124] The author then extols the primate at the time and some other prominent scholarly monks belonged to various *mūlas* (āyatanas).[125] This and other information given in the work will be useful in tracing the history of *mūlas* in their period of decline.

Apart from the sources examined above there are a number of literary works of lesser importance belonging to the period of this study. Among them the *Buduguṇālaṃkāraya,* composed by Vīdāgama Maitreya, in the reign of Parākramabābu VI, is a noteworthy work.[126] This poem is the story of the Buddha's visit to Visālā (Pali.Vesālī), the city of Licchavis, to remove the threefold pestilences of famine, diseases and evil spirits in that city. The poet has used this anecdote to extol the virtues of the Buddha and to point out that Brāhamnical gods and priests were of no avail. In this respect the work is significant because it depicts the attempts by some members of the Sangha in this period to decry the worship of numerous gods, a practice which had attracted as adherents even some distinguished monks of the day. It is worthwhile to investigate whether the author's ruthless condemnation of the Brahmins emerged as a result of their influence on the society of this period.

To this period also belongs the *Kāvyaśekharaya,* composed by Śrī Rāhula of Toṭagamuva, considered the second *mahākāvyaya* of the Sinhalese literature.[127] This poem gives valuable information regarding the author's biography and an insight into his scholarship. Besides, a careful examination of this work may help us to collect useful references regarding the monastic education of this period. Another work, the *Guttila-kāvyaya,*[128] whose authorhip is uncertain (though the work is attributed to *Vättāvē),* is noteworthy because of its information in connection with the religious works carried out by *Salāvata Jayapāla,* one time chief minister of *Parākramābahu VI.* [129] A prose work, the *Kuveṇi-asna,* belongs to the occult literature, written for the purpose of being used at *bali* ceremonies is considered to have been written in this period. It is a text of magical incantation composed to obtain victory and blessings for Parākramabāhu VI.[130] The work is attributed to a Buddhist monk who bore the title Ṣaḍbhāṣāparameśvara Uttaramūla Mahāthera.[131] Some scholars believe that the *thera* referred to is no other but Śrī Rāhula of Toṭagamuva.[132] The *Padasādhana-ṭīkā,* also called *Buddhippasādinī-ṭīkā,* a Pali grammatical work of Śrī Rāhula is valuable for us in tracing his relationship to Parākramabāhu VI.[133] One of Śrī Rāhula's Indian pupils, Śrī Rāmacandra Bhārati, wrote in Sanskrit the *Vrittaratnākara-pañjikā,* an eulogy of a monk named Rammuṅgoḍa Dīpaṅkara, which is helpful in deciding some factors regarding the kinship relations of some hierarchs in this period.

A later work, the *Mandārampura-puvata,* is useful in tracing the Hindu influence on society of this period.[135] This was written by Vikum Äduru in the seventeenth century and later continued by a monk named Unambuve Yati and another person in the eighteenth century. The *Mandārampura-puvata* mostly deals with local history and is the nature of the *Rājāvaliya,* so that its authenticity is not free from doubt. Certain historical incidents which appear to be based on rumours or legends dealing with Buddhism and Kandyan kingdom are debatable. However, in certain aspects the book's importance is noteworthy and useful to a research student. This is the only work that refers to a revolt against Vimaladharmasūriya I of Kandy by a Hindu priest, and this has been verified by a copper plate of Padiyapälälla.[136]

We are fortunate to have a considerable number of epigraphic sources relevant to our period of study. Although they are not regular as literury sources, at times they provide information more accurate and useful than that given by literary sources but often shed a new light on them. They are of immense value to us regarding the administration of religious institutions of this period. Since our period belongs to comparatively recent times the script is not much different from that of today.[137] Due to the fact that the majority of these records were issued to record the endowments of rulers towards religious institutions they are sometimes longer than those of the ancient period, for much care has been taken in clarifying boundaries of the particular grant of land or other properties endowed.

The royal grants known as *sannasas* (charters) became more and more abundant in this time. The purpose of such charters also was to donate land to the Sangha or to individual officials. They were usually inscribed on copper plates but sometimes on gold or silver plates. Palm leaf copies of the documents however are not rare.

The donors of these grants, who had the inscriptions made, were reigning monarchs, and therefore, they provide evidence concerning the duration of particular reigns. However, they sometimes exhibit confusion identifying a particular monarch.

There were five Parākramabāhus and three Bhuvanekabāhus in this period. Because these records always use quite similar titles such as Tribhuvanādhipati, Śrī Saṅghabodhi in mentioning the reigning monarch we have to be very careful in distinguishing one from another. Fortunately literary sources of the period often used epithets such as Dharma, Vīra in mentioning these kings. Therefore we are able to compare these two kinds of records and draw conclusions. On the other hand, apart from a few instances, every epigraphic record gives the date of the accession of the reigning king in the Śaka era or Buddhist era, which helps us to determine the reign in which the grant was issued.

As an introduction to the epigraphic records of the period we may examine three documents which are of special significance for the religious activities of the period.

Of these, the Päpiliyāna inscription, referred to in this study as the Päpiliyāna document I, issued in the 44th regnal year of Parākramabāhu VI (1415-1467), contains very valuable information with regard to the religious works of the monarch, and, especially, the monastic administration of the period.[138] The object of the document is to give an account of the construction of the Päpiliyāna monastery undertaken by the king, and to declare the lands and other endowments made by him to the monastery. The document as it stands, when read side by side with the *Maha Saman Dēvālaya Sannasa,* supplies the fullest particulars on record- except for the stone slabs of Mahinda IV (975-991) at Mihintale [139] regarding the administration and revenues of Buddhist monasteries in Sri Lanka, richly endowed and supported by royal aid and munificence. In some respects the contents of the document are very similar to those of the *Daṁbadeṇi Katikāvata* of Parākramabāhu II of Daṁbadeṇiya.[140] Therefore it can be regarded, to some extent, as a code of *vinaya* rules of the Buddhist Sangha.[141]

The *Maha Saman Dēvālaya Sannasa* issued in the 39th regnal year of Parākramabāhu VI,[142] is significant, for it gives the description of the administration of the Maha Saman Dēvālaya of Ratnapura and the Buddhist monastery attached to it at the same time.

The *sannasa* specifies extensive repairs and additions effected by Nīlaperumāl, the grandson of a brāhmaṇa named Aryakāmadeva, to the institution in pursuance of the order given by the king. It further names the chief incumbent appointed to the Buddhist monastery attached to it, as Maṅgala *tera-sāmi,* a pupil of the Hierarch Galaturumula Medhaṅkara. This particular instance shows us the prevalence of popular religion side by side with Buddhism in this period.

This record enumerates 26 villages dedicated to the god Sumana, besides other benefits. Apart from that, it notifies the apppointment of specifically titled officers over the *devālaya* and villages belonging to it. It also describes the display of the revenues of the institution for the maintenance of the three Bodhis [143] at the monastery as well as for the service to Saman *deviyō,* his queen and the prince god. Thereafter follow the rules and regulations regarding the general administration of the establishment.

The *Munneśvaram Dēvālaya* inscription, another valuable document of the period, supplies the details of the administration of a purely Hindu *kōvila* (dēvālaya) of the time.[144] This was issued in the 38th regnal year of Parākramabāhu VI, one year earlier than the *Maha Saman Dēvālaya Sannasa.* Although in details it is also similar to the former, the titles of the officers of the *dēvālaya* given here differ from those of the *Maha Saman Dēvālaya Sannasa.* For instance, the chief officer of the Maha Saman Dēvālaya bears the title Baṇdāranāyaka but here it takes a Tamil form 'Modanmoyi' . The full contents of these epigraphic sources will be dealt with in a later stage of this study.

Apart from the sources so far considered, several foreign accounts dealing with the period under review will be utilised in this study. Among them mention may be made of a Pali chronicle from Chieng Mai (Thailand), the *Jinakālamālī,* [145] written by *Ratanapañña Mahāthera of Rattavanavihāra of Chieng Māi.* Although the bulk of it was written in 1516 A.D., this work was completed in the year 1528 A.D.[146] The *Jinakālamālī* is a collection of legends and stories relating to Buddhism. The author uses his material to narrate the history of Buddhism from its very beginning to the date of composition of the work. It mainly deals with the spread of Buddhism into Sri Lanka and subsequently into parts of South East Asia. Since the author has extracted his information from a wide range of sources of different value one has to exercise the utmost caution in accepting his statements. Besides, we have to be careful about the chronological difficulties arising from the work. Jayawickrama has drawn attention to these difficulties in his English translation of the work.[147]

The *Jinakālamālī* is more useful for us in examining the religious intercourse between Sri Lanka and South East Asia, especially, Thailand, since an account of the Sīhaḷa Sāsana in North Thailand is its main theme. It gives a long account of a *Sīhaḷa-paṭimā* which is stated to have been secured for Rocarāja of Sukhothāi by King Siridhamma of Siridhammanagara.[148] According to some scholars this episode has bearing on Sri Lanka's relations with the kingdom of Tamaliṅga in the Malay Peninsula in the time of Parākramabāhu II of Daṁbadeniya.[149]

The section of this work most relevant to our period is its account of the introduction of the Mahāvihāra tradition of Sri Lanka into Thailand and the neighbouring kingdoms. It is in this section that the work describes the religious mission of the Elder Medhaṅkara who came to Sri Lanka to receive higher ordination. This mission, consisting of Thai, Kamboja and Burmese monks, arrived in 1424 A.D. in the reign of Parākramābāhu VI (1414-1467). The contents of the account on this mission will be dealt later in this survey. What is to be borne in mind here is that this remarkable event in the relations between Sri Lanka and South East Asia is not mentioned in Sri Lankan chronicles and other literary sources. This event had initially no significance for Sri Lanka's religious history but in the eighteenth and nineteenth centuries it became a matter of immense importance for the re-establishment of the higher ordination in Sri Lanka. Therefore, this work is certainly a very useful source for a study of Sri Lanka's relations with Thailand and the neighbouring kingdoms in the medieval period.

Another interesting work useful to students of the religious history of this period is *Kalyāṇipakaraṇa* contained in the *Kalyāṇi* inscriptions of Dhammaceti of Pegu. The *Kulyāṇi* inscriptions were erected in 1476 A.D. at Zainggnaing, the western suburb of Pegu.[150] The text of these inscriptions was independently preserved in the *Indian Antiquary* entitled 'A Preliminary Study of the *Kalyāni* Inscriptions of Dhammaceti[151] Taw Sein Ko used the manuscripts of the texts which were available in Burma. The Sri Lankan version of the inscriptions, the *Kalyāṇipakaraṇa*, was especially preserved in the monasteries belonging to the Amarapura Sect which had close contact with Burma since the beginning of the nineteenth century. This was edited by Gintota Medhankara in 1924.[152]

The *Kalyāṇi* inscriptions were intended to give an authoritative ruling of the *vinaya* rules of the Buddhist Sangha and to prescribe a ceremonial for the consecration of a *sīmā* called *Kalyānisīma*.[153] The *Kalyāṇisīmā* derives its name from the fact that it was consecrated by the Talaing (Mon) monks, who had received their *upasampadā* for the second time at the hands of the successors to the Mahāvihāra fraternity, the spiritual successors of Mahinda at an *udakukkhepa-sīmā* upon the *Kalyāṇi* river near Colombo.

They have an immense value for this study because they narrate the mission of Mon monks to Sri Lanka in the reign of Bhuvanekabāhu VI (1470- 1478) of Kōṭṭē. This higher ordination ceremony, at which the primate and the high dignitaries of the Sinhalese Sangha officiated, was held in 1474 A.D. Since there is no reference to this religious ceremony in the chronicles of Sri Lanka, we are indebted to the *Kalyāni* inscriptions for the information given regarding the relations between Sri Lanka and Pegu during the period of this study.

Among other foreign accounts, which require our attention is the *Sāsanavaṃsa,* written in Burma in 1861 A.D. by a monk named Paññāsāmi. He was the tutor of the then reigning king Men-dun-Meng of Burma, and himself a pupil of the Head of the Order at Mandalay.[154] The text of the *Sāsanavaṃsa* was edited by Mabel Bode for the Pali Text Society.[155] She has also published a thoughtful study of the work under the litle *A Burmese Historian of Buddhism.*[156] More recently an English translation of the *Sāsanavaṃsa* has been published by B.C.Law under the title *History of the Buddha's Religion.*[157] In studying the text one may derive some benefit by consulting the *Sāsanavaṃsa-dīpikā*[158] and the *Sāsanavaṃsa- padīpaya,*[159] two later works published in Sri Lanka, mainly based on the *Sāsanavaṃsa.*

The table of contents given in the text promised a general history of Buddhism drawn from such well known Pali works as *Aṭṭhakathās, Vinaya Piṭaka, Mahāvaṃsa* and *Dīpavaṃsa.* Events are brought up to the time of the Third Council in the time of Aśoka and the sending forth of missionaries by the Elder Moggaliputta. The later history of religion consists of nine chapters, which falls into two parts. The first consists of a few lengends strung together with quotations from ancient commentaries as well as Buddhaghosa's commentaries, the *Dīpavaṃsa* and other texts. The accounts of Sri Lanka and Burma seem to be more reliable and complete than most topics. The second part covers three-fifth of the work and treats solely the history of Buddhism in Burma proper.

As far as our study is concerned these latter two parts of the work are very useful, for they help us to trace the religious intercourse between Sri Lanka and Burma in medieval times. In this context it is worth mentioning that Bode is of the opinion that the author's horizon seems to be limited, first by an orthodox desire to claim most of the early teachers for the southern countries, i.e. Sri Lanka, and secondly by certain feeling of national pride. Nevertheless, a careful study of the *Sāsanavaṃsa* will be very useful in a study of Sri Lanka's relations with Burma, as it contains information on this subject not given by the Sri Lankan chronicles.

# References


1. K. Wachissara, *Välivita Saraṇaṅkara and the Revival of Buddhism in Ceylon*, (unpublished thesis submitted for the degree of Doctor of Philosophy of the University of London), 1961): Sin. Tr. *Saraṇaṅkara Saṅgharāja Samaya*, Colombo, 1963.
2. ibid.
3. Unpublished thesis, University of London, 1968.
4. *University of Ceylon History of Ceylon*. Colombo, 1960, Vol. I, part. II, pp. 745-749.(UCHC).
5. *Sāhityaya*, Journal of the Ministry of Cultural Affairs, Vol. 1957, pp. 66-71.
6. Unpublished thesis submitted to the University of London, 1969.
7. Unpublished thesis submitted to the University of Lancaster, 1969.
8. *UCHC*. p. 52.
9. W. Geiger, 'The Trustwothiness of the Mahāvamsa',, Indian Historical Quarterly, Vol. VI, (1950), pp. 205-228.
10. *Cv.*, 99-100.
11. *Cv.*, 91-100.
12. *Cv.*, 99-100.
13. *Cv.*, 95-98.
14. Cv., 91-93.
15. Journal of the Royal Asiatic Society, (Ceylon Branch), *JRASCB*, Vol.XXIV, No. 68, p. 98. ff; Vol. XXVII, No. 68, p. 98 ff; Vol. XXVII, No. 73, p.31ff
16. *Cv.*, 91. 24.
17. *Girā sandeśaya*, ed.M. Kumaranatunga, Colombo, 1955, v. 124 ff.
18. *Saddarmaratnākaraya*, ed. K. Nanavimala, Panadura, 1931, p.299.
19. *UCHC.*, pp. 669-70; *Political History of the Kingdom of Kotte*, p. 173 ff.
20. *Cv.*, 91.24.
21. *Cv.*, 91.28-35.
22. *Cv.*,95.5.
23. P.E.Peiris, *Ceylon ; the Portuguese Era, Vol. I, pp. 373-391.*
24. *Cv.*,95.4-7.
25. *Cv.*, 93.3.
26. See, for the *Puññapotthakas* used by the author of the *Mahāvaṃsa, Mahāvaṃsa*, ed., W.Geiger, (PTS), London, 1908, 35.25 f.
27. *Cv.*, 92.24-30; cf. *Rajaratnākaraya*, p. 54 ff.

28. *Mädavala Vihāre Pinvattoruva;* the purpose of the document was to record the benefits the temple at Medavala received from Kīrti Srī Rājasinha. *Epigraphia Zeylanica,* Vol. V, No.48. p.65.

    *Moratota Dinapota;* the purpose of this document was to record the meritorious-deeds of the Elder Moratota Dhammakkhandha of Malvatu Vihāraya of Kandy, who was the Mahānāyaka of the Malvatta Chapter of the Siyam Nikāya. Ceylon Government Archives, Or. Ms. 125. (N).
29. C.E.Godakumbura, *Sinhalese Literature,* Colombo, 1955, p.127; see also H.W.Codrington, 'Some Documents of Vikramabāhu of Kandy', *JCBRAS* Vol. XXXII, No. 84, 1931, pp.64-75.
30. *Rājaratnākaraya,* ed. Simon de Silva, Colombo, 1930, p.1.
31. *Rjrt.,* p. 56ff.
32. C.E.Godakumbura, 'Historical writings in Sinhalese', *Historians of India, Pakistan and Ceylon.,* ed. C.H. Phillips, London, 1962, p.76.
33. *Ibid.* p.76.
34. *Rājāvaliya,* ed. B. Gunasekara, Colombo, 1953 (reprinted;tr. B. Gunasekara, Colombo. 1954, (reprinted)
35. *Rājāvaliya,* ed. Vatuvatte Pemananda, Colombo, 1945.
36. Alakeśvarayuddhaya, ed. A.V. Suraweera, Colombo, 1956.
37. Diego do Couto, *Da Asia, Dos fei tos que os Portuguez fizeram na conquistae descombimento das larrase mare do Oriente,* Decadas, IV-XII, 10 parts in 15 Volumes. Lisbon, 1778-1788; the parts concerning Sri Lanka were translated by Donald Ferguson in *JCBRAS,* XX, No. 60, 1908, p.56 ff; Valentijn.F. *Oud en niew Cost Indian, Amsterdam,Vol. 5, 1726. An English translation of Valentijn's account pertaining to Sri Lanka has been published in* *JCBRAS,* XXII, No. 65, p.36 ff. An abbriviated translation of Valentijn's account is given in A.M.Philatethess *History of Ceylon,* ch.III and IV London, 1817.
38. Edward Upham, *The Mahāvansī, the Rājaratnākarī* and *the Rājāvalī,* London, 1833. The published version of Gunasekara will be reffered to hereinafter in this study for the sake of convenience.
39. C.E.Godakumbure, *Historians of India, Pakistan and Ceylon,* p.76.
40. R.S.Hardy, Manual of Buddhism, London, 1880, p. 539; G. Turnour, *Epitome of History of Ceylon,* London, 1896, p.4; *UCHC.,* P.53.
41. *Rjv.,* p.48. and p.69.
42. *Rjv.* p.53.

43. C.E.Godakumbure, *Sinhalese Literature*, Colombo, 1955, p.129.
44. *Rjv.*, p.37.
45. Somaratna, *op.cit.* p. 35 ff.
46. *Rjv.*, p.47.
47. E.W.Perera, 'Age of Śrī Parākramabāhu VI, *JCBRAS*, XXII, No.63. 1912, p.12; H.C.P.Bell, *Report on the Kegalle District, Sessional papers*, Colombo, 1892, XXI, p.91.
48. *Vrittaratnākara-pañjikā*, ed. C.A. Seelakkhandha, Bombay, 1908, p.20; K.D.P. Wickramasingha *Koṭṭe Yugaye Siṁhala Sāhityaya*, Colombo, 1960, p.33 ff.
49. *Sdhrt.*, p. 24.
50. *Pärakumbā Sirita*, C.de. Silva, Kandy, 1957, v. 27.
51. Simon de Silva, 'Vijayabāhu VI', *JCBRAS*, XXII No. 65, 1912, pp. 312-318.
52. *Rjv.*, p.48.
53. *The History of Ceylon, from the Earliest times to 1000 A.D., as related by Joan de Barros and Diego Do Couto*, , tr. and edited by Donald Ferguson, JCBRAS, XX, No. 60. 1908, p.56 ff.
54. *Rjv.*, p. 57.
55. *Saddharmaratnākaraya*, ed. K. Nanavimala, Panadura, 1931.
56. *Sdhrt.*, p. 501.
57. *Sdhrt.*, p.72.
58. C.E.Godakumbure, *Sinhalese Literature*, p. 96.
59. *Sdhrt.*, p. 499 ff.
59.
60. *Nikāyasaṅgrahaya*, ed. D.P.R. Samaranayaka, Colombo, 1960; of .*Sdhrt.*, p. 253 ff.
61. JCBRAS., XXIV, No. 68, p.13; *UCHC.*, P. 664; Somaratna., *Political History of the Kingdom of Kōṭṭē*. p.94,
62. *Sbhrt.*, p.294; *UCHC.*, p.664.
63. *Sdhrt.*, p.71.
64. *Sdhrt.*, p. 296
65. *Vidyodaya.*, Vol. III, No. 8. 1931, p. 37 ff.
66. *Katikāvat Saṅgarā*, ed. D.B.Jayatilaka, Kelaniya, 1955, pp.40-43.
67. *Ceylon Antiquary and Literary Register*, Vol. II. part. I., p.42 f.
68. *Vidyodaya.*, Vol.III, No.8, p.238 ff; Vol.III, No.9, p.269 ff.
69. *Sdhrt.*, p.499 ff.
70. *Alutnuvara Dēvālē Karavīma*, Br.Mus. Ms. No. Or. 6606 (125)
71. D.B.Jayatilaka, *Siṁhala Sāhitya Lipi*, Kelaniya, 1959, (reprinted), pp. 70-71.
72. This work is not mentioned in the *Catalogue of Manuscripts in the Temple Libraries in Ceylon*, compiled by K.D.Somadasa, Colombo 1959.

73. H.W. Codrington, *A Short History of Ceylon*, Colombo, 1947 (reprinted) p.87.
74. A Liyanagamage, *The Decline of Polonnaruva and the Rise of Dambadeniya*, Colombo, 1968, p.29.
75. A.D.K., folio. kau(a).
76. Cf. *Rjv.*, p.50 ff.
77. *A.D.K.*, folio. ki (a)
78. *Nikāyasaṅgrahaya*, ed. D.P.R. Samaranayaka, Colombo, 1960.
79. *UCHC.*, P. 57.
80. *Nks.*, p.96.
81. *Sdhrt.*, p.500.
82. *Nks.*, p.96.
83. *Ibid*
84. *Mayura-sandeśaya*, ed. W.F.Gunawardhana, Colombo, 1938, introduction, p.4
85. P.B.Sannasgala, *Siṅhala Sandeśa Sāhityaya*, p.10 ff.
86. C.E.Godakumbure, *Sinhalese Literature*, p.189.
87. *Hamsa-sandeśaya*, ed. C.E.Godakumbure, Colombo, 1953, v.201 f.
88. The authorship and date of this poem have been discussed by Godakumbure in his edition of the text. See, *Hms.*, intr. p.XIV.
89. *Hms.* v.48 ff.
90. *Parevi-saneśaya*, ed. M. Kumaranatunga, Colombo, 1942, introduction, p.XIV and v.208; C.E.Godakumbure, *Sinhalese Literature*, p.191.
91. *Prs.*, v.203.
92. *Prs.*, v.201-202.
93. *Prs.*, v. 165 ff.
94. Sälaḷihiṇi-sandeśaya, K.D.P. Wickramasingha, Colombo, 1956, v. 109.
95. *Sls., vv.93-107.*
96. *Sls.*, vv.60-71.
97. *Girā-sandeśaya*, ed. M.Kumaratunga, Colombo, 1944, vv. 250-252.
98. *Grs.*, vv.250-252.
99. *Grs., introduction, p.4; P.B.Sannasgala, Sandeśa Sāhityaya*, p.24.
100. *Grs.*, v.40 ff; *UCHC.*, P.675.
101. *Grs.* vv. 126-156.
102. *Grs.*, v.69.
103. *Grs.* vv. 217-227.
104. See chapter five.
105. *Kokila-sandeśaya*, ed. H. H. Pannatissa, Colombo, 1945.
106. *Kks.*, v.291.
107. *Kks.*, v.268; *UCHC.*, p.675.
108. *Kks.*, v.44.

109. *Kks.*, v.101.
110. *Kks.*, v.118.
111. *Kks.*, v.185
112. *Kks.*, v.198.
113. *Sävul-sandeśaya*, ed. U Dhammasiri and S. Gamage, Delgoda, 1968.
114. P.B.Sannasgala, *Siṅhala Sāhitya Vaṃsaya*, Colombo, 1961, p.297.
115. *Svls.* v.122 and 170.
116. See chapter four.
117. *Vuttamālā-sandesa-sataka*, R.Batuvatudave, Colombo, 1923.
118. *Vss.*, v.103.
119. G.P.Malalasekara, *Pali Literature of Ceylon*, London, 1928, p.254; A.P.Buddhadatta, *Theravādī Bauddhācāryayō*, Colombo, 1960, p149.
120. *Tisara-sandeśaya*, ed D.B.Jayatilaka, 1935, v. 179 ff.
121. Sannasgala, *Siṅhala Sandeśa Sāhityaya*, p.13 f.
122. *Tss.*, v. 177 ff.
123. *Sdhrt.*, p.296; *Vidyodaya.*, Vol.I, No.8, p. 295; *Vṛttaratnākara-pañjikā*, p.13.
124. *Vas.* 31 ff.
125. *Vas.*, v.42 ff.
126. *Budugunālaṅkāraya*, ed. D.B.Jayatilaka Kelaniya, 1948.
127. *Kāvyaśekharaya*, ed. R.Sri. Dharmarama, Kelaniya, 1935.
128. *Guttila-Kāvyaya*, ed. D. Sumanajoti, Kelaniya, 1956. Sannasgala, *Siṅhala Sāhitya Vaṃsaya*, p.435.
129. *Guttila-kāvyaya*, v.16.
130. *Kuveṇi-asna.* p.7.
131. Sannasgala, *Siṅhala Sāhitya Vaṃsaya*, p. 249.
132. D.M.de.Z. Wickramasingha, *Catalogue of the Sinhalese Manuscripts and Printed Books in the British Museum*, London, 1901, vol. II, p.101.
133. *Padasādhana-tīkā*, ed. Srī Dharmarama, Kelaniya, 1937., vv. 1-7.
134. *Mandārampura-puvata*, ed. L.Lankananda, Panaduara, 1956.
135. *Epigraphia Zeylanica*, Vol.V.part III, p.113 f
136. P.E.E.Fernando, 'Development of the Sinhalese Script from the 18th century A.D. to the 15th century A.D.', *University of Ceylon Review* Vol.III, pp. 222-242.
137. The Päpiliyāna Inscription which bears the two documents refered to in this study as Päpiliyāna document I and Päpiliyāna document II, has been destroyed by the Portuguese, but their texts are available in palm leaf manuscripts. For the document I, see *Vidyodaya*, Vol. I, No. 6. 1931, pp. 295 ff and, Vol. I, No. 10, p.374ff; for the document

II, *Katikāvat Sañgarā*, pp.40-43 and *Vidyodaya*. Vol.I, Nos. 11,12, p.413 ff.

138. *EZ.*, I, p.85 ff.
139. *Kts.* p.7 ff.
140. The inscription of this *sannasa* has also been destroyed by the Portuguese, but the text is extant in palm leaves. See. *Ceylon Antiquary and Literary Register*, 1924, Vol. II, part. I. pp.42-49.
141. See chapter seven.
142. *Vidyodaya*, III, No.8, p.230 f. and No. 9. p.269 f.
143. *Jinakālamālī*, ed. A.P.Buddhadatta, (PTS), London, 1962.
144. The Sheaf of Garlands of the Epochs of the Conqueror, (Being a translation of Jinakālamālīpakaraṇam), translated by N.A. Jayawickrama, (PTS), London, 1968, introduction, p.XXIX. (referred to hereafter as *Epochs of the Conqueror*)
145. *Epochs of the Conqueror*, pp. XI-XIV.
146. *Jkm.*, p.86 ff.
147. S. Paranavitana, *Ceylon and Malaysia*, Colombo, 1966, p.54.
148. *Epigraphia Burmanica*, III, part.II, 1928, Rangoon, pp.76 ff.
149. *Indian Antiquary*, XXII, 1893 January, p.13 ff.
150. *Kalyaṇipakaraṇa, ed. Gintota Medhankara, Colombo, 1924.*
151. *IA*, XXII, p.13.
152. M.H.Bode, *The Pali Literature of Burma*, London, 1909, p.91.
153. *Sāsanavaṃsa*, ed. M.H.Bode (PTS), London, 1897.
154. *A Burmese Historian of Buddism*, Londoon, 1898
155. *B.C.Law, The History of the Buddha's Religion*, London, 1952.
156. *Sāsanavaṃsa-dīpikā*, ed. K. Saddhammavamsa, Colombo, 2474 B.E.
157. *Sāsanavaṃsa-padīpaya*, ed. A. Vimalasara, Colombo, 2473 B.E.
158. B.C.Law, *op.cit.* introduction, p.ix.
159. M.H.Bode, *op.cit.* p.51.

# Chapter Two

# Political Background

The capital of the Sinhalese kingdom during the period of this survey was *Kōṭṭē* (Jayavardhanapura) in the south-western part of Sri Lanka. This city was founded, during the fourteenth century, by Alakeśvara, a semi- independent ruler, who had shifted his residence there from Peradeṇiya in the Kandyan hills.[1] The *Cūlavaṃsa* gives a description of the building of Kōṭṭē by Alakeśvara.[2] According to Paranavitana, who traced the pedigree of the Alakeśvaras, this ruler, the greatest to bear that name, may be called Alakeśvara III.[3] The *Saddharmaratnākaraya* of Vimalakīrti, belonging to the first part of the fifteenth century, describes how Kōṭṭē was built by Alakeśavara III during the reign of Vikramabāhu III (1356-1374) of Gampola.[4] All the sources for the period are unanimous in recording the motive for the construction of this south- western stronghold of the Sinhalese. According to them, it was intended to be a fortress to oppose the threat of Aryacakravarti, the Tamil ruler of Jaffna.[5] It is also possible that it was built to protect Colombo which had become an important port by this time and had occasionally been controlled by Muslim traders.[6] The *Nikāyasaṅgrahaya* and the *Rājāvaliya* give considerable details of the building of *Kōṭṭē* and the military success achieved later by Alakeśvara III over the Tamil ruler.[7]

Apart from this, these accounts help us to study a significant feature of the political history of the country on the eve of the foundation of the Kōṭṭē kingdom, namely the Alakeśvaras coming to the forefront of the political scene, pushing the reigning monarch to the background. The Alakeśvaras in this manner practically ruled the Sinhalese kingdom for over half a century.[8]

The builder of the city of Kōṭṭē, Alakeśvara III, was the most powerful figure in Sri Lanka in the latter part of the fourteenth century though he was not crowned a king. As the *prabhurāja*[9] or the provincial ruler of Vikramabāhu III of Gampola he was able to inspire confidence in his people and check the aggressive Āryacakravarti. By fortifying Kōṭṭē and driving away the armies of the Āryacakravarti from the western seaboard towns of the Island he paved the way for a united Sri Lanka under an able Sinhalese king. This future unifier of Sri Lanka was Parākramabāhu VI who ascended the throne in 1415 A.D.

In studying the political events of this period the *Cūlavaṃsa* is of little value. It is for this reason that we have to use other sources, especially the *Saddharmaratnākaraya*. This work gives a brief but more precise account of the political events of the country before the accession of Parākramabāhu VI. According to the *Saddharmaratnākaraya*, Vikramabāhu III was succeeded by Bhuvanekabāhu V in Gampola. It states that by the fifteenth year of Bhuvanekabāhu V, one thousand nine hundred and fifteen (1915) years had elapsed after the passing away of the Buddha.[10] Therefore he must have ascended the throne in 1371-2 A.D. Bhuvanekabāhu's relationship to Vikramabāhu is not known. Wickramasinhe thinks that he was probably related to Senā Laṅkādhikāra the Great.[11] It is not unlikely that Bhuvanekabābu was associated in the government with Vikrambābu III in the last two years of the latter's reign, Alakeśvara being the real power in the country. The Vēgiriya Dēvālē inscription, dated 1415, gives details of dedications made by Bhuvanekabāhu V to the *dēvālaya* in his 20th, 34th and possibly 36th regnal years.[12] He would thus have ruled the country until at least 1407/8 A.D., even if only in name. Though he was the crowned king, the real political power of the country during this period was in the hands of the successors of Alakesvara III, first his son Kumāra Alakeśvara. Before long another Alakeśvara, named Vira Alakeśvara, the son of a sister of the great *prabhurāja* captured power. We have no information to ascertain how long Kumāra Alakeśvara remained in control of affairs, and in what manner he was put out of the way.

However immediately after there arose another Alakeśvara, named Vīrabābu Ādipāda, the younger brother of Vīra Alakeśvara, who made a bid for power. After an armed struggle between these two brothers, the younger gained the ascendancy.

According to the *Nikāyasaṅgrahaya,* in the 20th year of Bhuvanekabābu, Virabāhu Ādipāda became his co-regent,[13] though the former continued to hold the title of king for about fifteen years. During this time Vīrabāhu was faced with the task of countering the hostile schemes of the Tamils and Muslims, and also with opposition from his own brother, Vīra Alakeśvara, who fled to South India after his defeat.[14] He is praised in the *Nirkāyasaṅgrahaya* in the conventional language of the time, as having brought the three *Siṅhalas* under one umbrella, but it is very doubtful whether his writ-ran in the extreme north of the Island, which continued to be ruled by the Aryacakravarti dynasty. The last mentioned date of this ruler is 1939 B.R. (1396 A.D), the year in which a purification of the Sangha took place under his patronage.[15]

The *Saddharmaratnākaraya* records that Vīrabāhu Ādipāda was succeeded by his two sons Vijaya Āpā and Tunayesa.[16] Their authority over the Sinhalese was limited to three years. We are told by the chronicle that after this period Vīra Alakeśvara returned to the Island and seized power after spending nearly twenty years in South India. It has been observed by Somaratna that Vīra Alakeśvara was able to ensure the help of Vijayanagara kings in his struggle for political power.[17] This second period of Vīra Alakeśvara's rule continued for twelve years at the end of which, in the words of *Saddharmaratnākaraya,* 'he went away being caught in the Chinese strategem through his *karma* of a previous existence.[18] It is known from Chinese sources that the ruler of the country was taken captive to China early in 1411 A.D.[19] According to the *Pien-i-Tien,* the king of the Island during this time was A-lie-kou-nai-oul, who observed heretical practices and did not respect the sacred Tooth of the Buddha. He was cruel to his subjects and did not honour the law of the Buddha. When Cheng-ho, the Chinese Admiral, arrived in the country with pious offerings he made an attempt to persuade A-lie-kou-nai-eul to honour the teachings of the Buddha and give up heretical practices. The king felt irritated and seemed determined to use force against Cheng-ho. However, after a hard struggle, Cheng-ho succeeded in capturing the king, taking him captive to China.[20] The person mentioned as *A-lie-kou-nai-eul* in this work and *Ya-lieh-k'u-nai-elh* in the *Minh-Shih*, another Chinese source, can easily be identified as Vīra Alakeśvara of the *Saddharmaratnākaraya*, for the latter work mentions that it was he who had dealings with the Chinese.[21]

It has been assumed that the accusation made by the *Pien-i-tien* concerning Vīra Alakeśvara's attitude towards religion is perhaps based on facts.[22] As we noticed earlier, Vīra Alakeśvara was forced by his brother Vīrbāhu Ādipāda to leave the country. Vīrabāhu, if we are to give credence to the *Nikāyasaṅgrahaya* whose author received the patronage of that prince, was a great benefactor of Buddhism.[23] In fact, during Vīrabāhu's rule of more than eight years Vīra Alakeśvara lived exile in South India. The latter possibly adopted a policy opposed to that of his rival after he recaptured power in 1400 A.D. Paranavitana is of the opinion that the estimate of Vīra Alakeśvara's character, formed by the Chinese, was probably not unjust, for nowhere in Sinhalese writing does one find a good word said about him.[24] This may be partly due to the fact that Vīra Alakeśvara lost against the Chinese. Still, it is hard to understand that this was a sufficient reason for Cheng-ho to capture and take him as a prisoner to China. Although we do not possess sufficient evidence to be sure of the movements and motives of Cheng-ho in Sri Lanka, from the manner in which he treated the kings in South East Asia it can be assumed that the Admiral arrived in the Island in the hope of reopening seaborne trade, and of developing Chinese commercial contacts.[25] However, the misfortune that befell Vīra Alakeśvara marks the end of the supermacy of the Alakeśvaras established by the great *prabhuāja*, Alakeśvara III.[26]

The political instability and chaotic conditions of the country which had prevailed since the decline of the Daṁbadeniya dynasty in the latter part of the thirteenth century came to an end with the accession in 1415 A.D. of Parākramabāhu VI of

Kōṭṭē. According to our sources he was offered the throne because there was no king in the country after Vīra Alakeśvara had been taken captive to China.[27] His long reign (1415-1467) marked an important period not only in the political history of Sri Lanka but also in the cultural history of the Sinhalese. Politically it was the period in which for the last time till the present age the entire Island was brought under one sovereign Sinhalese power.

We have no information about the means adopted by Parākramabāhu VI to consolidate his power. The contemporary sources are silent on this point, and do not mention any event which took place during his reign before the suppression of the Vanni chieftaincies and the conquest of the Jaffna kingdom. On the other hand, we have a number of inscriptions issued by this ruler scattered in many parts of the Island, such as the *Beligala Sannasa* dated 1958 B. E.[28] There is an inscription found at Mahayyāva in Kandy, issued in the fourth regnal year of this monarch, and there are others among the fragmentary inscriptions at the Gaḍalādeṇiya temple, which seem to have been issued in his fifth regnal year.[29] The *Saddharmaratnākaraya* refers to some repairs undertaken by him in places such as Päpiliyāna, Gaḍalādeṇiya, Attanagalla and Mahiyangana.[30] We do not know whether the king extended his suzerainty over these territories by his own effort or inherited it from the last Alakeśvara. However, it is apparent that from his early years he held sway over most of the country excluding the Vanni areas and Jaffna kingdom, which he subsequently conquered.

Contemporary poems like the *Girā-sandeśaya* indicate that after a hard struggle he forced the Vanni chiefs to acknowledge his sovereignty.[31] The subjugation of these chiefs may have been necessary as a prerequisite to the expedition to Jaffna because they ruled in areas lying between the Sinhalese and Jaffna kingdom. After achieving this end, Parākramabāhu despatched an expedition against the Tamil ruler under the command of Prince Sapumal.[32] According to the *Rājāvaliya*, before the main expedition was undertaken, Prince Sapumal raided a number of villages in the vicinity of Jaffna, captured prisoners and brought them to Kōṭṭē.[33] Not very long after this, Sapumal conducted the final expedition which led to the capture of Jaffna. The *Rājāvaliya* states that the Āryacakravarti was killed in this expedition,[34] but all contemporary writings agree that he managed to escape to South India.[35] This victory made Prince Sapumal a national hero in the eyes of the Sinhelese, though he himself was not Sinhalese. The feeling of exultation and rejoicing among them is echoed in the poems like the *Säḷalihiṇi-sandeśaya* and *Kōkila-sandeśaya.*[36] According to the *Säḷalihiṇi-sandeśaya,* the subjugation of the Jaffna kingdom took place in the 33th regnal year of Parākramabāhu VI.[37] This conquest of the Jaffna kingdom led to the unification of the Island under a Sinhalese ruler for the last time in the history of Sri Lanka.

Apart from a short lived rebellion led by Jōtiya Siṭu in the Kandyan provinces,[38] the long reign of Parākramabāhu VI appears to have been free from internal disturbances, and thus created a favourable atmosphere for a revival of Sinhalese culture. Parākramabāhu VI was undoubtedly one of the greatest kings of Sri Lanka and, for the last time since Parākramabāhu the Great and Nissaṅkamalla, in the latter part of his reign Sinhalese sovereignty was acknowledged throughout the Island.

The death of Parākramabāhu VI in 1467 A.D. left the country again in a state of insecurity. At his death his daughter Ulakuḍaya-dēvi's son for whose accession he had cleared the path, ascended the throne at Kōṭṭē as Jayabāhu II. Hardly had he ruled for two years when Prince Sapumal, the Commander in Chief at Jaffna, marched to Kōṭṭē, killed Jayabāhu, and had himself consecrated as king of Sri Lanka under the name of Bhuvanekabāhu VI. The conflicts and chaos that arose in the country at the death of Parākramabāhu VI can be seen from the account given in the *Rājāvaliya.*[39] The accession to the throne by Jayabāhu and subsequently by Bhuvanekabāhu is mentioned very briefly at one place in the *Cūlavaṃsa.*[40]

The murder of Jayabāhu II, the grandson of Parākramabāhu VI, seems to have aroused considerable resentment among the subjects. The Dädigama inscription amply reflects the general opposition Bhuvanekabāhu VI had to face in a number of provinces for many years.[41] The rebellion in the provinces from the Kalu- *gañga* up to the Valavē-gañga[42] was generally known as the *Sinhala- sange* or *Sinhala-peraliya*[43] (the revolt of the Sinhalese subjects against the king, who may have been of Tamil (South Indian?) origin. When Prince Ambulugala, the younger brother of the king, was sent to suppress the revolt in the provinces, the four Kōralēs[44] over which he ruled also rose in revolt. This uprising was suppressed by the king himself but he seems to have been unable to prevent the secession of Uḍaraṭa from the Kōṭṭē kingdom. The affairs of Uḍaraṭa referred to in the Dädigama inscription were the secession of that territory from the sovereignty of Kōṭṭē under a prince who proclaimed his independence and assumed the title Sēnāsammata Vikramabāhu.[45] This event marks the beginning of the Kandyan kingdom.

Furthermore, the Dädigama inscription gives clear indications not only of the widespread opposition that the Sinhalese showed to the rule of Bhuvanekabāhu VI but also of the disappearance of the peace and prosperity that had prevailed during the reign of Parākramabāhu VI.

Bhuvanekabāhu seems to have considered himself a son and legitimate heir of Parākramabāhu VI, for in the Dädigama inscription he calls himself 'Śrī Parākramab-āhu-mah-ārājād-hirāja-nandana' (the son of Śrī Parākramab- āhu-mahā- rājā-dhirājā-nandana' (the son of Śrī Parākramab?hu, the great emperor).[46] Further, he reckoned his reign from the death of Parākramabāhu, for this inscription is dated in the eighth year of his reign, whereas the *Cūlavaṃsa* and the *Rājāvaliya* ascribe to him only a reign of seven years, assigning two years to the reign of Jayabāhu II.[47]

In spite of these troubles in the Sinhalese areas, Bhuvanekabāhu VI appears to have kept the allegiance of Jaffna after he became king of Kōṭṭē.[48] However, it seems that at the close of his reign this part of the Island again became independent.[49] Thus the unity of Sri Lanka achieved during the reign of Parākramabāhu VI ended within a few decades of that monarch's death and, at the close of the reign of Bhuvanekabāhu VI, there were three independent kingdoms in the Island though the ruler of Kōṭṭē claimed the overlordship of three *siṅhalas* in his official documents.

Bhuvanekabāhu VII,[50] who did not rule long, being slain by his uncle, Prince Ambulugala, the younger brother of Bhuvanekabāhu VI, who claimed the throne for himself and ascended it as Vīra Parākramabāhu VIII. Couto gives him a reign of only three years,[51] According to the *Rājāvaliya*, however, he reigned for twenty years.[52] Vīra Parākramabāhu had constant trouble with his relatives; internal dissension was the besetting sin of the dynasty which ultimately led to its downfall. During this ruler's reign the Island was for the first time visited by the Portuguese in 1505.[53] The impression made on the people of Colombo by their appearance is dramatically recorded in the *Rājāvaliya*.[54]

Vīra Parākramabāhu was succeeded by his son Dharma Parākramabāhu IX in 1509.[55] Except with regard to his relations with the Portuguese, this king is of little importance. He was succeeded by his brother Vijayabāhu VI in 1513 A.D. From several of Vijayabāhu's inscriptions we know that he was already king of Kōṭṭē in 1518 A.D., contrary to the claim of Queyroz who writes that at that time the ruling monarch was Paṇḍita Parākramabāhu, and that he was poisoned by Vijayabāhu.[56] Paranavitana has demonstrated that this particular part of the work of Queyroz is erroneous.[57]

Vijayabāhu VI, instigated by the Muslims who were known as 'Moors' and helped by the Samorin of Calicut, the suzerain of Malabar, then at war with the Portuguese, attacked the Portuguese fort of Colombo, which had been built shortly before.[58] The Sinhalese and their allies were beaten off, and the king's long struggle to expel the Portuguese proved unsuccessful. Having lost his prestige in the ensuing war, he ultimately lost his thorne and life in the 'Vijayabā Kollaya' (the sacking of Kōṭṭē and assasination of Vijayabāhu) in 1521. This happened, according to the *Rājāvaliya*, because he intended to disinherit his own sons in favour of a young prince whom he had adopted.[59] The revolt which caused the death of the king was led by his own sons: Bhuvanekabāhu, Rayigam Baṇḍāra and Māyādunne. After the death of the king, the kingdom of

Kōṭṭē was divided among the three brothers. The eldest, Bhuvanekabāhu, was given the administration of the seaports and the conduct of foreign trade. The prestige and the power held by the previous kings of Kōṭṭē were vested in him. The next prince, Rayigam Banḍāra, received the Valallāvity, Pasdun and Rayigam Kōrales in the Galle and Kalutara districts. The youngest prince, Māyādunne, established his seat at the city of Sītāvaka. He obtained the territory now comprising the Provinces of Sabaragamuva which included Sītāvaka, Denavaka and Satara Kōralēs. Thus, practically, there came to exist five kingdoms in Sri Lanka including the Jaffna and Kandyan kingdoms although the nominal suzerainty of the country was vested in the king of Kōṭṭē.[58]

Bhuvanekabāhu VII did not reign in peace because of the aspirations of his youngest brother, the ruler of Sītāvaka, to the throne of Kōṭṭē and the overlordship of the Island. In the year following 1526 an almost continuous conflict was waged between the two brothers. During this period of struggle Māyādunne was aided by the Portuguese in Colombo.[59] In 1539, however, Māyādunne was forced to conclude peace, which lasted until 1547.

This long struggle between the two brothers provided an opportunity for the Portuguese to interfere in the political affairs of the country. With the object of making his position more and more secure against Māyādunne, Bhavanekabāhu sent an embassy to Lisbon in 1540 with a golden image of his grandson Dharmapāla, requesting that the prince should be installed by the king of Portugal as the heir-apparent of the kingdom of Kōṭṭē. This unprecedented request shows that Bhavenekabāhu VII openly held himself out as the Vassal of Dom João III of Portugal.[60]

The two brothers were again at war in 1548, the Portugese now favouring Māyādunne. This policy of the Portuguese did not last. In 1550 Kōṭṭē forces took Sītāvaka with the help of the Portuguese. In November of that year the new Viceroy of Goa, Dom Affonco de Noronnha, on his way to Goa, arrived in Colombo, having been driven off course by adverse winds. He did not trust the good faith of the king, and before leaving

Sri Lanka directed the king and his brother, Māyādunne, to keep peace, and to send envoys to Goa.[61] But in the middle of 1551 the king was shot while looking out of a window in his palace at Kelaniya. This sudden death of Bhuvanekabāhu VII brought about a profound change in the relations between the Portuguese and Kōṭṭē.

The youthful Dharmapāla had been proclaimed king of Kōṭṭē immediately after the death of his grandfather, Bhuvanekabāhu VII. He was but a puppet in the hands of the Portuguese. The hostility of Māyādune and his son Rājasinha I of Sītavaka led the new king to be more and more dependent on foreign help. In 1557 Dharmapāla was baptised under the name of Dom Joao Periya Banḍāra, while his queen, who was baptised at the same time, took the name of Dona Catherina, after the queen of Portugal.[62] This was followed by the conversion of many of Dharmapāla's courtiers.[63] The king's enthusiasm for his new faith was confirmed by a *sannasa*, 'grant', by which he offered the Daḷaḍā Māligāva, the Tooth Relic temple of Kōṭṭē, the two great shrines at Kelaṇiya, and all the temple revenues in the Island for the maintenance of the Colleges which the Catholic missionaries proposed to found in Sri Lanka.[64]

Dharmapāla could not rule long at Kōṭṭē, which was constantly attacked by the Sītāvaka kings. After a heavy struggle in 1564, Dharmapāla and his protectors decided that the continued maintenance of Kōṭṭe was detrimental to them. Consequently, in July 1565, to the distress of the Sinhalese of the Kōṭṭē kingdom, this capital was abandoned.[65] In 1580, Dharmapāla bequethed his kingdom to the king of Portugal.[66] In the later years of his reign Dharmapala came to such a pitiful condition under the power of the Portuguese that he had to make constant appeals to King Philip of Portugal to safeguard the dignity of his person.[67] King Philip commanded his Viceroy in Goa that Dharmapāla should be treated with every consideration. With all his appeals and orders from the king of Portugal, Dharmapāla could not regain his royal prestige, and died in 1597. This was the end of the Sinhalese kingdom in the south- western part of Sri Lanka and the introduction of Portuguese rule over that area.[68]

As has already been mentioned the kingdom of Sītāvaka came into existence as a result of the division of Kōṭṭē in 1521. Although it played a prominent part in the history of the country in the sixteenth century, Sītāvaka was never regarded as an independent kingdom. None of our sources refers to the coronation of the Sītāvaka kings as independent rulers, although they mention them as *rajas* or kings.[69] For the entire period of its existence it was considered a principality of the Kōṭṭē kingdom. This is proved by the fact that the grant of Dharmapāla, by which he transferred the kingdom to the king of Portugal in 1580, included Sītāvaka, even though the ruler of that kingdom, Rājasiṁha I, was alive.[70]

Form the very beginning the history of Sītāvaka is marked by constant warfare with either Kōṭṭē or Uḍaraṭa. Māyādunne, the first ruler of Sītāvaka, expanded his authority over the Rayigama principality in 1536 after the death of its ruler, Rayigam Banḍāra.[71] In 1539, he waged war against his suzerain, Bhuvanekabāhu VII, but suffered a heavy defeat, which forced him to surrender to the king all he had annexed and conquered, and to pay a heavy war indemnity, while pledging never again to take up arms against his suzerain.[72] After the death of Bhuvanekabāhu VII in 1551, Māyādunne again tried to conquer the Kōṭṭē kingdom, but this attempt was suppressed with the aid of the Portuguese. However, the conversion in 1557 of Dharmapāla strengthened the cause of Māyādunne. The *Rājāvaliya* states that on the eve of the conversion of Dharmapāla, Buddhist monks of the Kōṭṭē kingdom fled to Sītāvāka and to Kandy.[73] Eventually there was a great uprising of the people, which enabled Māyādunne to enlist great support for himself. The abandonment in 1565 of Kōṭṭē was a triumph for Māyāḍunne who now became the acknowledged sovereign of the lowlands. He was the master of Sītāvaka and of the territories of Kōṭṭē, Rayigama, Denavaka, and the Four and Seven Kōralēs; in fact of everything except Colombo. Neverthless, with all his efforts to oust Dharmapāla and expel the Portuguese from the country, Māyādunne never achieved a lasting success.

Māyādunne was succeeded by his son Rājasiṁha I, a great warrior. Continuing the policies of his father, Rājasiṁha turned his attention to Kandy in about 1580, and succeeded in conquering that kingdom, annexing it, after which he expelled the royal family.[74] He thus became master of all Sri Lanka except the North and the area dominated by the Portuguese. From his accession to his death in 1593, Rājasiṁha I was involved in a constant struggle with the Portuguese in Colombo, but never succeeded in expelling them. Rājasiṁha I was a great warrior, and was unfavourably regarded by the Portuguese for his persistent hostility towards them, and by the Buddhists for his rejection of their faith and his adoption of Hinduism. After his death in 1593, the Sītāvaka kingdom ceased to exist, and without a rightful heir it passed into Dharmapāla's hands.

Under Parākramabāhu VI (1415-1467) the Kandyan provinces were under the control of a prince of Gampola who acted as a viceroy.[75] In the 52nd regnal year of the king, a provincial ruler named Jotiya Siṭu, paying nominal allegiance to the Gampola prince, revolted and ceased to pay annual tributes to Kōṭṭē.[76] The king dispatched prince Ambulugala with the task of subduing Jotiya Siṭu. The Prince entered Uḍaraṭa with a powerful force, gained victory over the rebels, captured a number of relatives of Jotiya Siṭu and brought them as prisoners to Kōṭṭē, after having placed the government of Uḍaraṭa in the hands of the prince of Gampola. Jotiya Siṭu himself seems to have escaped, for the words used in the panegyric are that 'he fled in fear to the confines of the other *cakravāṭa*.'[77] As has been stated above, during the reign of Bhuvanekabāhu VI (1470-1478) there was a widespread rebellion in the kingdom. Taking advantage of this rebellion in the kingdom, Prince Vikramabāhu, then at Gampoln, again raised a revolt in the highlands in 1473, and succeeded in establishing himself as an independent ruler there.[78]

The two rebellions of Jotiya Siṭu and Vikramabāhu illustrate the ambition of these rulers to establish a separate and independent kingdom in the Kandyan hills in the fifteenth century.

Vikramabāhu came to be known as Vikramabāhu *cakravarti*.[79] He is probably identical with the king named Vīravikrama referred to in the *Cūlavaṃsa*[80] The *Rājaratnākaraya* gives a long account of his benefactions towards the Sangha.[81]

Although the kingdom of Vikramabāhu originally consisted of the *kanda-uḍa-pas-raṭa*, 'the five districts in the hills', [82] he utilised the existing political confusion in Kōṭṭē to bring the Vanniyārs of Batticalao, Trincomalee, Vellassa and Pānama under his rule, and also extended his authority over the prince of the Seven Kōralēs.[83]

Vikramabāhu was succeeded by his son Jayavīra Astāna, who also took the name of Vikramabāhu.[84] During his reign several attempts were made by Bhuvanekabāhu VII (1521-1551) of Kōṭṭē and Māyādunne of Sītāvaka to bring the Kandyan kingdom under their influence. Because of these threats Jayavīra turned to the Portuguese for help so as to defend his sovereignty. On one of these occasions Bhuvanekabāhu VII and Māyādunne directed a combined attack on the Kandyan kingdom. Though Jayavīra appealed to the Portuguese for help, his appeal proved unsuccessful as the reply of the Portuguese fell into the hands of the Kōṭṭē king.[85] The low-country rulers took over the passes giving access to Uḍaraṭa and prepared for an offensive. Jayavīra with his governors again appealed for Portuguese help, even promising to become converts to Christianity. Neverthless, in 1546, before Jayavīra could obtain help, Bhuvanekabāhu VII and Māyādunne succeeded in obtaining a large indemnity from him.[86] In 1547, Bhuvanekabāhu VII compelled Jayavīra to come to terms with him and to marry his daughter to his grandson, Dharmapāla. In these circumstances Jayavīra refused to become a Christian and to accept Portuguese help.[87]

Jayavīra died in 1549, and was succeeded by his son Karalliyadde Banḍāra. Rājasiṅha I of Sītāvaka, pursuig his father's ambition, aimed at the annexation of the Kandyan kingdom. In this he received assistance from Vīrasundra Mudaliyār of Perādeniya, who turned against his ruler Karalliyadde. This help enabled him to fulfil the life-long ambition of his father by annexing the Kandyan kingdom.

Karalliyadde, expelled from Kandy, took refuge with the Portuguese at Trincomalee.[88]

Elated by his success in Kandy in 1587-88 Rājasiṁha laid the greatest of his sieges to Çolombo. The Portuguese realized during this siege how difficult it was to take the full force of Rājasiṁha's attack on Colombo alone. It was therefore thought that a second front might divert a part of his forces and thus reduce the pressure on the city. The presence of the heirs of the king of Kandy with the Portuguese in Manner suggested that the division might take the form of an attack on Kandy on behalf of the heirs of the late king. When it was known that Rājasiṁha was planning another attack on Colombo, it was decided to launch the project. An expeditionary force entered Kandy from Mannar and put Don Philip Yamasiṁha Baṇḍāra, the nephew of the late king, on the throne. The new king, however, died soon after, and the Sinhalese Commander in Chief, Konappu Baṇḍāra, who had accompanied the Portuguese force from Goa[89] seized power, drove out the Portuguese force and ascended the throne under the name of Vimaladharmasuriya I. With his accession, Kandy got not only a new dynastic line, but also a new role in the history of Sri Lanka.

## References

1. *Cv.*, 91.2 f.
2. *Cv.* 91.5-7-
3. *UCHC.*, p.654.
4. *Sdhrt.*, p.292.
5. *Nks.*, p.34; *Sdhrt.*, p.294; *Rjv.*, p.47.
6. S.F.de Silva, 'The Historical Geography of Some of the Capital Cities of Ceylon', *Ceylon Historical Journal*, I, July 1951, No. I, p.20.
7. *Nks.*, p.34 f; *Rjv.*, p.94.
8. Somaratna, *Political History of the Kingdom of Kotte*, p.94.
9. The title *prabhurāja* has the same connotation as *patirāja* which denoted a member of the feudal nobility, but seems to have

taken at this time and later as a designation indicating the unique position in the state occupied by Alakeśvara III. No one after him assumed the title. See, 'UCHC., p.735.

10. *Sdhrt.*,p.297.
11. EZ III, p.33.
12. *JCBRAS* XXII, No. 65, 1912, p.366.
13. *Nks.*, p.94.
14. *Sdhrt.*, p.294.
15. *Nks.*, p.95.; *Ṣdhrt.*, p294.
16. *Sdhrt, p.294.*
17. Somaratna, *Political History of the Kingdom of Koṭṭē*, p. 113.
18. *Sdhrt.*, p.294.
19. *JCBRAS*, XXIV, No. 68,1914, pp.96-102; J.E.Tennent, *Ceylon*, I, pp. 622-626; *UCHC* p.665.
20. *JCBRAS.*, XXIV, No.68, 1914, pp. 98-119.
21. *Sdhrt.*, p. 317; *JCBRAS*, XXIV, No. 68, 1914, pp. 119-120.
22. *JCBRAS*, XXIV, No 68., p98; Se-yih-ke-choo quoted in Tennent, *Ceylon*, I, p.622; S. Beal, *Buddhist Records of the Western World*, II, pp. 294 and 282; *UCHC*, P.651; C.W.Nicholas and S.Paranavitana, *A Concise History of Ceylon*, Colombo, 1962, p.303.
23. *Nks.*, p.94.
24. *UCHC.*, P.651; *Sdhrt.* p.317.
25. D.G.E. HALL, *A History of South-East Asia*, New York, 1970, (third edition), p. 201; J.F. Cady, *South-East Asia*, New York, 1964, p.155.
26. *UCHC.*, p.665.
27. *Rjv.*, p.47; *JCBRAS*, XX, No. 60, 1907, p.62. n.3.
28. *Rkd.*, p.94.
29. *Ceylon Journal of Science*, Section G., II 1957, p.195.
30. *Sdhrt.*, 296.
31. *Grs.* vv.137-138.
32. *Grs.*, v.136.
33. *Rjv.*, p.49
34. *Rjv.*p.49
35. *Grs., v.188 ff* ; *Kks.*, vv. 8. and 263.
36. *Sls*, v. 29; *Kks.* vv.8.and 81.
37. *Sls.*, v. 29.
38. *Rjv.*,p.49.
39. *Rjv.*, pp.49-50.
40. *Cv.*, 92.1.1

41. *EZ.*, III, p.278 f.
42. This province, known as Mātara Disāva, was the populous and the richest of all the provinces that directly ruled by the kings of Koṭṭē.
43. *R;v.*, p.49.
44. The four *korales*, known as Hatara Koralē Disāva, lay to the north-east of Colombo and terminated in the foothils of the Kandyan plateau.
45. *UCHC.*, p.680.
46. EZ., p.278
47. *Cv.* 92.2; *Rjv.*, p49.
48. *UCHC.*, p.682.
49. S.Pathmanathan, *Kingdom of Jaffna.*
50. *Cv.*, 92.2; *Rjv.*, p.49.
51. Couto records that Pandita Parākramabāhu was "not crowned more than four times' which means that his reign was confined to four years. See, *'JCBRAS'*, XX, No.60, p.70.
52. *Rjv.*, p.49.
53. *SHC.*, P.94; *UCR.*, XIX, P.18.
54. *Rjv.*, p.51.
55. Fernão Queroz, *The Temporal and Spiritual Conquest of Ceylon*, 5 books, Tr. and ed. S.G. Perera, 1930, Colombo, p.6.
56. *Queroz.*, p.5.
57. S. Paranavitana, 'The Emperor of Ceylon at the time of the Arrival of the Portuguese in 1505.' *UCR*, XIX, 1961, p.16.
58. *SHC.*, p.96.
59. *Ibid.*, p.96.
60. *CPE.*, P.113.
61. *ibid.*.p.113.
62. P.E.Peiris-M.AEitzler, *Ceylon and Portugal*, Leipzirg, 1927, Vol. I, p.3.
63. *Rjv.*, p.58; P.E.Peiris, *Ceylon and the Portuguese*, Colombo, 1935, p.77.
64. *Queroz.*, p.330.
65. Peiris, *Ceylon and the Portuguese, p.135; see also, Rjv.*, p.65.
66. *Queroz.*, p. 140.
67. Peiris, *Ceylon and the Portuguese*, p. 135.
68. After the death of Dharmapāla, the kingdom of Koṭṭē with all its assets passed to Philip I, king Portugal by vitue of a deed of gift. This donation, first made in 1580 to Dom Henrique, was renewed and ratified in 1583, after the death of that

monarch, in favour of Philip and his successors. It is stated in this deed that the kingdom of Koṭṭē consisted of the kingdoms known as Koṭṭē, Sītāvaka, Raigama.. Kanda Uḍaraṭa and of the provinces of the Four and Seven Korales, Mātara, Denavaka, Velevara, Kosgama, Pālugama, Batticaloa, Kottiyar, Trincomalee and Puttalam See. *Queroz*, p.428.

69. *Rjv.*, p. 55 ff.
70. *Queyroz.*, p.428.
71. *Rjv.*, p.56; *CPE.*, I, p.234.
72. *CPE* p. 234.
73. *Rjv.*, p.58.
74. *Rjv.*, p.65.; *CPE.*, I, p. 245.
75. *Rjv.*, p.49.; *Pärakumbā-sirita*, v.48.
76. *Rjv.*, p.49.
77. *Pärakumbā-sirita*, v.48.
78. *EZ.*, IV, p.276.
79. H.W. Codrington, 'Some Documents of Vikramabāhu of Kandy' *JCBRAS*, XXXII, No.84, 1931, p.67.
80. *Cv.*, 92.,
81. *Rjrt.* p.47.
82. The central highlands of the Island, which were usually known as *udarata* in the medieval Sinhalese writings are sometimes denoted as *kanda-uda-pas-kaṭṭuva* (the confederation of the five provinces of the hill country), *kanda-uḍa-pas-kaṭṭuva pas-raṭa* (the five districts in the hills) or simply as *kanda-uḍaraṭa* (the country on the mountains). *EZ.* IV, p.226. The usual *pas-raṭa* are reckoned as *Udunuvara, Yaṭinuvara, Dumbara, Hevāhäṭa* and *Hārispattuva*. See, C.R.de Silva, *Cylon Under the British Occupation*, Colombo 1945, p.293.
83. *EZ.*, IV, p. 268.
84. *EZ.*, IV, p.270.
85. *CPE.*, I, p.267.
86. *Ibid.*
87. Peiris, *Ceylon and Portugal*, I, p.5.
88. *CPE.*, p.267.
89. Konappu Bandāra was the son of Vīrasundara Mudali of Peradeniya, who had helped Rajāsiṅha I in his annexation of Kandy, but was killed afterwards by treachery on Rājasiṅha's instigation. Konappu thereupon fled to the Portuguese in Colombo. He was banished to Goa for some offence commited while in Colombo. At Goa, he aquired a reputation for skill in the use of arms, and was known as Dom Joao of Austria,

after the brilliant illegitimate brother of King Philip IIof Spain who had sixteen years before destroyed the naval strenght of the Turks at Lepanto.

90. See, *Rjv.*, pp. 64-65; *Mandārampura puvata,* vv. 65-72; J.H.O. Paulusz, 'Some Sinhalese Royal Families' *CBRAS.*, XX, 1952, PP.21-30.

# Chapter Three

# The Sangha

As a result of the unification of the Sangha in the twelfth century and the subsequent 'purifications' of the Sangha in the Daṁbadeni period sectarian differneces were no longer recognized. Hence during the period of this study all members of the Sangha in the Island claimed to be the spiritual heirs of the Mahāvihāra of Anurādhapura.[1] The author of the *Saddharmaratnākaraya* while mentioning this fact requests the rulers of the country to do their utmost to afford requisites for the maintenance of the purity and prestige of this *theriya-nikāya* tradition of the Mahāvihāra.[2] However, the Sangha of this period had certain differences based on fraternities *(vāsas)*, institutions *(āyatanas)* and lineages *(paramparās)*. The following discussion is an attempt to trace these differences as far as our sources warrant.

At the end of the Anurādhapura period the three *nikāyas* of the Sangha, i.e. Mahāvihāra, Abhayagiri and Jetavana,[3] suffered a general decline. This situation prompted Vijayabāhu I (1070-1110) to invite Buddhist monks from Rāmaññadesa in order to restore the higher ordination.[4] But before long sectarian differences developed to such an extent that Parākramabāhu I (1153- 1186) was compelled to take steps to unify the Sangha, and to have disciplinary rules laid down for the monks.[5] He was assisted in this task by Diṁbulāgala Mahā Kāśyapa, a leading hierarch of the time. These new measures put an end to the division of the Sangha into *nikāyas*. Although the Sangha was united into a single body other differences among its members, particularly in the stress laid on certain aspects of their spiritual life and training, gradually brought about other divisions. By this time we hear of two fraternities of the Sangha, namely the Vanavāsa (Forest-dwelling Fraternity) and Gāmavāsa (Village-dwelling Fraternity).[6]

The origin and the gradual development of the two Fraternities up to the end of the fourteenth century have been discussed by Dhammavisuddhi.[7] Hence, the present discussion concerns mainly the activities and monastic life of these two Fraternities during the period under review.

## *The Vanavāsi Fraternity*

There was a general tendency that the Vanavāsi Fraternity established their residential quarters mainly in the forests and engaged themselves in meditation.[8] But this did not lead them to spend a life altogether cut off from the centres of population. This is evident from the fact that they always had to change their headquarters whenever the capital was transferred. Thus the centre at Diṁbulāgala of the Vanavāsi Fraternity in the Polonnaru period had been shifted to Palābatgala[9] with the rise of Daṁbadeniya as the capital of the Sinhalese kingdom. Throughout the thirteenth and fourteenth centuries, it appears that Palābatgala retained its position as the centre of the Vanavāsi Fraternity. But with the gradual drift of the greater part of the Sinhalese population towards the south- western plain of the country, and the abandoning of ancient capitals and founding of new ones, the centre of the Vanavāsa was moved to those areas. Nevertheless, even in the fifteenth century the monks of the Vanavāsi Fraternity perpetuated the memory of Palābatgala as their centre in the early medieval period.[10]

In the fifteenth century the Vanavāsi Fraternity had their headquarters at Kāragala in the Western Province of the Island. This village was about 30 miles north of Kōṭṭē, the capital during the fifteenth and sixteenth centuries. The *Haṃsa-sandeśaya* gives an account of the educational establishment attached to the monastery at Kāragala the head of which was Vanaratana *mahāsāmi.*[11] Besides Kāragala, the Vanavāsi monastery at Vattala achieved its fame on account of its former incumbent Nāgasena *mahāthera,*[12] said to have lived in the Daṁbadeni period.[13] It shows that this monastery can be dated back to the thirteenth century. However, neither the

*Hamsa- sandeśaya* nor the Kāragala inscription, which refer to this place as the residence of Nāgasena, gives information about its contemporary incumbent or its significance. It can be conjectured that owing to the rise of Kāragala the monastery at Vattala may have lost most of its importance.

The next residence of the Vanavāsi Fraternity was at Bentota in the Southern Province of the country. This institution has been mentioned in a number of literary works of this period.[14] Even though our sources do not allow us to identify the contemporary incumbent of this monastery they mention it as a flourishing centre of the Vanavāsa Fraternity.

A brief account of life in the Kāragala monastery is given in the *Hamsa-sandeśaya,* the author of which appears to have been a monk who had a great admiration for Vanaratana *mahāsāmi* of Kāragala. [15] According to this account the monastic life of the establishment seems to have been well regulated. Exemplary conduct in accordance with the *vinaya* was the primary concern of the monks who dwelt there. [16] Furthermore, they consistently developed the *vipassanādhura,* 'life devoted to true insight'. It has been formulated in the *Dambadeni Katikāvata* that the primary concern of the Vanavāsi monk should be the *Vipassanādhura.* [17] The emphasise given to the *Vipassanādhura* by the Vanavāsi Fraternity can be seen from certain references in the *Saddharmaratnākaraya* of Vimalakīrti, who was the famous scholar of that Fraternity in this period. In dealing with the disappearance of the five-fold constituents of Buddhism (*pañnca-antardhāna)* Vimalakīrti requests all beings to meditate on the impermanence of life while the teachings of the Buddha still shine.[18] After giving a description of the wealth of a *cakravarti,* Vimalakīrti admonishes devotees to develop good thoughts, one of the means of achieving *bhāvanā* (meditation), in order that they may themselves gain similar wealth in after-life.[19]

However, the attention paid to *vipassanādhura* by the monks of the Vanavāsi Fraternity did not prevent them from being engaged in learning and literary activities. There were monks of the Vaṇavāsi Fraternity who earned fame more as scholars than as monks devoted to meditation. For instance, it may be cited that the monks of the lineage of Dharmakīrti of

Palābatgala, to which Vimalakīrti himself belonged, are reputed as scholarly monks who made learned contributions to the literature of the country.[20] An account of the scholars of the lineage of Dharmakīrti and their contributions is given in the colophon of the *Saddharmaratnākaraya.*[21]

It has been suggested by some writers on this period that the literary works of the monks of the Vanavāsi Fraternity were almost always confined to doctrinal compendia or *dhammasaṅgaha.*[22] They further point out that the monks of the Vanavāsa never engaged themselves in learning or producing books on secular arts and sciences such as poetics, drama and astrology.[23] But a close examination of the literary works of the monks of this Fraternity in this period furnishes evidence to show that this was not so. The author of the *Haṃsa-sandeśaya,* who eulogised Vanaratana *mahāsāmi* of Kāragala, shows his ability on these secular subjects not second to his counterparts in the Gāmavāsa.[24] He never failed to follow the Sanskrit *kāvyālaṅkāra* so as to produce a standard *sandeśa* poem.[25] In his poem the author extols the Elder Vanaratana as a monk well versed in secular subjects such as poetics, drama and astrology.[26] In his account of the Kāragala Padmāvati Pirivena the author writes that some student- monks of the institution learnt secular subjects including poetics and drama (*kav- nalusatara*) in addition to religion.[27] A detailed account of the curriculum of this institution will be given later.[28] It is evident from these references that the monks of the Vanavāsi Fraternity in this period not only learnt secular subjects but also produced books on them.

It has also been suggested that monks of the Vanavāsi Fraternity rejected both Mahāyānic and popular beliefs while their counterparts in the Gāmavāsa freely adopted them.[29] This is again a supposition that does not seem to receive much support from facts. As has already been shown the *Saddharmaratnākaraya,* the sole prose work on the Dhamma in the fifteenth century, was composed by Dhammadinna Vimalakīrti, a high dignitary of the Vanavāsi Fraternity. This work refers to the Buddha as having a fourfold body : *rūpa-kāya, dharma-kāya, nimitta-kāya,* and *śūnya-kāya.*[30] The author proceeds to explain these terms. *Rūpa-kāya* is said to be the human form of the Buddha which could be seen by all persons having the faculty of sight. From the description of the *dharma- kāya* as given in the text it can be conjectured that the reference is to the inner enlightened body or Dhamma of the Buddha. *Nimitta-kāya* is explained as the state of *sopadhiśesa-nirvāṇadhātu, nirvāṇa* with corporeal residue, which is visible only to the clairvoyant. Śūnya-kāya is described as his state in *anupadhiśesa-nirvānadhātu i.e. the bliss of nirvāna* without any corporeal residue.[31]

The doctrine of the three bodies of the Buddha is a Mahāyānistic one. The early Mahāyanists, whose doctrines are mostly to be found in the *Aṣṭasāhasrikā Prajñnāpāramitā* along with the school of Nāgārjuna postulated two *kāyas*: *rūpa-kāya* and *dharma-kāya*.[32] At a later stage, the Vijñnānavāda school of philosophy introduced a third *kāya, sambhoga-kāya,* into the *tri-kāya* of the Mahāyānists.[33] Of these, *dharma- kāya* or *dharma-dhātu* "the Body of the Law" is the essence of all the Buddhas and is described as "the one permanent reality underlying all phenomena and individuals." *Sambhoga-kāya* "the body of bliss" is the radiant and superhuman form in which Buddhas appear in their paradises or when otherwise manifesting themselves in celestial splendour." The *nirmāna-kaya* of the Mahāyānists, the body of the transformation", is the human form of the Buddha.[34] The word *dhamma-dhātu* is not unknown in the Pali literature in the sense of "the nature of things",[35] but the other two terms are totally unknown in the sense in which they are used by the Mahāyānists.[36] A close examination of the *tri- kāya* doctrine of the Mahāyānists and the description of the fourfold body of the Buddha given in the *Saddharmaratnākaraya* would show us that Vimalakīrti was familiar with the doctrine of *tri-kāya* of the Mahāyānists.

Rūpa-kāya of this description appears to be identical with their *nirmāṇa- kāya*. The Mahāyānist theory of *dharma- kāya* may be compared with the description of *dharma-kāya* given in this text.

*Nimitta-kāya* of the *Saddharmaratnākaraya* seems to be an elaboration of the *sambhoga-kāya* of the Mahāyānists. As we have seen the author of the *Saddharmaratnākaraya* adds another *kāya* to the *kāya* doctrine. The description of this *kāya* given in the work is identical with the elaboration of *śunyatā* by Nāgārjuna.[37] Thus it can be seen that Vimalakīrti was familiar with the texts of the Mahāyānists, especially those of Nāgārjuna.

The fifth chapter of the *Saddharmaratnākaraya*, which is entitled Maitreya-saṅgrahakathā, gives the prophecy of the Buddha concerning the future Buddha Maitreya, which he is said to have proclaimed at the request of Sāriputta, the chief disciple of the Buddha, on the occasion of the *ruvansakmaṇa*.[38] One of the chief differences between Mahāyāna and Theravāda is the great importance attached by the former to the cult of *bodhisattvas*, the future Buddhas. The Mahāyānists recognize the existence of an innumerable number of *bodhisattvas*.[39] In addition to Siddhārtha, i.e. Gautama the Buddha before his enlightenment, the only *bodhisattva* common to all schools of Buddhism is Maitreya. The belief in this *bodhisattva* constitutes one of the principle tenets of the religion of the Sinhalese Buddhists. Thus the reference to the *bodhisattva* Maitreya in the *Saddharmaratnākaraya* can be considered in keeping with this belief. Nevertheless, the prophecy attached to him has its origin in that of the Mahāyānists.[40] Since the later Anurādhapura period the kings of Sri Lanka were looked upon as *bodhisattvas* owing to Mahāyāna influence.[41] The Jetavanārāma slab inscription of Mahinda IV (956-972) testifies to this when it says that none but *bodhisattvas* would become kings of prosperous Laṅkā.[42] This Mahāyānist cult has been amplified to such an extent in the fifteenth century that Parākramābahu VI is referred to as the great *bodhisattva* or *bodhisattvāvatāra* (an incarnation of a *bodhisattva*) in the *Oruvala Sannasa*.[43] The author of the *Saddarmaratnākaraya* also referred to him as a *bodhisattva*.[44] It is evident from this references that Vimalakīrti himself admitted this popular belief by referring to the king as a *bodhisattva*.

The author of the *Haṃsa- sandeśaya* requests the Elder Vanaratana to bring under obedience the gods Upulvan, Saman and Vibhīṣaṇa by chanting the *Ratana- sutta*,[45] so that they may shower their blessings on Parākramabāhu VI. It seems that early Theravāda was free from these cults. They were so popular in medieval Sri Lanka that even Elders like Vanaratana could not neglect their influence on the society. Upon the foregoing data, we may conclude that Mahāyāna doctrine and popular beliefs were known to the learned monks of the Vanavāsi Fraternity like the authors of the *Saddarmaratnākaraya* and the *Haṃsa-sandeśaya* and that they drew inspiration, to a certain extent, from their knowledge of Mahāyāna texts.

The monks of the Gāmavāsi Fraternity usually lived in *vihāras* situated in towns and villages, and naturally devoted themselves to religious affairs of the people. The main centre of the Gāmavāsa was invariably the *vihāra* in the capital. During the Daṁbadeni period this Fraternity had its headquarters at the Vijayasundarārāmaya at Daṁbadeniya.[46] The *Vuttamālā -sandesa-sataka*, a Pali poetical work composed in the fourteenth century, gives a description of a monastery at Dädigama which is said to have been built by Parākramabāhu V (1344- 1339).[47] According this text, in this monastery there lived the primate of the time with *mahātheras* belonging to both fraternities.[48] Although we are not certain whether this monastery was the main centre of the Gāmavāsa at that time, it may be assumed that this establishment was the administrative centre of the Sangha after the decline of the Daṁbadeni dynasty. At the beginning of the fitteenth century Parākramabāhu VI is said to have some monasteries built in his new capital, Kōṭṭē.[49] It may be conjectured that these were meant for the Gāmavāsi Fraternity whose members used to stay in the centres of population.

Nearly every *sandeśa* poem of this period refers to a magnificent monastery at Kōṭṭē, generally called Raja Mahavihāraya,[50] the 'King's Monastery', probably the most important of the monasteries built by Parākramabāhu VI in the early part of his reign. This establishment retained its position as the centre of religious affairs of the country for nearly one and a half century, but the time of Bhuvanekabāhu VII (1521-1551) we hear no more about it. It is possible that owing to the growing influence of the Portuguese and the Catholic missionaries at the court of Bhuvanekabāhu VII this place may have lost its power and prestige. At the beginning of the reign of Dharmapāla (1551-1597) the final blow fell upon the Raja Mahavihāraya. On the eve of the king's baptism the monks living in this institution left and took refuge in Sītāvaka and Kandy.[51] As has already been mentioned earlier the king's enthusiasm for the new faith was confirmed by a *sannasa* by which he offered all the temples in the Island, especially the lands belonged to them, including the Raja Mahavihāraya and their revenues, for the maintenance of the colleges which the Franciscans proposed to found in the country.[52]

Apart from the Raja Mahavihāraya, a considerable number of monasteries belonging to the Gāmavāsa are mentioned in the literary works of this period. Of these, mention may be made of the monasteries at Kelaṇiya, Väligama, Delgamuva, Attanagalla, and Totagamuva. Some of these came into prominence in this period not only because of their historical significance but also owing to the high reputation of their contemporary incumbents as scholarly monks.[53]

The main duties of a Gāmavāsi monk were the study of the Dhamma, recitation of the texts, preaching, and attending day-to-day religious needs of the people. This is in accordance with *grantha- dhura*[54] (studying the Scriptures) described in the *Aṭṭhakathās*[55] and the *Katikāvatas*. It has been elucidated in the *Polonnaru-Katikāvata* that one of the purposes of the promulgation of that *Katikāvata* was to implement a scheme according to which monks had to follow the *grantha- dhura* and the *vipassanā-dhura* for the advancement of the Sāsana.[56] The *Dambadeni Katikāvata* further confirms that the main duties of the monks who followed the *grantha-dhura* were teaching, learning and preaching the Dhamma[57] However this may not warrant the conclusion that the monks of the Gāmavāsa did not practise or were debarred from meditation. It is advised in the *Dambadeni Katikāvata* that the Gāmavāsi monks should practise meditation in addition to learning the Dhamma and performing the duties laid down for them.[58] In a fragmentary *Katikāvata* attributed to the reign of Parākramabāhu VI it is regulated that the monks of the Gāmavāsa should keep in mind that their primary duty is that of studying and preaching the Dhamma.[59] It is quite evident that in performing this main duty they had to keep in close contact with lay society. Their contact and dealings with the laity conditioned the life and thought of the monks of the Gāmavāsa in a manner completely different from that of the Vanavāsa, who believed in as much detachment from the laity as was possible and desirable. This close relationship between the Gāmavāsi monks and lay society gradually led to certain laxities, even corruption. For this reason, our sources describing the purifications of the Sangha said to have taken place at various times, mention that corruption in the Sangha was more apparent among the Gāmavāsi than among the Vanavāsi monks.[60] Close contact between the Gāmavāsa and society led to another significant deveopment in that Fraternity. This was the prevalence among these monks of some practices and beliefs wholly in conflict with the teachings of the Buddha. They apparently attempted to effect a synthesis between Buddhism and popular practices and beliefs, leading to the increase of popular influence on Buddhism.

It is natural to expect that the monks who were drawn from a society which believed in the influence of local cults such as *yakkhas* would ensure the persistance of these beliefs even within the community of monks. This is evident in the *Sumaṅgalavilāsini* which prescribes measures to be taken if a monk were to be 'possessed' by a *'yakkha'*.[61] The *Dambadeni Katikāvata* forbids monks to offer sacrifices to *yakkhas* or to take part in exorcism.[62] During the period under discussion the rites and performances connected with exorcism became widespread among the Gāmavāsi monks. It has been suggested that Śrī Rāhula was an exponent of these practices.[63] This attitude in him is clearly portrayed in his literary works. The *Kuveṇi-asna*, a text of magical incantation composed to obtain victory and blessings for Parākramabāhu VI, is attributed by some scholars to Śrī Rāhula.[64] On the other hand, Vidāgama Maitreya levelled his attacks at these in his *Buduguṇālaṅkāraya*.[65] The worship of gods such as Upulvan and Vibhīṣaṇa besides that of the Mahāyāna *bodhisattva* Avalokiteśvara (Nātha) side by side with the Buddha became widespread in the temples that belonged to the Gāmavāsa. It will be seen later that the history of some of these cults in Sri Lanka goes as far back as to the early Anurādhapura period.[66] Suffice it to mention here that neither the literature nor the inscriptions after the tenth century up to the thirteenth century make any reference to these cults. During this period they commended in the literary works produced by the monks of Gāmavāsa.[67] The Vijayabāhu Pirivena and its monastery at Toṭagamuva became the centre of the cult of Nātha at this time.[68] The temples at Devinuvara and Kelaṇiya had since long been regarded as the abodes of the gods Upulvan and Vibhīṣaṇa respectively[69] Śrī Rāhula was a votary of Vibhīṣaṇa, and his devotion to Upulvan is proved by his own work, the *Parevi- sandesaya.*[70] Similarly the monk who was the principal of Tilaka Pirivena at Devinuvara was a votary of Upulvan as is revealed by his work. the *Kokila-sandeśaya.*[71] Unlike in the case of *Haṃsa-sandeśaya,* where the Elder Vanaratana of Kāragala is requested to bring under obedience the gods, both Śrī Rāhula and the Principal monk of the Tilaka Pirivena address their prayers direct to the gods with feelings of reverence and awe.[72] It was inevitable that the Gāmavāsi Fraternity, on account of their close contact with the laity, should have adopted and observed popular religious practices, thereby working out a compromise between these popular beliefs and Buddhism.

The monks of the Gāmavāsa not only supported popular practices but they were also influenced by popular beliefs. Like the laity, they believed that gods such as Upulvan and Vibhīṣaṇa could grant boons such as a prospective royal husband for a princess or a baby boy to the king's daughter who had long been childless. This belief led Śrī Rāhula to the writing of the *Parevi-sandeśaya* and the *Säḷalihini-sandeśaya.* In the *Parevi- sandeśaya* a dove is used as a messenger to carry to Upulvan at Devinuvara a prayer to grant Princess Candrāvati, daughter of Parākramabāhu VI, a suitable husband.[73] His *Säḷalihiṇi-sandeśaya* contains a message to Vibhīṣaṇa at Kelaṇiya on behalf of Nannurutunayyār, the husband of Ulakuḍayadevi, another daughter of Parākramabāhu VI, entreating Vibhīṣaṇa to endow this princess with a son. His message to the god is as follows :-

> O, lordly God, the eye of the three worlds, whose illustrious feet are wet with the fragrant flower juice of the garlands of the crowns of the gods. May you grant to this princess (Ulakuḍayadevi) in the proper manner a worthy gem of a son delightful to the mind and endowed with longevity, prosperity, intelligence and fame. The son whom your honour was pleased in abounding the lovable queen Ratnāvali, became the ruler of this country, Laṅkā, as king *Parākramabāhu* the Great. Nothing more is necessary for manifestation of your worthy majesty and power. Therefore the merits and the wealth of fame of the god would increase if the gem of a son is gifted to this noble princess, who honours the illustrious feet of the noble god with offerings of jasmines and lillies.

The very nature of this message of Śrī Rāhula may help us to realize the extent of the influence of popular beliefs on the monks of the Gāmavāsi Fraternity. This tendency among the Gāmavāsi Fraternity led to a new development in the monastic establishment in this period. In earlier times there is no evidence for monasteries attached to the *dēvālayas* of popular gods. In the Gampola period, however, we see that the Laṅkātilaka temple contained images of Hindu gods outside the sanctum between the inner and outer walls of the building.[74] In the fifteenth century this practice had grown to such an extent that we come across a number of *dēvālayas* having Buddhist monasteries as their appendages. It has been mentioned in the *Alutnuvara Dēvālē Karavīma* that there was a monastery attached to that *dēvālaya;* and it was one of the duties of the incumbent of the monastery to chant *pirit* in front of Upulvan every day.[75] The document further describes how these services were to be carried out by members of the Galaturumula *vihāra,* belonging to the Gāmavāsi Fraternity.[76] Land and other endowments offered towards the incumbents of this monastery in lieu of their services are enumerated in the document. The chief incumbent of the monastery who organized these services is called *vidānasāmi*.[77] There was the same procedure in the Maha Saman Dēvālaya of Ratnapura. It also had a monastery attached to it, while its incumbent belonged to the same Galaturumula monastery. According to the *Maha Saman Dēvālaya Sannasa* the main duty of the monks of this monastery with regard to the *dēvālaya* was that of chanting *pirit* every day in front of the god Maha Saman.[78]

Literary works of the members of the Gāmavāsi Fraternity, such as the *Parevi-sandeśaya* and the *Säḷalihiṇi-sandeśaya*, provide evidence for their familiarity with astrological auspicious signs. In the *Parevi-sandeśaya* Śrī Rāhula gives the auspicious time for the dove to start on its journey as Monday morning under the asterism *hata*[79] when Mercury is in Virgo.[80] The *Säḷalihiṇi-sandeśaya* contains a list of good omens.[81] Śrī Rāhula advises the messenger to look out these on starting its journey, for they are more important even than the auspicious asterisms.[82] There is evidence to show that Śrī Rāhula was not only a believer in occult practices, spells and charms but also an active participant in such practices. As has been mentioned earlier, he believed to be the author of the *Kuveṇi- asna* the "ritual of Kuveṇi" which is said to have been composed in order to confer blessings on Parākramabāhu VI.[83]

Legend has it that Śrī Rāhula won the favour of Skanda by having recourse to a *mantra* called the *skanda- varaprasāda*.[84] It is said that as a result of this *mantra* this Elder was able to acquire a vast knowledge of the arts and sciences that earned him the title *ṣāḍbhāṣā-parameś-vara*.[85] Śrī Rāhula himself claims in his Parevi-sandeśaya that he acquired the favour of Skanda at the age of fifteen.[86] A grandfather (in monastic succession)[87] of Śrī Rāhula, also a monk belonged to the Uturumula (Pali. Uttaramūla), is also said to have been a favourite of Skanda. This was one of the chief institutions of the Abhayagiri monastery at Anurādhapura.[88]

The last reference to the Vanavāsa and the Gāmavāsa is found in the *Rājaratnākaraya* in connexion with the purification of the

Sangha carried out under the auspices of Sēnāsammata Vikramabāhu of Kandy at the end of the fifteenth century.[89] It has been recorded in the work that the monks of the Gāmavāsi Fraternity were so corrupt that none could purify the Sangha satisfactorily.[90] This situation became worse with the political instability all over the country which set in the early part of the sixteenth century. Preoccupied by internal political struggles and foreign interventions the rulers of the country after Vikramabābu were not able to pay attention to the affairs of the religion. Deprived of royal patronage both the Vanavāsa and the Gāmavāsa not only failed to retain their identity but even to continue to perform the higher ordination. At the end of the sixteenth century this situation had become so serious that Vimaladharmasūriya I (1594-1606) of Kandy had to invite monks from Arakan in order to re-establish the higher ordination.[91]

The sources pertaining to the period of our study make occasional references to some ecclesiastical institutions called *āyatanas* or *Mūlas*. These institutions are frequently mentioned in the literature and inscriptions before the fifteenth century.[92] They came to be places of centres of learning during the early medieval period, especially, in the Polonnaru period. Their origin and early development have been discussed in detail by Gunawardhana.[93] It has been observed that the early sources mention eight *āyatanas* or *mūlas* i.e Uttaramūla, Selantaramūla (also called Upalantaramūla) Kappūramūla, Senāpatimūla, Pañcapariveṇamūla or Pañcapariveṇa-samūhaūmula. Sara-sigāmamūla (also called Sarogamamūla), Vāhadīpakamūla and Dakkhiṇamūla.[94] The *Dhampiyāaṭuvā-gāṭapadaya,* an eigth-century Sinhalese work, uses the Sinhalese derivation of the term *mūla, mula,* to denote these institutions.[95]

In their early phase these institutions occupied an important place in the organization of the Sangha. Each one was presumably led by a *mahāthera.*[96]

Apart from being organization of monks, they were bodies which owned property including land and villages. It is set out in the *Dambadeni Katikāvata* that the rich endowments possessed by the *āyatanas* belonged to two categories: estates for their maintenance *(daru- gam)* and regular provisions made for the supply of the requisites of the *bhikkhus (vaṭanā-pasa).*[97] The document further stipulates that the heads of these institutions had, therefore, to be persons who were not attached to material gain, so that there was a reasonable prospect of the income being properly used. It is regulated that the candidates for these ecclesiastical offices should be descendents of the families named Saṅgamu and Gaṇaväsi. No detail is given as to how these rich endowments should be administered.

The history of the *āyatanas* does not furnish evidence of their relationship to the two fraternities, Vanavāsa and Gānavāsa. Neverthless, it is apperent that like the latter these institutions had to change their sites with the shift of capitals. Thus with the rise of Polonnaruva these institutions were moved there from Anurādhapura.[98] The *Pūjāvaliya* and the *Cūlavaṃsa* state that Parākramabāhu II (1236-1270) had monasteries built for monks including the *mahātheras* of the eight *āyatanas.*[99] This suggests that with the rise of Daṁbadeniya as the centre of Sinhalese political power the *āyatanas* had to change their sites. However, during the Daṁbadeni period, although the customary number of eight *āyatanas.* is mentioned, there were only six such institutions with the Dakkhiṇamūla and Vāhadīpakamūla left out.[100] They have not been mentioned in the literature after this period. It is mentioned in the *Daṁbadeni Katikāvata* that at the time of its promulgation, the heads of *āyatanas* came next to the *mahāsāmi* of time in order of importance in the hierarchy.[101] Paranavitana suggests that every *bhikkhu* of this time appears to have belonged to one or another of these institutions.[102]

After the Daṁbadeni period the history of the *āyātanas* is obscure. In the period of this study no mention is made of the prevalence of the *āyatanas* as separate religious bodies apart from occasional references to some scholarly monks who were members of one of these institutions. The *Vuttamālā sandesa-sataka,* written in the reign of Parākramabāhu V (1341-1359) of Dädigama, which refers to the Raja Mahavihāraya in the capital where the Primate of the time lived with the *mahātheras* of various *mūlas,* does not mention any separate monasteries associated with these institutions.[103] It is noteworthy that this

Sen- āpatimūla, Sarasigāmamūla and Mahānettapasādamūla[104] thus leaving out the Uttaromūla and Vāhadīpakamūla.

It has been suggested by Dhammavisuddhi that the change of capitals resulted in the decline of the *āyatanas* after the Daṁbadeni period.[105] Although this seems to be a strong reason for the disappearance of *āyatanas*, it is also highly probable that the development of the *pariveṇas* as centres of learning and education from the fourteenth century onwards would have caused the *āyatanas* to recede to the background.[106] For, as mentioned earlier, the *āyatanas* functioned as ecclesiastical colleges at the early stages of their existence and do not seem to have been distinguished in that field in the later centuries. It is stated in the *Cūlavaṃsa* that the Uttaromūla initially had six hundred members as a *pariveṇa*.[107] Thus the Kappūramūla had well over three hundred members when it flourished as a separate institution. The Pañcapariveṇamūla, as its name implies, may have been inaugurated as an educational institution or as a group of five *pariveṇas* which provided educational facilities to their members. It can be inferred from the account dealing with the origin of the Selantaramūla that it had a large number of monks as followers.[108] These references would suggest that at least some of the *āyatanas* provided for the educational needs of their members in addition to their being monastic administrative bodies. However, our sources do not furnish satisfactory evidence to ascertain the period in which the *āyatanas* gave way to the *pariveṇas* as educational establishments. It will be seen from the chapter dealing with monastic education that the *pariveṇas* began to flourish as separate educational institutions from about the first half of the fourteenth century onwards.[109] From the circumstanital evidence it would not be unjustified to assume that the development of the *pariveṇas* as specialised educational institutions would have been one of the major reasons for the disappearance of the *āyatanas*.

Even though the *āyatanas* disappeared as separate religious bodies their significance was perpetuated by the monks of the fifteenth century by the use of *āyatana* names in titles. It seems that this custom came into use from about the Daṁbadeni period. the *Pūjāvaliya* states that Parākramabāhu II (1236-1270) had special ceremony held to award titles to the heads of the *āyatanas.*[110] It is stated in the *Dambadeṇi Katikāvata* that these appointments should be made with the unanimous assent of the Sangha, and required the approval of the king.[111] Vijayabāhu IV (1270- 1272) is also said to have followed the same custom as his father by awarding various titles, including *mūla-padavi,* to prominent monks in connexion with an *upasampadā* ceremony instituted by him.[112] The last mentioned rulers who awarded the titles of *āyatanas* were Bhuvanekabāhu II (1293-1392)[113] and Vīrabāhu, who functioned as a co-regent of Bhuvanekabāhu V (1372-1408).[114] None of the sources of this period mentions a similar ceremony in which titles of *āyatanas* were awarded, although there were a number of prominent monks who used some of these names as prefixes to their names. It will be seen from the following pages that we are left with only four such titles: Uturumula (Uttaromūla), Galaturumula (Selantaramūla or Upalantaramūla), Mahanetpāmula (Mahānetta- pasādamūla) and Seneviratmula (Senāpatimūla).

Of these, the Uturumula was one of the most important and influential institutions of monks in the Polonnaru period.[115] The *Cūlavaṃsa* presents an account of the origin of this institution in its chapter dealing with the life of Vijayabāhu I (1070-1110).[116] From that period onwards it wielded much influence as the place where the Tooth and Bowl Relics were kept. These played an important part in the religious as well as the political life of the country.[117] More information on this institution is given in the *Daḷadāsirita,* a fourteenth century Sinhalese prose work.[118] It is stated in the work that the casket containing the Tooth Relic was taken out in the presence of the head of the Uturumula and the representatives of the Gaṇaväsi and Kiling families. It further states that the seals of the casket were broken in the presence of the king, the head of the Uturumula, the two representatives of the Gaṇaväsi and Kiling families and the guardians of the Temple.[119] From this information it may be assumed that the association with these relics helped the

Uturumula to gain much influence among the people as well as the rulers.

The concluding verses of the *Padasādhana- ṭīkā* **mention a** *mahāthera* named Uttaromūla Rāhula whose grandson, in pupilary-succession was *Vācissara saṅgharāja*.[120] The latter may be identified with Śrī Rāhula of Toṭagamuva who claims in his *Kāvyaśekharaya* that he was the grandson of Uturumula *mahateriňdu*.[121] Although there is no further information about the former it can be assumed that he was the person referred to in the both sources. Buddhadatta is of the opinion that the Elder Rāhula was the Galaturumula *mahāsāmi* who had been extolled in the *Vimuktisaṅgaha* as the chief incumbent of the Tīrthagrāma (Totagamuva) monastery[122] and that the term Uturumula was derived from Galaturumula. But there is no evidence to justify such an identification. The statement of particular interest occurs in the *Parevi-sandeśaya* of Śrī Rāhula. As mentioned earlier, here, Śrī Rāhula claims to have obtained a boon at the age of fifteen from the god Skanda.[123] This reminds one of the legends about the founder of Uturumula, who is also described as a devotee of the same god.[124] It is extremely difficult to determine the true significance of these two statements though they seem to suggest that the Uturumula was associated with the cult of Skanda. Besides Śrī Rāhula, there are no records of other monks of this period claiming to be associated with the Uturumula. The Uturumula possibly declined in importance after Śrī Rāhula.

Galaturumala, like the Uturumula, had become one of the most important centres of religious life during the Polonnaru period.[125] The *Cūlavaṃsa* gives a long account of the origin of the Galaturumula.[126] It has been suggested by Nicholas that the original site of this institution was near Māgama, the capital of ancient Rohaṇa.[127] Even in the fifteenth century, there existed a well-known monastery at Devinuvara called Galaturumulapāya.[128] We have no evidence to determine whether this monastery had any connexion with the original Galaturumula.

The *Vuttamālā-sandesa-sataka* refers to a monk called Upalantaramūla *mahāthera*, evidently the Head of Galaturumula at the time, who was living at the Raja Mahavihāraya at Dädigama with the Primate of the Sangha of the time.[129] He is extolled as a monk bent on service, pure in mind and endowed with many virtues. The *Nikayasaṅgrahayu*, composed in the latter part of the fourteenth century, states that Maitreya *mahāthera*, another monk of the Galaturumula, assisted the hierarch Dharmakīrti, the Head of the Sangha at the time *(tatkāla-śāsnānuśāsaka)*, in carrying out reforms in the Saṅgha under the patronage of Vīrabāhu Āipāda who was the *de facto* ruler of the country during the latter part of the reign of Bhuvanekabāhu V (1372-1406).[130] The *Vṛttamālā*, a fifteenth century Sanskrit eulogy, mentions the Selantarasamūha (Gaḷaturumula) *mahāsāmi* as the teacher of Dīpaṅkara, the hero of the eulogy.[131]

There is enough evidence to show that monks who claimed connexion with the Galaturumula lived in monasteries situated in various parts of the country in this period. As has already been mentioned, the monastery attached to the Upulvan shrine at Alutnuvara was a residence of monks descended from the Galaturumula[132]. The monastery attached to the Maha Saman Dēvālaya of Ratnapura also had its incumbents from the same institution.[133] It is stated in the Päpiliyāna document I, that the monastery and the educational establishment attached to it, which had been built by Parākramabāhu VI (1415-1467) in memory of his mother, were offered to Maṅgala *sāmi*, the chief disciple of Galaturumula Medhaṅkara *mahāsāmi*.[134] This *mahāsāmi* is said to have lived in the fourteenth century. The *Vimuktisaṅgrahava*, written in the eighteenth year of Vikramabāhu III (1357-1374) of Gampola, extols the literary achievements of this *mahāsāmi* who was the chief incumbent of the monastery at Toṭagamuva.[135] But we have seen earlier that the monastery at Toṭagamuva was under the incumbency of Śrī Rāhula, who claimed his relationship to the Uturumula institution, in the reign of Parākramabāhu VI. Apart from these monasteries, as its name implies, the Galaturumulapāya at Devinuvara may have been another centre of the monks who claimed their relations with the Galaturumula.[136]

Some literary works of the fifteenth century refer to another institution called Mahanetpāmula. According to the *Cūlavaṃsa*, this institution also had its origin at Anurādhapura in the eighth century.[137] The *Pūjāvaliya* records that Vijayabāhu IV (1270-1274) had a monastery built on the summit of the Vātagiri, modern Vākirigala in the Kegalle district,[138] for the *mahāthera* of Mahanetpāmula. The *mahāthera* of Mahanetpāmula, who lived in the Raja Mahavihāraya at Dädigama with the Primate of the time, is commended as a teacher of renown and a monk of great virtue in the *Vuttamālā-sandesa-sataka.*[139] The *Vṛttamālā* of Śrī Ramacandra Bhārati was written to eulogise Rammuṅgoḍa Dīpaṅkara who held the title of Mahanetpāmula, presumably in the early part of the fifteenth century[140]. It is stated in the work that he was the chief incumbent of the two monasteries, i.e. Rammuṅgoḍa and Galapāta, at the time when he was awarded the title of Mahanetpāmula[141]. It is noteworthy that although he held the title of Mahanetpāmula, Dīpaṅkara had his ordination under the tutorship of Galaturumula *mahāsāmi.*

Buddhadatta holds the opinion that this Dīpaṅkara was the same monk who is said to have invited Śrī Rāhula to compose his *Padasādhana-tīrkā*[142]. This opinion has no sound basis, for it is clearly stated in the Padasādhana-tīkā that the latter was a descendent of Gañgatatan-Karambavatan family and the principal of Saptaratna Pratirāja Pirivena at Erabattoṭa, Kōṭṭē,[143] whereas the former is said to have been a member of Vikramasiṅha family and the principal of Śrīnivāsa Pirivena at Rammuṅgoda Kelaṇiya.[144] After Dīpaṅkara the title of Mahanetpāmula was held by Vīdāgama Maitreya. In the *Kavlakuṇumiṇimala,* a work on prosody written in the 54th regnal year (1465 A.D.) of Parākramabāhu VI, Maitreya refers to himself as Mahanetpāmula *mahateriñdu.*[145] He maintained this position in the next reign; the *Buduguṇālaṅkāraya,* another poetical work of his, composed in the third regnal year (1472 A.D) of Bhuvanekabāhu VI (1470-1476) also refers to this title.[146] In the *Aramkäle Sannasa,* this king records a grant of land made to Mahanetpāmula *mahāsāmi.*[147] As shown in this document the king showed great devotion to this monk, who held an esteemed position in his reign.

The institution called Seneviratmula is mentioned for the first time in a slab inscription from the grounds of Jetavana monastery of Anuradhapura[148]. This inscription is assigned to the reign of Mahinda IV (718-736). According to the description given in the document the institution belonged to the Jetavana monastery. It is possible that the Seneviratmula mentioned in the inscription was the same as the Senāpatimūla mentioned in the *Vuttamālā-sandesa- sataka.*[149] The *Cūlavaṃsa* mentions a monk called *Senānātha-parivenatthera* who lived in the reign of Parākramabāhu II (1236-1270).[150] We are not certain whether the *Senānātha-parivena* was the same institution called Seneviratmula in the slab inscription and Senāpatimūla in the *Vattamālā -sandesa-sataka*. The last mentioned work refers to the *mahāthera* of Senāpatimūla as a devout ascetic and a kind monk.[151] No literary or epigraphic source in the fifteenth century mentions this institution. However, the *Palkuṁbura Sannasa,* a copper plate granted by the last king of Kandy, Śrī Vikrama Rājasiṅha (1798-1815), refers to a *thera* called Seneviratmula *mahāsāmi.*[152] According to the history of succession of the *Palkuṁbura Vihāraya* given in this document, the hierarch referred to lived in the reign of a monarch called Bhuvanekabāhu. Codrington identifies this king with Bhuvanekabāhu of Kōṭṭē.[153] As the date of the original grant is Śaka 1446, this identification is acceptable. The hierarch referred to in the document was also known by the name of Bhuvanekabāhu as he was a brother of the king. The *Sannasa* further records that on the death of the king, he migrated to the hill country with several of his brothers and settled down at Urulāvatta in Uḍunuvara of the Central Province. After this time neither the title 'Seneviratmula' nor the institution is mentioned.

There was another division of the Sangha, viz. that into *gaṇas,* but the precise meaning of this term in this period is not certain. Originally the term *gaṇa* was used to denote a group of monks living together. The rules relating to *gaṇa- bhojana* (communal meal of members of a *gaṇa*) were modified seven times according to circumstances.[154]

As to the Anurādhapura period, it is reported in the *Aṭṭhakathās,* that it was a custom among monks to recite *suttas* in a *gaṇa* (a group). This recitation is called *gaṇa- sajjhāyana.*[155] This kind of recitation is still practised in Sri Lanka, especially at a *paritta* ceremony. Besides that, there were, according to the *Visuddhimagga,* also certain groups of monks *(gaṇas)* who specialised in a particular branch of the doctrine. For instance, the *suttantika-gaṇa*[156] was a group or a class of monks who specialised in the *Sutta- piṭaka,* whereas the *ābhidhammika-gaṇa* specialised in the *Abhidhamma-piṭaka.*[157] In the sense of a body of monks in general the term is used in the *Săratthadīpanī, the Dharm- apradīpikā,* the *Pūjāvaliya* and the *Saddharmālaṃkāraya.*[158] The contexts, however, do not indicate the strength of a *gaṇa* nor its exact nature. According to the *Mahāvagga* and the *Cullavagga* the strength of a *gaṇa* varied from two or three monks to five or ten and perhaps even more.[159]

The *Cūlavaṃsa* uses the term *gaṇa* to refer to a single congregation or a group of monks living together in a monastery. The monks forming such a group are called *gaṇavāsino.*[160] Based on these reference, it has been suggested by Geiger that the term *gaṇa* represents the *bhikkhus* who live together in a monastery, perform ecclesiastical acts *(dhamma-kamma),* as one group.[161] The *Saddharmaratnāvali,* a Sinhalese prose work attributed to the Daṁbadeni period, also contains a reference according to which *gaṇa* signifies a group of monks living in one monastery.[162] The same source uses the term to denote a *vihāra* in another context.[163]

The position of the *gaṇa* seems somewhat more precise and different in the later Polonnaru period. During this time there were seven organizations or *gaṇas* of monks each headed by a *mahāthera.* Some rulers of this period offered endowments to these *gaṇas* specially set apart for their maintenance. One inscription records that at the time of Queen Kalyāṇavati a certain Pirivatubim Vijayānāvan and his wife gave alms and robes to the monks of the Ruvanvāli monastery of Anurādhapura led by the *theras* of the seven *gaṇas.*[164] On the strength of this evidence, it has been observed by Paranavitana that the Buddhist Sangha of Sri Lanka was divided into seven *gaṇas* in the later Polonnaru period.[165] But this scholar adds that he does not know of any place where the seven are enumerated.

It is relevant in this connexion that the *Nikāyasaṅgrahaya* refers to *viyatpat-aṭagaṇaya* as an institution restored by

Parākramabāhu.[166] Medhananda in his introduction to the *Anāgatavaṃsaya* states that the eight *gaṇas* referred to in the *Nikāyasaṅgrahaya* were the *mūlas* Uttara, Senāpati, Dakkhiṇa, Mahānettappasāda, Selantara, Saroggāma and the two fraternities, Vanavāsa and Gāmavāsa.[167] This identification has also been accepted by Buddhadatta.[168] However, it must be mentioned here that the reference to *gaṇas* in the *Nikāyasaṅgrahaya* occurs in connexion with the administrative machinery of Parākramabāhu I. On this basis, Ariyapala suggests that the term here no doubt meant some secular divisions of his administration.[169] Codrington interprets it as divisions of the army, i.e. eight corps of skilled foot-soldiers.[170] It has been suggested by Gunawardhana that the *viyatpat-aṭagaṇaya* in the *Nikāyasaṅgrahaya* may have been a' group of eight learned men' or 'eight groups of learned men', who attended on the king at his court.[171] Paranavitana takes it as an equivalent of 'the eight corporations of those who had scholarly attainments'.[172] He further states that the *viyatñā* referred to in the same work[173]' was probably the representative of these eight colleges of experts in various branches of knowledge. Whatever the case, it is apparent that *genehi* in the Ruvanväli inscription of Kalyānāvati and the *viyatpat- aṭagaṇaya* in the *Nikāyasaṅgrahaya* do not refer to one and the same institution.

The Alutnuvara inscription of the fifteenth century also refers to seven *gaṇas*.[174] Paranavitana here observes that the same seven organizations recorded in the inscription of Kalyāṇavati may have continued till the sixteenth century. In addition to this, the *Daṁbadeni Katikāvata* lays down that at the Higher Ordination *Katikāvata* be read amidst the assembly of the respective *gaṇas* prior to the admission of a candidate into the Higher Order.[175] This text further stipulates that the monks belonging to each *gaṇa* should go to their teacher or preceptor and perform the act of *uposatha*. This implies that there were several *gaṇas* in one monastery. This may further show that the Sangha in the thirteenth century was also divided into *gaṇas*. Nevertheless, it should be mentioned here that the *Katikāvata* does not mention the number of the *gaṇas*.

The *Saddharmaratnākaraya* records that Parākramabāhu VI (1415-1467) offered the requisites *(pariṣkāra)* of monks taking into account the order of *gaṇapradhānas*, the chiefs of the *gaṇas* [176] The chief incumbent of the Kelaniya monastery in the reign of this king is referred to in the *Haṃsa-sandeśaya as gaṇa-nāyaka.*[177] Again he is mentioned in the Raja Maha Kelaṇi inscription as *geṇehi nāyaka* which gives the same meaning.[178] It is not clear whether the title has been used to denote his chief incumbency of the monastery or to mention his being a head of a special group of monks. There is another interesting reference in this connexion in the *Alutnuvara Dēvālē Karavīma.* It records that there were thirteen successive *gaṇas* of the incumbency of the monastery attached to the Upulvan *dēvālaya* at Alutnuvara from the Dambadeni period to the date of composition of the work.[179]

The *Rājāvaliya* uses the term *gaṇa* on various occasions to refer to the residence of monks. For instance, it states that Vīdāgama *mahāsāmi* protected Prince Parākrama by giving him asylum in the *gaṇa-pantiya,* 'monks' quaters'.[180] On another occasion it mentions that Māyādunne and his brothers took refuge in the *gaṇa- pantiya* so as to evade the wrath of their father, Vijayabāhu VI.[181] It is not clear, in this connexion, whether the term *gaṇa* has been used to denote the whole community of monks. However, these references should not lead us to conclude that the meaning of the term which it had in the early Anurādhapura period disappeared completely. For, it has been used even this period to represent a group of monks who specialised in a particular section of the Scriptures. In the Vijayabāhu Pirivena at Toṭagamuva there were such groups of student monks who specialised a particular section of the Scriptures such as Sutta, Vinaya and Abhidhamma.[182]

The *Saddharmaratnākaraya,* written in the reign of Parākramabāhu VI (1415-1467), contains an account of the religious and literary activities of the lineage of Dharmakīrti of the Vanavāsa at Palābatgala,[183] to which the author Dhammadinna Vimalakīrti himself belonged. According to this work, the author was the third member of this lineage to make contributions to the literature of the country. Apart from Vimalakīrti, there were some prominent figures of the Sangha of this period who claimed their relationship with some well known hierarchs of the preceding centuries. The following discussion deals with this teacher-pupil relationship of the Sangha which had some significance not only in monastic property but also in the literary activities of the country.

An mentioned above, Vimalakirti was the third member of the lineage of Dharmakīrti, which descended from the Palābatgala Vanavāsa, to engage in literary activities. The inauguration of this dwelling for the Vanavāsi monks under the leadership of a monk named Dharmakīrti is given in the *Cūlavaṃsa* and the *Pūjāvaliya*[184] According to the sources, Parākramabāhu II (1236-1270) arranged for the monks devoted to *patipatti* to be sent to the Palābatgala Vanavāsa. This took place soon after the unification of the Sangha in about 1250 A.D.; for the *Cūlavaṃsa* account gives the impression that it was a part of the series of religious works including the unification of the Sangha. Mudiyanse[185] and Dhammavisuddhi[186] identify the founding member of the Vanavāsa of Palābatgla with Dharmakīrti of 'Tambaraṭṭha' who was brought to Sri Lanka by Parākramabāhu II because of his fame as a saintly monk.[187] They are of the opinion that after this hierarch the monks of the Palābatgala fraternity came to be known as 'Dharmakīrti'. A line of eminent scholars sprang up from this fraternity and produced some of the best known literary works of the medieval period.

The first member of the Palābatgala Vanavāsa to make valuable contribution in literature was Sīlavaṃsa Dharmakīrti. The *Saddharmaratnākaraya* traces the descent of Sīlavaṃsa from the monks in the Mahāvihāra which was built in the Mahamevnā park in Anurādhapura.[188] As will be seen later, Silavaṃsa Dharmakīrti was the first member of the lineage of Dharmakīrti to hold the title *māhimi*. He was a descendant of the Gaṇaväsi family,[189] and responsible for some religious monuments in India and Sri Lanka.[190] The *Saddharmaratnākaraya* does not give the date of the *māhimi*, but according to a fragmentary inscription at Gadalādeniya, attributed to the reign of Bhuvanekabāhu IV, it may be concluded that he lived in the first part of the fourteenth century.[191] The epigraph informs us that a *mābimi* named Dharmakīrti was a descendant of the Gaṇaväsi family and responsible for building and renovating some religious buildings in India and Sri Lanka. His connexion with these religious works and the fact that he, too, belonged to the Gaṇaväsi family prove that the hierarch referred to in the *Saddharmaratnākaraya* was the same person as that mentioned in the epigraph. He composed two Pali poems, named the '*Pāramī-mahāsataka* and the *Janānurāga- carita.*[192] In addition to the data found in the *Saddharmaratnākaraya,* the *Saddhar-mālaṃkāraya* of his pupil Devarakṣita Jayabāhu states that the *māhimi* lived in Mālatīmālasela-Vihāra in Gañgasiripura (Gampola), and wrote another Pali poem, the *Sujanappasāda.*[193] The *māhimi* Dharmakīrti, in the colophon of one of his other works, the *Pāramīmahāsataka,* says that he lived in Laṅkā which was ruled by a monarch named Vijayabāhu who was 'a lamp to the world as well as to the religion'.[194] This king is identified with fifth of that name,[195] the predecessor of Bhuvanekabāhu IV(1341-1351).

The teacher (ācārya) of Vimalakīrti was Devarakṣita Jayabāhu, the second member of the lineage of Dharmakīrti to hold the title *māhimi.*[196] He was the author of the *Nikāyasaṅgrahaya,* the *Saddharmālaṃkāraya,* the *Bālāvatāra-sankṣepasannaya* and the *Jinabodhāvalī.*[197] He calls himself *Saṅgharāja* both in the *Saddharmālaṃkāraya* and the *Nikāya-saṅgrahaya.*[198] The *Saddharmaratnākaraya* mentions that Devarakaṣita Jayabāhu, otherwise called Dharmakīrti II, was a descendant of the Mahadäliyā-vaṃsa and presided over the convocation of the Sangha held under the auspices of Vīrabāhu Ādipāda.[199]

The last of the well known members of the lineage of Dharmakīrti was Dhammadinna Vimalakīrti, the author of the *Saddharmaratnākaraya.* Among the writers of the fifteenth century in Sri Lanka Vimalakīrti occupies a unique position as he was the only prose writer of any significance.[200] Vimalakīrti was the pupil of Devarkaṣita Jayabāhu, Dharmakīrti II. The *Kokila- sandeśaya,* the last of the *sandeśa* poems written in the reign of Parākramabāha VI, mentions a *māhimi* Dharmakīrti who was living in the Pohoyage- vihāraya of Kōṭṭe.[201]. One writer identifies him with Devarakṣita Jayabāhu.[202] The *Kokila- sandeśaya* is ascribed to a date between 1460 and 1457.[203] It is apparent that Jayabāhu was *māhimi* in 1396 A.D. when the Convocation of the Sangha over which he presided took place in the reign of Bhuvanekabāhu V (1372-1408).[204] There is no doubt that as *māhimi* he would have been a somewhat elderly monk. It is rather unlikely that he should have been alive at the time when the *Kokila-sandeśaya* was written, i.e. nearly seven decades after the date he is known to have held the title *māhimi*. It seems possible, therefore, that the *māhimi* Dharmakīrti referred to in the *Kokila-sandeśaya* was no other but the last member of the lineage of Dharmakīrti of Palābatgala Vanavāsa, i.e. Dhammadinna Vimalakīrti. According to the description of the *sandeśaya*, the *māhimi* Dharmakīrti III belonged to the Vimalakula, a sub-division of the Solar dynasty (*rivikula*, Skt. *ādityavaṃsa*).[205]

Śrī Rāhula of Toṭagamuva claims in his *Padasādhana- ṭīkā* that he was the grandson of a hierarch named Uturumula Rāhula who hailed from the lineage of Sāriputta *mahāsāmi* of Polonnaruva.[206] As has already been mentioned, apart from his devotion to Skanda, little is known about the Elder Rāhula of Uturumula. However, Śrī Rāhula's claim seems to be an allusion to his connexion with the lineage of Sāriputta, which included highly reputed scholarly monks like Sangharakṣita of Daṃbadeniya.[207] Although it is not clearly stated whether the term *nattā* (grandson) denotes a relationship in monastic succession, considering the teacher-pupil relationship among the Sangha in this period, it is not impossible to assume that this was so. But this assumption leads us to another issue. Nowhere in his literary works does Śrī Rāhula mention his teacher's name, although two of them contain references to his affiliation to the Elder Rāhula of Uturumula.[208] There is strong tradition that Śrī Rāhula was a pupil of the Elder Vīdāgama who played a prominent role in installing Parākramabāhu VI on the throne of Kōṭṭē.[209] Buddhadatta suggests that as the Elder Vīdāgama was not a descendant of the royal family, Śrī Rāhula, being a member of Kañdavurukula (Skandavara- vaṃsa),[210] which had connexion with the royal family, preferred to mention his teacher's teacher, the Elder Rāhula of Uturumula, who, according to this scholar, was another member of that family.[211] None of our sources mentions that Elder Vīdāgama was a pupil of Rāhula of Uturumula; there is hardly any evidence regarding the family connexions of the Elder Vīdāgama. We do not know whether Rāhula of Uturmula was a member of the Kañdavurukula. The *Kañdavuru-sirita,* a thirteenth- century Sinhalese prose work, mentions a village called Kañdavuru-pura in the Daṁbadeni period[212], but we do not know whether this had any connexion with the Kañdavurukula, nor do we know whether either of these had anything to do with Skanda, whose famous temple was at Kataragama, nearly 150 miles south of Daṁbadeniya. As has been mentioned earlier in this study,[213] both Rāhulas were devotees of Skanda. If we assume that this god has some connexion with the origin of Kañdavurukula, it is possible that both Rāhulas belonged to it, but this conclusion remains conjectural.

According to tradition the author of the *Guttila- kāvyaya,* one of the most popular poems of the Kōṭṭē period, was a monk called Vättäve, a pupil of Śrī Rāhula.[214] It is said that Vātve left the temple of his teacher when he found that the teacher was not well disposed towards him. Tradition also says that Vättäve composed the *Guttila-kāvyaya* to show that he was aware of the evils that befall a pupil who disrespected his teacher, as is shown in the story of the *Guttila-jātakaya.*[215] We have no evidence in the contemporary literature to corroborate this tradition.

The author of the Sinhalese paraphrase of the *Bhakti- śataka* of Rāmacandra Bhārati, a monk called Sumaṅgala, calls himself a pupil of Śrī Rāhula of Toṭagamuva.[216] It is not clear whether Sumaṅgala had his education in the Vijayabāhu Pirivena at Toṭagamuva where Śrī Rāhula was the principal, or was a pupil of the hierarch in monastic succession.

According to the Päpiliyāna document I of Parākramabāhu VI, Maṅgala *thera-sāmi,* the principal of the Sunetrādevi Pirivena at Päpiliyāna, was a pupil of a hierarch called Medhaṅkara *mahathera-sāmi* of Galaturumula.[217] The *Maha Saman Dēvālaya Sannasa* of the same king also states that the monastery attached to the *dēvālaya* was offered to Maṅgala *thera-sāmi,* the chief disciple of the Elder Medhaṅkara of Galaturumula.[218] Another pupil of this hierarch, a monk named Rammuṅgoda Dīpaṅkara, is the hero of the *Vṛttamālā* of Rāmacandra Bhārati.[219] None of these sources dates the lifetime of the Elder Medhaṅkara. According to the *Vimuktisaṅgrahava*, a prose work attributed to the reign of Vikramabāhu III (1371-1374)[220], a certain Galaturumula *mahāsāmi* had a pupil called Vilgammula who is eulogized for his intellectual attainments.[221] Some scholars are inclined to believe that the Elder Galaturumula referred to in the *Vimuktisaṅgrahava* was the hierarch referred to in the Päpiliyāna document I and the *Maha Saman Dēvālaya Sannasa.*[222] But, if the monk Vilgammula can be identified with the *mahāsāmi* by that name referred to in the Kitsirimevan Kelaṇi inscription, it seems possible that the *mahāsāmi* Galaturumula lived in the first part of the fourteenth century. For, according to the inscription, the *mahāsāmi* Vilgammula was living in 1344 A.D. On the other hand, there is no mention whatsoever of a monk called Vilgammula in the literary works of the fifteenth century. This may help us to conclude that the *mahāsāmi* Galaturumula mentioned in the *Vimuktisaṅgrahava* lived prior to 1344 A.D. for it is clear from the Kitsirimevan Kelaṇi inscription that his pupil Vilgammula held the title *mahāsāmi* in about 1344 A.D. On the basis of this assumption, it is not difficult to decide that Medhaṅkara *mahathera-sāmi* referred to in the Päpiliyāna document I and the *Maha Saman Dēvālaya Sannasa* was a monk different from the *mahāsāmi* Galaturumula. It is generally believed that the principal of the Tilaka Pirivena at Devinuvara also belonged to the Galaturumula.[223] But it is not certain whether he was a pupil of Galaturumula Medhaṅkara in monastic succession. Yet, as has been discussed before, it seems likely that the Elder Medhaṅkara had a large number of pupils who held important ecclesiastical and educational posts in the reign of Parākramabāhu VI (1415-1467)

Some senior members of the Sangha of this period seem to have been inclined to mention their family connexions in addition to their affiliations to certain religious institutions or lineages. The responsibility of a monk towards his parents is acknowledged even in the Vinaya.[224] However, it was not customary for members of the Sangha to continue or mention their caste or clan connexions after their entry into the Order. In fact all such distinctions are lost once a person enters the Order. The Buddha says in the *Pahārāda Sutta* :-

Just as the great rivers Gaṅgā, Yamunā, Aciravatī, Sarabhū, and Mahī, entering the mighty ocean, lose their former names and identities and are termed simply the ocean, even so these four castes Kṣtriyas, Brahmaṇas, Vaiśyas and Śudras, going fourth from the world into the homeless life, into the discipline of Dhamma proclaimed by the Tathāgata, lose their former names and lineages and are reckoned simply recluses, sons of the Śākya....[225]

According to the *Mahāvaṃsa*, the place where those who entered the Order of monks from noble families, became Issarasamaṇaka,[226] and the place where those who entered the Order from the Vaiśya caste, became Vessagiri.[227] Rahula doubts whether these references give any indication of the prevalence of caste and class differences among the Sangha in the early Anurādhapura period.[228] Although we have no further evidence to prove this hypothesis, it is apparent that the enthusiastic patrons went to the extent of patronising the kinsmen of the monks they respected. Kassapa V (914-925) distributed rice and clothing among the kinsmen of *paṅsukūlika* monks.[229] Vijayabāhu I (1070-1110) granted 'maintenance villages' to the relatives of monks who practised ascetism[230]. These instances may indicate that the admission of a person into the Sangha brought social recognition to his family. But it is more probable that it reflects the failure of monks to completely sever the ties of obligations which bound them to their kinsfolk.

In the Daṁbadeni period, it seems that new rules were laid down in the Sangha, especially regarding ordination and appointment to high ecclesiastical posts. In the *Dambadeni Katikāvata* it is stressed that great care should be exercised in the selection of novices. Only those who were temperamentally and socially fitted for the religious vocation should be admitted.[231] Commenting on this rule of the *Katikāsvata* Rammandala says that it clearly shows that caste and class differences entered the Sangha during the Daṁbadeni period.[232] But it is not certain whether this rule implied any discrimination regarding the ordination. Nevertheless, in later centuries it seems that efforts were made to encourage men of noble families to seek ordinations. The *Nikāyasaṅgrahaya* states that Vīrabāhu Ādipāda, who took several steps to uplift the Sāsana at the end of the fourteenth century, procured ordination to sons of noble families including his own son.[233] According to the *Cūlavaṃsa* and the *Rājaratnākaraya*, Sēnāsammata Vikaramabāhu, who ordered a purification of the Sangha by the end of the fifteenth century, brought about the ordination of 350 sons of noble families.[234] However, we are not certain whether these instances, which indicate ordination ceremonies held under the patronage of the then rulers, represent a general tendency of the Sangha towards caste and class discriminations. We read in the *Cūlavaṃsa* that from the sixteenth century onwards much care was taken to ordain only persons from noble families. For instance, Vimaladharmasūriya I (1592-1604), who re-instituted the higher ordination with the help of monks from Arakan, had a ceremony of admission performed on many of the sons of noble families.[235] Vimaladharmasūriya II (1687-1706) also encouraged the ordination of 33 young noblemen.[236]

Another rule of the *Katikāvata* stipulates that candidates for the headship of *āyatanas* should be scions from the families named Saṅgamu and Gaṇaväsi.[237] As it seems that these families held a considerable influence on the religious affairs of the country during the medieval period, a brief discussion is necessary. According to Paranavitana the word *'gamu'* (lit.villages) in Saṅgamu denotes families, and the names of these families indicate that 'they were originally tenants or administrators of the land and estates of the monastic foundations', and must, therefore, 'have had traditions of attachments to the Sangha, and were well versed not only in the details of monastic administration but also about the needs of the members of the Order'.[238] Vimalakīrti, noting the resemblance of Saṅgamu of Pali *saṅghagāma,* suggests that it may have derived from the latter by the following stages : *saṅghagāma-saṅggam- saṅgama-saṅgamu.*[239] Analysing the term *saṅghagāma* as *saṅghassagāmo,* Dhammavisuddhi interprets it as 'the villages of the Sangha'.[240] On the basis of these interpretations, it may be concluded that Saṅgamu denotes a category of villages, or families living there, which had a close relationship with the Sangha. The *Cūlavaṃsa* account of the unification of the Sangha in the reign of Parākramabāhu I (1153-1186) mentions the unholy elements of the Sangha living in *saṅghagāmas.*[241] According to the chronicle there were many such villages. It may be suggested that Saṅgamuva,[242] where the text of a peace settlement between Gajabāhu II (1132-1153) and Parākramabāhu I (1153-1186) was found, descended from one of the villages or group of such villages called *saṅghagāmas*. But this does not exclude the possibility of the name of this village being ḍerived from *saṅgama* 'meeting' (of the two kings).

As to the second type of villages it may be suggested that they also belong to a similar category and may perhaps be connected with the Gaṇaväsi-vaṃsa or Gaṇaväsi-kula.[243] Paranavitana takes *gaṇa* as 'monastery' and *väsi* as 'employee'.[244] He translates *gaṇaväsi* as 'temple official' and observes that the family would have had its origin in some officials in monastic administration who acquired great political influence and had connexions with royalty. The origin of the Gaṇaväsi family, which produced some of the greatest figures in the history of Sri Lanka during the fourteenth century, is given in the Sagama inscription of Bhuvanekabāhu V (1372- 1408).[245] According to the *Saddharmaratnākaraya,* which gives an account quite similar to that of the epigraph, Gaṇaväsi is another name for the Lämäṇi (Lambakarṇa) family, which had as its progenitors the Śākya princes Sumitta and Bodhigupta who were sent to Sri Lanka by Asoka to accompany the branch of the sacred Bo-tree.[246] The work adds that the name Gaṇaväsi was given to that *vaṃsa* as it gradually became bigger; and it is called Lämäṇi (Lambakarṇa) because it was pure on 'both sides' and the scions of this lineage had long ears.[247] It has been observed by Paranavitana that the connexion between the Lämäṇi clan of the fourteenth and fifteenth centuries and the Lambakarṇas of the early Anurādhapura period, and through them with the kinsmen of Asoka, is a very tenuous one, but was accepted as a self- evident truth by the panegyrists of those days and by the people as a whole who were not permitted to entertain doubts with regard to such matters.[248]

The *Cūlavaṃsa* informs us that Parākramabāhu I donated several villages in Koṭṭasāra to the Gaṇaväsi.[249] Sirima Wickramasinha holds that the term is used in this connexion for Valaikkāra soldiers.[250] The precise meaning of Gaṇaväsi in this context is not clear, but it may be taken either as 'monks living in a *gaṇa*', i.e. a group of monks or as 'scions of the lineage called Gaṇaväsi'. As has been mentioned before, according to the *Daḷadāsirita,* the Gaṇaväsi family was connected with the rituals and ceremonies in the Tooth Relic Temple.[251]

According to the Sagama inscription, Alakeśvara III belonged to the Gaṇaväsi family on his mother's side.[252] The *Saddharamaratnākaraya* states that Parākramabāhu VI was also a scion of this family.[253] As mentioned above, although these two sources trace the origin of the Gaṇaväsi family from the early Anurādhapura period, no Sinhalese king before the Gampola period claimed to have belonged to it. Ellawala, on the basis of account given in the Sagama inscription and the *Saddharmaratnākaraya,* observes that the Gaṇaväsi family may have been a branch of the Vaiśya caste.[254]

The foregoing account shows us that the Saṅgamu and Gaṇaväsi families had close connexions not only with the administration of monastic property but also with the royalty of the country. It is possible that the villages where these families lived, or which were administered by them, were called Saṅgamu and Gaṇaväsi. The fact that the above cited regulation of the *Dambadeni Katikāvata* emphasises that the candidates for the office of heads of *āyatanas* should be scions of these families clearly shows the influence they had on the religious affairs of the country in the medieval period. It is therefore possible that this regulation of the *Katikāvata* would have resulted in caste and class differences among the Sangha in the later periods, at least regarding high ecclesiastical posts. On the other hand, this shows the influence of particular clans on the religious affairs of the country.

We have seen above that the *māhimi* Sīlavaṃsa Dharmakīrti was one of the greatest figures in the Sangha in Sri Lanka during the fourteenth century. In the Gaḍalādeniya inscription he claims descent from the Gaṇaväsi family.[255] The *Saddharma-ratnākaraya* also informs us that the *māhimi* was a descendant of that family.[256] It is quite probable that the *māhimi* and his posterity preferred to mention his family connexions owing to the privileges assigned to it in the *Dambadeni Katikāvata* in respect of high ecclesiastical posts.

The close relations that monks maintained with their kinsmen would have made it difficult for them to dissociate from the social strata of their lay life. At least the monks from the leading families of the upper castes of the society would not have been too keen to forget their status in lay life. Several hierarchs of this period did not hesitate to mention their relationship with certain influential families of the time. It is stated in the *Saddharmaratnākaraya* that the *māhimi* Devarakṣita Jayabāhu, Dharmakīrti II, was 'a lamp to the family called Mahadä-liyā-vaṃsa'.[257] Although little is known about this family, the passage quoted above and the account related to it in the *Saddharmaratnākaraya* imply that it was closely connected with the Mehenavara-vaṃsa to which Sēnā Laṅkādhikāra and Vīrabāhu Ādipāda belonged. Śrī Rāhula of Toṭagamuva claims to be descended from the *Kañdavuru-kula* of Demaṭānagama in his *Kāvyaśekharaya* and *Parevi-sandeśaya*.[258] Although it is traditionally believed that the parents of Śrī Rāhula were Vikramabāhu, a prince of Kañdavuru-kula, who met an untimely death, and Sīlavatī, who took refuge in the harem of Parākramabāhu VI after her husband's death,[259] there is no record of this fact in any contemporary work. But it has been often mentioned in his own works as well as in the contemporary writings[260] that Śrī Rāhula was adopted from his childhood as a son of Parākramabāhu VI. In his inscription at the premises of Kitsirimevan Kelaṇi Vihāra the *māhimi* Vilgammula claims that he was a descendant of a family called Gañgatalān Karaṁbavalān.[261] Śrī Rāhula was invited to compose his *Padasādhana- ṭīkā* by a monk named Dīpaṅkara of the Gañgatalān Karaṁbavalān family.[262] No further information is found on this family. The author of the *Kokila-sandēśaya* called himself the crest-jewel of the *Irugal* family in the colophon of this work.[263] This reference is obviously in keeping with the traditional practice of old Sinhalese writers who some times preferred to remain anonymous. However, the old *sanne*, 'inter-verbal commentary', of the *sandeśaya* which was written in the sixteenth century, gives references to the author's life as a monk, and to his lay life.[264] The work states that the author belonged to the *Irugal-kula* which was associated with the Sinhalese royal house. The queen of Parākramabāhu II (1236-1270) and Alakeśvara III, the all- powerful minister of Vikramabāhu III (1357-1374), were both members of this family.[265] The chief incumbent of the Kelaṇi Vihāraya towards the beginning of the fifteenth century was a descendant of the Ekanāyaka family of Kosgama.[266] At the same time, one member of this family held an influential position in the court of Parākramabāhu VI.[267]

The family connexions of the Sangha seem to have led to a new development regarding monastic property. In this period we have references to *bandhu* or *jñāti- śiṣya-paramparā*, 'kindred-pupil succession', in the Sangha, according to which the ownership of property of a religious institution passed on from teacher to pupil, the latter being a relative of the former. The earliest document mentioning this spiritual-cum-temporal succession is the Kitsirimevan Kelaṇi Vihāra inscription of B.E. 1887 (1344/5 A.D.).[268] As mentioned before, in the epigraph the *Māhimi* Vilgammula claims descent from the Gañgatalān Karaṁbavalān family, while the monastery is described as a property of his family for ten generations. Furthermore, he mentions Gatārā-piriventāna, 'the incumbent of the Gatārā

Pirivena', as his successor of the *bandhu- paramparā*. We learn from the *Vuttamālā-sandesa- sataka* that the author of the work, Gatārā Upatapassi, was a nephew of the Sarasigāmamūla-mahāsāmi, 'the *mahimi* of Vilgammula'.[269] There is no doubt that the both sources refer to the same persons. We have no further evidence to ascertain whether Gatārā Upatapassi succeeded his uncle, the *māhimi* Vilgammula, as the chief incumbent of the Kelaṇi Vihāraya. Nevertheless, it is apparent that the custom of *bandhu* śiṣya- *paramparā* was well established before this period, for the inscription mentions ten generations before the *māhimi* Vilgammula. The naming of his successor by Vilgammula shows that the basis of this custom was still preference, and not a rule as in the Kandyan period.

The *Haṃsa-sandeśaya* of the fifteenth century takes great pains to trace the family connexions of the *māhimi* Vanaratana, who was the chief incumbent of Kāragala monastery.[270] The description given in the work is quite similar to that of the Kāragala inscription II.[271] According to both sources, the monastery at Kāragala was founded by Arthanāyaka Dalasengamu Migantaru, who was the grandnephew of Nāgasena *mahāthera* of the Vanavāsa monastery at Vattala. Reference is made to a princess called Padmāvati (Piyamavvan), sister of Arthanāyaka, who lived in his household and was related to Alakeśvara III. She married Maha Lē Siñgāna, and their grandson was the *māhimi* Vanaratana. Neither of these sources mentions the parents of Vanaratana. But Paranavitana, tracing the history of Alakeśvara family, observes that Vanaratana, being a grandson of Sudasun Mahalēna (Sudasun Maha Lē Siñgāna), must have been a son of either Vīra Alakeśvara or Vīrabāhu Adipāda.[272] We know that the *Rājāvaliya* and Chinese sources, which give accounts of the political affairs of the country at the beginning of the fifteenth century, are unanimous in describing Vīra Alakeśvara's hostility towards the religion.[273] Therefore, it is unlikely that he should have allowed one of his sons to be ordained *bhikkhu*. On the other hand, the *Nikāyasaṅgrahaya* definitely tells us that Vīrabāhu Ādipāda made his eldest son adopt religious life.[274] It is, therefore, quite pobable that the *māhimi* Vanaratana of Kāragala was a son of Vīrabāhu Adipāda. The monastery was foundeded by Dalasengamu Migantaru to enable the princess Padmāvati to observe her religious duties without difficulty. It is quite proper that the incumbent of the monastery should have been vested in the hands of Vanaratana because he was a descendant of the Alakeśvara family to which Migantaru himself belonged, the founder of the institution. This is quite obvious by the fact that the Kāragala inscription II mentions that the monastery and its lands were a property of the family of Vanaratana from the Daṁbadeni period.[275]

The family connexions maintained by the hierarchs of the Sangha of this period may have led them to take great interest in the current political affairs of the country. We have seen earlier that Śrī Rāhula composed his two *sandeśa* poems, the *Sälaḷihiṇi-sandeśaya* and the *Parevi-sandeśaya*, as prayers to the gods that they might give a son to the princess Ulakudaya -devi and a husband to the princess Candrāvatī, the two daughters of Parākramabāhu VI.[276] At the beginning of the *Pañcikāpradāīpaya*, in two Pali stanzas, he prays for long life on Parākramabāhu VI, who had adopted him and brought him as as a son.[277] His association with the king and the royal family is quite evident from almost all his works. This close association with the royal family, to which he may himself have belonged, may have prompted him to take a keen interest in the current political affairs of the country. This over-enthusiasm of the hierarch in politics resulted in his deep indignation towards Bhuvanekabāhu VI who assassinated Jayabāhu II, the son of Ulakudaya-devi, and secured the throne for himself. Legend has it that Śrī Rāhula was so disappointed by this incident that he gave up public activities and led a secluded life afterwards.[278] This is proved by the fact that he did not participate in the higher ordination ceremony of foreign monks held under the auspices of Bhuvanekabāhu VI.[279]

## References

1. Sdhrt., p. 297.
2. *ibid.*

3. EZ., II, No. 6, Wickramasingha points out that according to a copy of *Dambadeṇi Kalikāvata* available at the British Museum, Or. 6680 (139), the *nikāyas* in question were the heretical sects called Dhammaruci, Sāgaliya and Vaitulya. EZ., II, No. 6, p. 275; The *Nikāyasaṅgrahaya* refers to the unification of the Sangha belonging to the three *nikāyas*, Dhammaruci, Sāgalika and Vaitulyavādi by Parākra-mabāhu I. *Nks.*, p. 22, But according to the description given in the *Cūlavaṃsa* the three well established *nikāyas* at this time were now other than the Mahāvihāra, Jetavana and Abhayagiri, Cv., 78, 12-22 and 77. 1-30, see also UCHC., P. 567 ff.
4. *Cv.*, 60-17 ff.
5. *Cv.*, 73. 12 ff.
6. *Kts.*, p. 8.
7. Y. Dhammavisuddhi, *The Buddhist Sangha in Ceylon*, (c. 1200-1400), (unpublished thesis submitted for the degree of Doctor of Philosophy of the University of London, 1970), p. 13 ff.
8. *ibid.*, p. 66.
9. Palābatgala is a mountainous locality in the Ratnapura District of the Sabargamuva Province, situated at a distance of about twelve miles from Ratnapura on the old route to Samanta- kūṭa See, *JCBRAS*, XXXI, p. 511-12.
10. *Sdhrt.*, pp. 72 and 501.
11. *Hms.*, 165 ff.
12. *Hms.*, v. 185 ff; H.W. Codrington, 'The Kāragala inscription', *JCBRAS.*, No. 86, 1925, p. 298 ff.
13. *Nks.*, p. 89.
14. *Tss.*, v. 65; *Prs.*, v. 69; *Grs.*, v. 105; *Kks.*, v. 90.
15. *Hms.*, v. 164 ff.
16. *Hms.*, v. 173
17. *Kts.*, p. 10.
18. *Sdhrt.*, p. 220.
19. *Sdhrt.*, p. 234.
20. *Sdhrt.*, p. 500 f.
21. *Sdhrt.*, p. 500 f.
22. Sannasgala, *Siṅhala Sandeśa Sāhityaya*, p. 179; M. Wickramasinha, *Siṅhala Sāhityaye Nägīma*, Colomb, 1954, p. 140.
23. Sannasgala, *Siṅhala Sandeśa Sāhityaya*, p. 179.
24. *Hms.*, v. 114 ff.; cf. *Grs.*, 166 ff.
25. *Hms.*, introduction, p. xxv.
26. *Hms.*, vv. 184-196.

27. *Hms.*, v. 181.
28. See Ch. V, p. 148 ff.
29. M. Wickramasinha, *op.cit.*, p. 120.
30. *Sdhrt.*, p. 14 ff.
31. *Sopadhiśesa- parinirvāṇadhātu*, the Arhat, whose impurities are all exhausted (*kṣīnāśrava*) while life remains, the series of great elements and secondary matter is not cut, and the series of thought resting on the five senses endures. As there are *upadhis*, the perfect exhaustion of all ties (*saṃyojanakṣaya*) that the Arhat obtains, takes, touches, realizes, (*prapti, prati, lamba, sparśana, sākṣātkāra*) is called *sopadhiśeṣa- nirvaāṇadhatu. Anupadhiśes-a-nirvāṇādhātu,* Arhat, whose impurities are all exhausted, life is extinct, the series of great elements and secondary matter is cut and thought resting on the five senses is not proceed further. As there are *upadhis* no longer, it is complete exhaustion of all ties and hence *nirupadhiśesa-nirvāṇādhātu*. See, *L'Abhidharmakoṣa de Vasubandhu*, Traduit et Annote par Louis De La Vallée Poussin, II, p. 284, VI, p. 211; Louis De La Vallée Poussin, 'The two Nirvānadhātus according to the Vibhāṣā, *Indian Historical Quarterly*, VI, pp. 39- 45.
32. N. Dutt. *Aspects of Mahāyāna Buddhism and Its Relation to Hīnayāna*, London, 1930, P. 96; M. Sasanaratana, *Lakdiva Mahāyāna Adahas*, Colombo, 1969, p. 217.
33. N. Dutt. *op. cit.* p. 117 ff; Har Dayal, *The Bodhisattva Doctrine in Buddhist Sanskrit Literature*, p. 28.
34. N. Dutt. *op. cit.*, p. 113 ff.
35. See, *Dīigha Nikāya*, (PTS), II, p. 8; *Majjhima Nikāya*, (PTS), I, p. 396.
36. S. Paranavitana, 'Mahayanism in Ceylon', *CJSc.*, (G), II, p. 43.
37. M. Sasanaratana, *Bauddha Darśana Sangrahaya*, Colombo, 1953, II, vv. 49-53.
38. *Sdhrt.*, p. 135 ff.
39. Bodhicaryāvātāra, ed. W. Medhananda, Colombo, 1953, II, vv. 49-53.
40. M. Sasanaratana, *Lakdiva Mahāyāva Adahas*, p. 213.
41. G.C. Mendis, *Early History of Ceylon*, Colombo, 1958, p. 54.
42. *EZ.*, IV, p. 242 ff.
43. *EZ.*, III, p. 66 ff.
44. *Sdhrt.*, p. 71.
45. *Hms.*, v. 201 ff.
46. D. Sumanajoti, Damabadeṇi Yugaya, II, p. 68; *Sāhityaya*, IV, 63.

47. *SSL.*, p. 104.
48. *Vss.*, v. 51 ff.
49. *JCBRAS.*, XXii, p. 15.
50. *Sāhityaya*, 1, 1957, p. 68.
51. *Rjv.*, p. 58.
52. *Queroz.*, p. 539.
53. *SSS.*, pp. 181-186.
54. *Grantha-dhura*; the burden of books, i.e. of studying the Scriptures, explained as one who knows by heart one, two or all *nikāyas*. Always combined with *vipassanā-dhura*, the burden of contemplation. See, *The Pali Text Society's Pali English Dictionary*, ed. T.W. Rhys Davids and William Stede, p. 73.
55. *Dhammapadaṭṭhakathā*, (PTS), ed. H.C. Norman, London, 1906, I, pp. 7, 8, 154; *Paramatthajotika*, (PTS), ed. H. Smith, London, 1916, pp. 194, 195, 306.
56 *Kts.*, p. 3.
57. *Kts.*, p. 13.
58. *Kts.*, p. 32.
60. *Nks.*, p. 96; *Rjrt.*, p. 17.
61. *Sumaṅgalavilāsinī*, (PTS), III, pp. 969-70.
62. *Kts.*, p. 19.
63. Wachissara, *Saraṇaṅkara Saṅgharāja Samaya*, p. 89.
64. See above, Ch. I, p. 23.
65. *Bdgnl.*, 134 ff.
66. See below, chapter vii.
67. *Prs.*, v. 178 ff; *Trs.*, v. 100; *Kks.*, v. 165; *Sls.*, vv. 77-92.
68. N. Mudiyanse, *Mahāyāna Monuments in Ceylon*, 1968, Colombo, p. 12.
69. *Prs.*, v. 178 ff; *Sls.*, vv. 77-92.
70. *Prs.*, v. 178 ff.
71. *Kks.*, v. 287.
72. *Prs.*, v. 178; *Kks.*, v. 287.
73. *Prs.*, v. 198.
74. *G. Varasambodhi*, *Gampola Ithihāsaya*, Colombo, 1948, p. 32. *AAGP.*, p. 64.
75. *ADK.*, folio. *klu*.
76. *ADK.*, folio. *klu*.
77. *ibid.*
78. K. Nanavimala, *Saparagamuve Pärani Liyavili*, p. 34.
79. Skt. Hasta, eleventh (or thirteenth) lunar asterism, *sv. Sanskrit-English Dictionary*, A.A. Macdonald, London, 1873.

80. *Prs.*, v. 43.
81. *Kuveṇi-asna*, ed. K. Nanavimala, Ratnapura, 1956, p. 11.
82. *Sls.*, v. 16.
83. *Kuveṇi-asna*, p. 11.
84. *Kvsk.*, p. 19.
85. For an account of ṣaḍbāṣā, see below, Ch. V. p. 152 ff.
86. *Prs.*, v. 203.
87. *SRS.*, p. 5.
88. *Rjrt.*, p. 56.
89. *Rjrt.*, p. 55.
90. *ibid.*
91. K. Wcchissara, *op. cit.*. p. 27.
92. M.B. Ariyapala, *Society in Medieval Ceylon*, Colombo, 1956, p. 233.
93. R.A.L.H. Gunawardhana, *Robe and Plough*, Monasticism and Economic Interest in Early Medieval Sri Lanka, The University of Arizona Press, 1979, p. 282 ff.
94. Sinh. Uturumula, Galaturumula, Kapurumula, Seneviratmula, Paspirivenmula, Vilgammula, Vahadumula, and Dakuṇumula, See, *Ssvp.*, p. 116.
95. *Dhampiyaāṭuvā-gäṭapadaya*, ed. D.B. Jayatilaka, Kelaniya, p. 200.
96. Gunawardhana, *op. cit.* p. 283.
97. *Kts.*, p. 13.
98. *Cv.*, 78. 32-33.
99. *Cv.*, 78. 32-33; *Pjv.*, p. 105.
100. Dhammavisuddhi, *op. cit.* p. 117.
101. *Kts.*, p. 13.
102. *UCHC.*, p. 247.
103. *Vss.*, vv. 42-45.
104. This institution is not mentioned in the list given by Vimalakirti in his *Sāsanavamsapradīpaya*, see, p. 166.
105. Dhammavisuddhi, *op. cit.* p. 96.
106. See below, Chapter V.
107. *Cv.*, 57.20-21.
108. *Cv.*, 57.31 ff.
109. See below, Ch. V.
110. *Pjv.*, p. 301.
111. *Kts.*, p. 13.
112. *Cv.*, 89.64.
113. *Nks.*, p. 90.

114. Nks; p. 96.
115. Gunawardhana, *op. cit.* p. 416.
116. *Cv.*, 57.
117. *CCMT.*, p. 213.
118. *Daḷadāsirita*, ed. W. Sorata, Colombo, 1953, p. 49 ff.
119. *Dls.*, p. 49 ff. An English translation of these regulations has been given in *ASCM*, III, pp. 34-37.
120. *Padasādhana-ṭīka*, ed. Dhammananda and Vacissara, Colombo, 1908, p. 134.
121. Kvsk., 1. v. 16.
122. *Theravādi* Bauddhācāryayo, A.P. Buddhadatta, Ambalangoda, 1960, p. 140.
123. *Prs.*, v. 203.
124. *Cv., 57.6. ff.*
125. Gunawardhana, *op. cit.* p. 446.
126. *Cv.*, 57. 31 ff.
127. *UCHC.*, p. 431.
128. *Prs.*, v. 148.
129. *Vss.*, 142.
130. *Nks.*, p. 96.
131. *Vṛttamālā*, Br. Mus. Ms. Or. 6611 (180), folio, *kī*.
132. *ADK.*,folio, *klu*.
133. *Vidyodaya*, III, No. 8, 1937, p. 230.
134. Vidyodaya; II, No. 9, 1936, p. 45; *Kts* p. 43 ff.
135. *Vimuktisaṅgrahava*, ed. H. Silaratana, Homagama, 1923, p. 215.
136. *Prs.*, v. 203.
137. *Cv.*, 48.2.
138. *Pjv.*, p. 139.
139. *Vss.*, v. 44.
140. *Vṛttamālā*, Br. Mus. Ms. Or. 6611 (178).
141. *Vṛttamālā, folio. kī*.
142. *Theravādi* Bauddhācāryayo, p. 147.
143. *Pdst.*, v. 6.
144. *Vṛttamālā, folio. kī*.
145. *Kavlakuṇu-miṇimala*, v. 8.
146. *Bdgnl.*, v. 4.
147. *SSL.*, p. 144.
148. *EZ.*, III, No. 25, p. 241 ff.
149. *Vss.*, v. 43.
150. *Cv.*, 88.85.
151. *Vss.*, v. 45.

152. *EZ.*, III, No. 25, p. 241 ff.
153. *ibid*
154. *Pācittiyapāli*, ed. Sri Ariyavamsa, Colombo, 1929, p. 74 ff.
155. *Majjhimanikāyṭṭhakathā*, ed. Sri Dharmarama, Colombo, 1917, pp. 150, 214, 354, 698.
156. *Suttapiṭaka* or *Suttantapiṭaka*, one of the three divisions of the Tripiṭaka. It consists of five *Nikāyas* : *Dīgha*, Majjhima, Samyutta, Aṅguttara and Khuddaka, See G.P. Malalasekara, *Dictionary of Pali Proper Names*, London, 1938, II, *Sv.*
157. *Suttanika*, versed in the Suttantas. A Suttanitika-bhikkhu is one who knows the *Suttas* (Contrast with *vinayadhara* who knows the rules of *vinaya*. PTSD, *Sv. Dhammadhara* was another name for *suttantika*, See, E.W. Adikaram, *Early History of Buddhism in Ceylon*, Colombo, 1946, p. 25.
158. *Sāratthadīpanī*, ed. B. Devarakkhita, Colombo, 1914, p. 36. Dharmapradīpikā ed. B. Vimalavamsa, Colombo, 1959, p. 284. *Pūjāvaliya*, ed. K. Nanavimala, Ratnapura, 1960. p. 311. *Saddharmālaṃkāraya*, ed. M. Nanesvara, Colombo, 1914, pp. 123.
159. *Mahāvagga*, ed. H. Oldenberg, London, 1879, 1.30, p. 58; 1.40, p. 74; 1.13, p. 197; *Cullavagga*, ed. H. Oldenberg, London, 1880, VI, p. 170.
160. *Cv.*, 89.18, 57.
161. CCMT., p. 198.
162. *Saddhrmaratnāvali*, ed. D.B. Jayatilaka, Kelaniya, 1946, p. 845.
163. *Sdrtl.*, pp. 237, 760.
164. *EZ.*, IV, pp. 253-260.
165. *EZ.*, IV, p. 254.
166. *Nks.*, p. 65.
167. *Anāgatavaṃsa*, ed. W. Medhananda, Colombo, 1934, p. viii.
168. TB., p. 101.
169. Ariyapala, *op. cit.* p. 232.
170. *CBRAS.*, XXXI, p. 398.
171. *Gunawardhana, op.cit.* p. 461.
172. *UCHC.*, p. 541.
173. *Nks.*, p. 85.
174. *EZ.*, IV, p. 266.
175. *Kts.*, p. 9.
176. *Sdhrt.*, p. 295.
177. *Hms.*, V. 104.
178. *CALR.*, 1, pt. III, p. 153 f.

179. *ADK.*, folio, *Ka.*
180. *Rjv.*, p. 47.
181. *Rjv.*, p. 53.
182. *Grs.*, V. 210.
183. *Sdhrt.*, p. 297.
184. *Cv.*, 84. 7-25; *Pjv.*, p. 145.
185. *AAGP.*, p. 11.
186. Dhammavisuddhi, *op. cit.* p. 49.
187. *Cv.*, 84. 11-16.
188. *Sdhrt.*, p. 500.
189. See below, p. 79.
190. See below, p. 79.
191. *Ez.*, IV, p. 93 ff; *UCHC.*, p. 636.
192. *Sdhrt.*, p. 297.
193. *Sdhrt.*, p. 778.
194. *Pāramīmahāsataka*, p. 97.
195. *UCHC.*, p. 637.
196. *Sdhrt.*, p. 298.
197. *Sinhalese Literature*, p. 122; *Pali Sāhityaya* p. 417; *PLC.*, p. 243.
198. *Sdhrml.*, p. 778; *Nks.*, p. 98.
199. *Sdhrt.*, p. 500; *Nks.*, p. 96.
200. *KYSS.*, p. 126 ff.
201. *Kks.*, V. 120.
202. W.F. Gunawardhana, *Kokila-sandesa- varṇanāva*, Colombo, 1934, p. 4.
203. K.T.W. Sumanasuriya, *A Critical Edition of the Kokila-sand-eśaya*, Colombo, 1955, p. 14.
204. *Nks.*, p. 94; *Sdhrt.*, p. 294.
205. *Kks.*, V. 120.
206. *Pdst.*, V.4.
207. *Nks.*, p. 89.
208. *Kvsk.*, canto, 1, V. 23; *Pdst*, V. 6.
209. *SRS.*, p. 126.
210. See below, p. 90
211. *TB.*, p. 160.
212. *SSL.*, p. 67 ff.
213. See above, p. 73 f.
214. *GTLK.*, p. iv.
215. *Pansiya Paṇas Jātaka Pota*, ed. N. Dhammananda, 1955, p. 13 oofff.
216. *Bhakti-Sataka-Sinhala Sannaya* ed., A.D. de. S. Batuvantudave, Colombo, 1914, p. 113.

217. *Kts.*, p. 41.
218. *Vidyodaya*, Vol. V, No. 11, p. 34.
219. *Vṛttamālā*, Br. Mus. Or. 6611 (180).
220. *SSV.*, p. 323.
221. *Vimuktisaṅgrahava*, ed. H. Silaratana, Homagama, 1923, p. 125.
222. *TB.*, p. 141; *Sañdakiñdurudā-kava*, ed. M. Piyaratana, Colombo, 1960, p. iii.
223. K.D.P. Wickramasinha, *Siṅhala Lekhaka Parapura*, Colombo, 1964, p. 384.
224. *Mhv.*, pp. 147-8, 297-8.
225. *Aṅguttara Nikāya* (PTS), London, 1899, part. IV, p. 202 ff; See also, *Dīgha Nikāya*, ed. T.W.Rhys Davids, London, 1947, 11, p. 72 f.
226. *Mv.*, xx, 14-15.
227. *Mv.*, xx, 60-62.
228. *HBC.*, p. 58.
229. *Cv.*, 52.27.
230. *Cv.*, 60.69.
231. *Kts.*, p. 9.
232. *Sāhityaya*, Dambadeṇi Kalāpaya, 1958, p. 92.
233. *Nks.*, p. 96.
234. *Cv.*, 92.22 ff; *Rjrt.*, p. 165.
235. *Cv.*, 94.15 ff.
236. *Cv.*, 97.14 ff.
237. *Kts.*, p. 9.
238. *UCHC.*, p. 748.
239. M. Vimalakirti, *Siṅhala Ānḍuva*, Colombo, 1956, p. 236.
240. Dhammavisuddhi, *op.cit.*, p. 125.
241. Cv. 87.3.
242. This village is situated two miles to the north-east of Gokarälla in the Häṭahaya Korale of the Kurunegala District. See *EZ.*, IV, No. 1, pp. 4-8.
243. *Vaṃsa* and *kula* in this context seem to have been used to denote a lineage or family. These two terms are often used so loosely in Pali nad Sinhalese sources that it is difficult to determine their exact meaning. cf. *SSSk*, S.V.; *PTSD.*, s.v.
244. *UCHC.*, p. 748.
245. *EZ.*, IV, pp. 310 ff.
246. *Sddhrt.*, pp. 294-295.
247. *ibid.*
248. *UCHC.*, p. 663.

249. *Cv.*, 74.48.
250. Sirima Wickramasinghe, *The Age of Parākramabāhu*, I, Unpublished thesis submitted for the Doctor of Philosophy of the University of London, 1958, p. 71.
251. *Dlds.*, p. 49 ff.
252. *EZ.*, IV, pp. 4-8.
253. *Sdhrt.*, p. 295.
254. H. Ellawala, Social Institutions in Ceylon from the 5th century B.C. to the 4th century A.D., Colombo, 1971, p. 36.
255. *EZ.*, p. 93 ff.
256. *Sdhrt.*, p. 500.
257. *ibid.*
258. *Kvsk.*, canto. 1, V. 23; *Prs.*, v. 203.
259. *SRS.*, p. 96; *KYSS.*, p. 64; *TB.*, p. 155.
260. *Pañcikāpradīpaya*, vv. 1-2; *Pdst.*, V. 1-4; *Kks.*, v. 81.
261. *CALR*, 1, p. 153.
262. *Pdst.*, V. 6.
263. *Kks.*,v. 291.
264. Sumanasuriya, *op. cit.*, p. VII.
265. *SHC.*, p. 54.
266. *Hms.*, v. 104.
267. *Hms.*, v. 48.
268. *CALR.*, 1, p. 153.
269. *Vss.*, VV, 51-58.
270. *Hms.*, V. 182.
271. *CBRAS.*, XXXII, No. 86, pp. 298-300.
272. *UCHC.*, p. 658.
273. *Rjv.*, p. 47; *JCBRAS.*, No. 68, pp. 96-102, & 110-111.
274. *Nks.*, p. 96.
275. *CBRAS.*, No. 86, p. 299.
276. *Sls.*, V. 103; *Prs.*, v. 198.
277. *Pañcikāpradīpaya*, vv. 2-3.
278. *SRS*, p. 34.
279. See below Ch. VI. p. 176 ff.

## Chapter Four

# The State and the Sangha

As has been discussed earlier the political condition of the country before the beginning of the Kōṭṭē kingdom was troubled by internal dissension and foreign intervention into the affairs of the country. Throughout this period of political instability, which had lasted from the decline of the Dam̆badeni dynasty at the end of the thirteenth century, the Buddhist Sangha faced various difficulties owing to the lack of royal patronage. The Sangha could not maintain its purity and prestige without such support. This situation gave an opportunity to imposters to gain a foothold in the Sangha. The *Nikāyasaṅgrahaya* states that such people brought discredit on the Sangha by their conduct and damaged the cause of Buddhism.[1]

In spite of these disastrous conditions there were occasional attempts to arrest the further decline of the Sangha. It is significant, according to the *Nikāyasaṅgrahaya* and *Saddharmaratnākaraya*, that these efforts, unlike those in the past, were made not by the reigning monarchs but by some members of the nobility of the country. It should be added that during this period certain noble families succeeded in becoming *de facto* rulers of the country by relegating the reigning monarch of the time to the background.[2] The first recorded attempt to prevent the decline of the Sangha was made by Sēnā Laṅkādhikāra, the prime minister of Bhuvanekabāhu IV (1341-1351) of Gampola, who called an assembly of the executives of the Sangha belonging to both fraternities, the Vanavāsa and Gāmavāsa, under the presidency of Vanaratana *mahāsāmi* of Amaragirivāsa.[3] In this assembly, an enquiry was conducted and the monks who led disreputable lives were expelled from the Sangha. This purge, according to the *Nikāyasaṅgrahaya*, took place in 1345 A.D., which is equated with the fourth regnal year of Bhuvanekabāhu IV.[4] Sēnā Laṅkādhikāra's service towards the religion was not confined to this purification of the Sangha, for the *Nikāyasaṅgrahaya* gives an impressive account of his religious activities afterwards. According to the text, he built a three-storeyed image-house at Devinuvara and a shrine at the Agrabodhi Vihāraya at Väligama.[5]

It has been suggested by Paranavitana that Sēnā Laṅkādhikāra was no doubt actuated by genuine religious fervour in undertaking these and other works, but the selection of these two seaports in the south as the recipients of his bounty must have been calculated to win the good-will of the people of that area which was under control of Rayigama, the rival royal house of the time.[6] However, he was successful in securing this end, for not long afterwards we find a religieux of Devinuvara composing a poem, the *Tisara- sandeśaya,* invoking the blessings of the local god on Parākramabāhu V (1344-1359) of Dädigama, the patron of Sēnā Laṅkādhikāra.[7]

Not very long after the purification of the Sangha, which was carried out under the patronage of Sēnā Laṅkādhikāra, it is reported in the chronicles that another attempt was made to check the decline of the Sangha. This time the patron was the semi-independant ruler (*prabhurāja*) Alakeśvara III, the founder of the Kōṭṭē kingdom. His achievements in the political field may have enabled him to turn his attention towards the uplift of the Sangha. The *Nikāyasaṅgrahaya* records that Alakeśvara found that it was highly necessary once again to put the affairs of the Sangha in order.[8] As was customary, he consulted the Primate at the time, Dhammakitti *mahāsāmi* and, acting in accordance with his wise counsel, expelled a number of monks who had been leading openly disreputable lives in the Sangha. Apart from this purification of the Sangha, Alakeśvara took various steps towards the well-being of the Sāsana.[9] Besides Alakeśvara's purification, there is another reference to a purge of the Sangha carried out under the patronage of Vīrabāhu Ādipāda, who ruled the country simultaneously with Bhuvanekabāhu V (1372-1408) of Gampola.[10] Although none of our sources gives details of these purifications, it is not difficult to understand that the political instability of the country caused great harm to the religion.

Roughly speaking, the period which followed the downfall of the Daṁbadeni dynasty at the end of the thirteenth century and preceded the accession of Parākramabāhu VI of Kōṭṭē in 1415 A.D. witnessed numerous petty rulers wielding independent power in various parts of the Island. As the kings of Gampola were generally weak, their chief ministers assumed supreme power.

In the inscriptions of the period, we find instances where the chief minister of the time is mentioned in terms more laudatory than those applied to the reigning monarch. In spite of this political weakness of the country, short intervals of peace and prosperity gave an impulse to the advancement of the religion. The inauguration of the Gampola kingdom was marked by the building of the famous Laṅkātilaka and Gaḍalādeniya temples, two monuments showing the influence of South Indian architecture.[11]

In addition to kings and ministers, some dignitaries of the Sangha were also instrumental in building religious monuments and making attempts to arrest the further deterioration of the Sangha. The hierarchs bearing the name of Dharmakīrti figure prominently in the religious history of this period. Of these, Sīlavaṃsa Dharmakīrti, the pupil of Dharmakīrti of Palābatgala, was responsible for the building of some religious foundations, even one in South India. The *Saddharmaratnākaraya* states that he arrived in India at Dhanyakaṭaka (Amarāvati), one of the most celebrated of Buddhist centres in ancient India, and had a stone *vihāra* called Śrī Dhanyakaṭaka erected there.[12] Having returned to Sri Lanka after some time, he lived for a while at Alavatura *vihāra* (also called Ganegoda *vihāra*) in the Kāgalla District. The reigning monarch at the time was Vijayabāhu, identified by Codrington as the fifth of that name.[13]

The hierarch Sīlavaṃsa later, presumably after the demise of his teacher, assumed the name of Dharmakīrti and composed the Pali poem *Pāramīmahāsataka*.[14] With the accession of Bhuvanekabāhu IV at Gampola, Dharmakīrti took up abode at the monastery called Mālatī-māla-sela built by the king on a rock in the neighbourhood of Ambuluvākanda. At this dwelling was composed the Pali poem *Janānurāga-carita.*[15] From Mālatīmāla-sela, the hierarch went to Gaḍalādeniya in Uḍunuvara and caused to be built there on the Dikgala a *vihāra* called Saddharmatilaka (otherwise called Gaḍalādeniya Vihāra), with the aid of some Indian architects headed by one Gaṇeśvarācāri.[16] The hierarch's inscription at the place is dated in the third year of Bhuvanekabāhu IV (1341- 1351).[5] He was the hierarch who presided at the Convocation of the Sangha of 1912 B.E. (1369 A.D.) held under the auspices of the great *prabhurāja* Alakeśvara III.[17] Tradition has it that the hierarch was a brother of a king called Parākramabāhu.

The pupil of the hierarch was Jayabāhu Devarakṣita or Dharmakīrti II, otherwise calledMahadāliyāvaṃsa Devarakṣita. He was the author of *Saddharmālaṅkāraya, Bālāvatārasanne* (Gaḍalādeni-sanne), *Jinabodhāvalī* and the *Nikāyasaṅgrahaya.* Together with Maitreya of Galaturumula, he presided over the Convocation of the Sangha of 1939 B.E. (1396 A.D.) convened under the patronage of Vīrabāhu Ādipāda.[18]

The last quarter of the fourteenth century witnessed chaos, political changes and disorganisation of the Sangha. It is likely that 1386/7 A.D. was the date of the passing away of the great Alakeśvara who established the harmony of the Sangha at the Convocation of 1869 A.D. None of the rulers who succeeded him nor any of the dignitaries of the Sangha who succeeded the first Dharmakīrti, is associated with religious foundations, but the shrines founded by their predecessors were to some extent maintained in good condition until Parākramabāhu VI of Kōṭṭē.

The accession of Parākramabāhu VI marks a new era not only in the political field but also in the cultural life of the country. The relationship between the state and the Sangha during his reign, which extends over more than half a century, was remarkable. We are informed by some of the sources pertaining to this period that during his childhood he enjoyed the protection of some of the high dignitaries of the Sangha. According to the *Rājāvaliya* and *de Couto*, Vīdāgama *mahāthera,* who was a powerful figure in the political affairs of the country at the beginning of the fifteenth century, gave Prince Parākrama and his mother protection against Vīra Alakeśvara, and finally installed him on the throne.[19] Apart from Vīdāgama *mahāthera*, there were a number of monks who were closely connected with the king. Śrī Rahula did not hesitate to mention in his literary works his close relationship with Parākramabāhu VI.[20]

Parākramabāhu VI had to devote much energy to preventing further decadence of the religion which had suffered through neglect or otherwise in the troubled times that preceded his reign. His determination towards this end follows from the *Maha Saman Dēvālaya Sannasa* of Ratnapura, which states that the king sat in the assembly with his regional rulers and ministers discussing ways and means of restoring and maintaining the monasteries and *dēvālayas* that were in a state of disrepair.[21]

It seems that the first step of the king's religious policy was to build abodes for monks in his capital. The *Rājāvaliya* records that the king caused a number of monasteries to be built for the Sangha in his capital.[22] Valentijn's version of the *Rājāvaliya* records :-

> He (Parākranabāhu VI) remained three years at Rayigama, then removed to Cotta (Kōṭṭē), and there he built a fine city entirely of solid blue stone, and a beautiful palace of the same stone, but with a number of devils, and of the idols that he worshipped. Here (in his new palace) he dwelt in a company of a priest whom he esteemed very highly, he preserved here (in the new capital) the relics of Budun, and built a special house or monastery for his priests.[23]

This account may help us to understand the king's service towards the Sangha in the early years of his reign. Apart from the monasteries for the Sangha, Parākramabāhu VI had a *pohoyagē* built as an assembly hall for the monks where they could regularly perform their *uposatha* ceremonies.

The holy Tooth Relic which was always kept by Sinhalese kings near their own palace, had become the palladium of the kingdom in medieval Sri Lanka. This new chapter of the history of the Tooth Relic begins in the twelfth century.[24] In the disastrous times that preceded the reign of Parākramabāhu VI, the Relic shared all the vicissitudes of the kingdom, and it was often necessary to protect the Relic against foreign invaders and usurpers of the throne. Parākramabāhu VI, realizing this and following the practice of his predecessors, caused the construction of a magnificent three-storeyed building (*tun-mahal-pahaya*) for the Relic adjacent to his royal palace[25]. Every poet of the day who described the city of Kōṭṭē mentioned the Daḷadā-Māligāva (the palace of the Tooth Relic) which was looked after with much care by the king himself.[26]

Parākramabāhu VI next turned his attention to repairing shrines and other religious buildings which had suffered through neglect in the past. Of these efforts, the first was that of restoring the Laṅkātilaka and Gaḍalādeniya shrines which had been built in the time of Gampola kingdom. The Gaḍalādeniya inscription, which mentions the repairs effected by the king, records that this was achieved immediately after the subjugation of the Uḍaraṭa kingdom which had been ruled by a prince called Sēnā Laṅkādhikāra, presumably the grandson of the great Sēnā Laṅkādhikāra.[27] Doubtless as a means of winning the loyalty of the people of Highlands, the king may have undertaken of restoration of the two shrines which had been held in great veneration by them.

A long list of the restoration works undertaken by the king is included in the *Saddharmaratnākaraya* and the *Cūlavaṃsa.*[28] According to these sources, the buildings renovated were the Mahiyaṅgaṇa, Kelaṇiya and Doraṇāgoḍa *cetiyas*. The image house at Saparagamu *vihāraya*, the five-storeyed mansion (*pas-mahal-pahaya*) and the image houses such as Saḷapiḷama-geya, Otpiḷima-geya, Nāmeṇevi-geya, Sätapena-geya, Telak-aṭāra-geya at Kelaṇiya were some of the edifices that were repaired and renovated by the king.[29] *The Sälalihiṇi-sandeśaya* gives a vivid picture of the Kelaṇiya temple, during the reign of Parākramabāhu VI.[30] It was after this restoration that this shrine flourished in all its glory. Having heard the hazards and hardships suffered by those who travelled to Samantakūṭa to worship the Foot-print of the Buddha, the king caused iron railings to be fixed at spots where the ascent to the mountain was difficult.[31] Besides, he built a resthouse at Gilīmalē, near

Samantakūṭa, where the pilgrims were supplied with free food and drink.[32]

In addition to constructing and restoring religious buildings, Parākramabāhu VI turned his attention towards the establishment and maintenance of educational institutions that were attached to the monasteries. Two of these may be mentioned here: first, the Pirivena built in memory of his mother Sunetrādevi, at Päpiliyāna;[33]; the Päpiliyāna document II gives details of the king's benefactions towards this institution.[34] The other establishment set up by the king is Mahapāya Pirivena at Ussāpiṭiya in the Kāgalla district.[35]

This institution is not mentioned in any of the literary works of this time. Besides these two institutions, there were a large number of ecclesiastical educational establishments which received the patronage of the king. They were the Padmāvati Pirivena at Kāragala, Vijayabāhu Pirivena at Totagamuva, Tilaka Pirivena at Devinuvara and Srighanānanda Pirivena at Vīdāgama. The extent to which the king extended his patronage to religious education may be seen from this large number of educational establishments that flourished during his reign. A detailed study on these institutions will be made in a later chapter of this study.[36]

The benefactions of Parākramabāhu VI towards the educational institutions were not confined to constructing buildings or granting lands for their maintenance. He no doubt realized the importance of books for the dissemination of knowledge as a necessary ancillary to these institutions. The ancient rulers of the country always valued a numerous, well-instructed clergy of blameless morals for the welfare of the Sāsana and the kingdom.[37] They therefore induced prominent monks to preach the doctrine, and they caused sacred texts to be copied and commentaries to be written on such books. Mahinda IV, in the tenth century, entrusted the learned *thera* Dhammamitta with the composition of a commentary on the Abhidhamma.[38] Parākramabāhu II (1236- 1270) sent many gifts to the Coḷa country and invited to Sri Lanka many respected Coḷa monks who were well known for their moral conduct and versed in the Tripiṭaka.[39] Following this ancient practice and realizing the necessity of religious books, Parākramabāhu VI took various steps to make available in great number books on the teaching of the Buddha. The scribes who daily copied the books on the doctrine were amply remunerated with grants of villages and the like. The Mädavala Sannasa of Vijayabāhu VI[40] records a bestowal of certain lands to a person called Dharmālaṅkāra Paṇḍita for his services in arranging the writing of religious books at Sunetrādevi Pirivena at Päpiliyāna.[41] There is also in the Päpiliyāna document II of Parākramabāhu VI an interesting reference to the articles that should be offered to a monk who would write one thousand *granthas*[42] of the Tripiṭaka.[43] Thus it will be seen that the king not only provided for scribes who could copy books continually but also had assigned officers to make arrangements for the writing of books. This indeed shows the meticulous care he took in ensuring a great supply of books on the religion for the purpose of disseminating religious knowledge.

After the purification of the Sangha carried out under the patronage of Vīrabāhu Ādipāda (1397/8) no attempt to reorganize the Order seems to have been made until the reign of Parākramabāhu VI (1415-1467). The political instability that prevailed in the country before his reign seems to have led to laxity among some members of the Sangha.[44] While their usual source of sustenance was absent or otherwise diminished, the monks who had to fend for themselves did not maintain their high standard of conduct and, by force of circumstances, were perhaps, even led them to practise secular arts for the purpose of gain.[45] While undertaking other activities for the advancement of Buddhism, Parākramabāhu VI did not fail to realize the importance of the reorganization of the Sangha as an essential condition for the furtherance of religion. A state of corruption in the Sangha is to some extent implied in the Päpiliyāna document II.[46] To check any further decline of the Sangha he took necessary steps with the wise counsel of the leaders of *gaṇas (gaṇa-nāyaka-tän)*. The Päpiliyāna document II and a fragmentary *katikāvata* (a code of *vinaya* rules)[47] record some of the rules pertaining to the conduct of the Sangha. These remaining rules of the *katikāvata* bear great resemblance to those of the *Dambadeni Katikāvata*. The author of the *Saddharmartnākaraya* advises the future rulers of the country to emulate the way in which Parākramabāhu VI purified and protected the *theriyanikāya*.[48]

The king took further steps to stabilize the Sangha by arranging for annual *upasampadā* festivals. We are told by the chroniclers that in the later medieval period from the end of the eleventh Century many Sinhalese kings, in order to invigorate the Sangha, arranged festivals in connexion with which the *upasampadā* ceremony was performed by monks. Vijayabāhu I (1070-1110) invited monks from Rāmañña (Burma) for that purpose,[49] caused to be held *upasampadā* ceremonies at several times. Similar ceremonies were instituted by Parākramabāhu I (1153-1186)[50], Vijayabāhu III (1232-1236) of Daṁbadeniya and his successor, Parākramabāhu II (1236-1270) who celebrated eight ceremonies of that kind, each of them lasting seven days.[51] By this procedure this ceremony assumed the importance of a state function in later centuries. Thus an *upasampadā* held by Bhuvanekabāhu I (1272-1284) is called a 'world festival' (*loka-maṅgala*).[52] Following the practices adopted by his ancient predecessors Parākramabāhu VI made necessary arrangements to hold annual *upasampadā* ceremonies. The *Saddharmaratnākaraya* states that the king performed a large number of *upasaṁpadā* ceremonies in order to ensure the continuity of pure Theravāda.[53] As has already been mentioned, the *Jinakālamālī* records a religious mission of the Elder Medhaṅkara who came to Sri Lanka to receive higher ordination under the guidance of the Sinhalese Sangha.[54] This mission included monks from Cambodia, Thailand and Burma.[55]

The foregoing discussion may help us to understand that the peaceful state of the country under Parākramabāhu VI (1415-1467) of Kōṭṭē inspired the Buddhists to intense activity in the promotion of their traditional religion. Under his patronage *vihāras* and scholastic establishments attached to them arose in many parts of the country. The Buddhist monks were well organized and well provided with their necessities. They found leisure and time for the fulfilment of the obligations attached to their vocation. Among the laity there was wide awakening of religious consciousness. Education greatly flourished and many literary works for the dissemination of religious knowledge were produced. In effect, it was a period of a great revivalist activity, a golden age in the history of the Sinhalese culture.

The peace and prosperity that existed under Parākramabāhu VI (1415- 1467) did not long survive his death. Immediately after his death the country was again troubled with internal dissension. The struggle for the throne between Jayabāhu II (1467-1469) and Bhuvanekabāhu VI (1469-1478) weakened the political stability of the country, and led towards the disintegration of the kingdom of Kōṭṭē. The Buddhist monks at this time did not seem to have been politically inactive, and it is possible that they took sides in the dispute between the two princes. We know that Śrī Rāhula was one of the closest well-wishers of Jayabāhu II. His *Sälaḷihiṇi-sandesaya* was written in order to offer prayer to Vibhīṣaṇa of Kelaṇiya for this prince's birth.[56] There are many stories showing how this hierarch looked forward to seeing Jayabāhu as king in succession to his grandfather, Parākramabāhu VI.[57] We can understand his disappointment when Bhuvanekabāhu VI killed the prince in order to gain the throne. The *Padasādhana-ṭīkā* written by Śrī Rāhula in his old age during the reign of Bhuvanekabāhu VI contains no reference to the reigning monarch.[58] The Kalyāṇi inscriptions refer to this hierarch as a virtuous monk, but the inscriptions do not mention him as having taken part in the higher ordination ceremony in 1476 A.D., during the reign of Bhuvanekabāhu VI.[59] It may be assumed that his political alignment and estrangement from the monarch were strong factors in his non- participation in this ceremony.

In contrast to the political ideas of Śrī Rāhula, there was another group of monks who were opposed to Jayabāhu's succession to the throne and favoured prince Sapumal (Bhuvanekabāhu VI) instead. The conquest of the Jaffna kingdom would naturally have marked him as the most outstanding prince of the period. We have seen above that the principal monk of the Tilaka Pirivena at Devinuvara composed his *Kokila-sandeśaya* seeking the blessings of the gods upon

Sapumal who was then residing at Jaffna as viceroy of Parākramabāhu VI.[60] Some writers take this as evidence to show that his most ardent supporters came from the southern-most part of the country, thereby even bypassing the king of Kōṭṭē, Parākramabāhu VI.[61] But this seems very doubtful because we have seen earlier that the strongest opposition to the accession of Bhuvanekabāhu came from the area comprising the Kalu-gaṅga to the Valavē-gaṅga which included even Devinuvara itself.[62] However, it is apparent that the sympathies of a group of monks, led by Vīdāgama Maitreya, were with Sapumal while Śrī Rāhula and his followers invoked blessings for the safety of the new king Jayabāhu II.[63] The *Aramkäkē* Sannasa bears evidence to the visit by Vīdāgama Maitreya to Yāpāpaṭuna, where Sapumal was residing.[64] Although it was ostensibly a visit for religious purposes it points to very close relations between Sapumal and the monks led by Vīdāgama Maitreya. The *sannasa* further mentions the endowments made towards Vīdāgama and his pupils by Bhuvanekabāhu VI, after he became king.

The close ralations between Vīdāgama Maitreya and Bhuvanekabāhu VI may be confirmed by the position held by this hierarch in the Kalyānī higher ordination ceremony in 1476 A.D. For this ceremony, held under the auspices of Bhuvanekabāhu VI, members of the Sangha were summoned by Vīdāgama Maitreya in accordance with the king's request.[65]

Both the *Cūlavaṃsa* and the *Rājāvaliya* make but a very brief reference to the reign of Bhuvanekabāhu VI and no mention whatsoever is made of his religious activities. The *Rājaratnākaraya*, however, mentions that he made a *karaṇḍuva* (casket) for the Tooth Relic at a cost of seven thousand *massas*,[66] made monthly and yearly offerings to the monks and distributed alms beyond calculation.[67] To Bhuvanekabāhu VI is also attributed the construction of the Galagama *vihāraya* at Galagama in the Central Province.[68] The *Aramkälē Sannasa* gives details of Bhuvanekabāhu's benefactions towards the Dharmarāja Pirivena at Erabattoṭa, Kōṭṭē, the principal of which was Niyaṅdavanē Phussadeva Sumaṅgala, the chief disciple of Vīdāgama Maitreya, and to the Vīdāgama fraternity of *bhikkhus*.[69] Apart from these limited religious activities, Bhuvaṇekabāhu VI's reign is marked by lively religious intercourse with present Burma. As will be seen later, Dhammaceti of Pegu sent a mission of Mon monks in order to have higher ordination conferred upon them by the Sinhalese Sangha. After suppressing the rebellion in the early part of his reign, with the help of Vīdāgama Maitreya's counsel the king was able to fulfil the aims of this religious mission, and thus reassured the fame of the country as the centre of Theravāda.

Popular cults then prevailing do not seem to have been neglected by Bhuvanekabāhu VI, for tradition ascribes to him the construction of the Doravaka *devāle* within the precincts of which he had constructed a small shrine dedicated to the goddess Pattini.[70] Bhuvanekabāhu VI, it is also said, endowed the Maha Saman Dēvālaya of Ratnapura with lands and gifted his own *cāmara* (whisk) and palanquin.[71] These limited religious activities of Bhuvanekabāhu VI (1470-1478) show us that, although he was not able to retain the overlordship of the whole Island, he was successful in continuing to some extent the religious policy that was carried out by his great predecessor, Parākramabāhu VI (1415- 1467).

After the death of Bhuvanekabāhu VI the political situation of the country deteriorated further. His immediate successor, Paṇḍita Parākramabāhu (VII) was slain by his uncle, Vīra Parākramabāhu (VIII), who then became king in his place. The Sinhalese chronicles are silent with regard to any religious activities of Vīra Parākramabāhu (1484- 1508) or his predecessor, Paṇḍita Parākramabāhu (1480-1484). Thus Vīra Parākramabāhu's twenty-four years' reign is not of much significance in the religious history of the country. However, tradition ascribes to him the rebuilding of the Galagama monastery.[72] Algama monastery, (also in the Kāgalla district), is said to date from the time of this king.[73]

The next ruler, Dharma Parākramabāhu (IX), could not do much for the cause of the religion because of the political unrest in his reign. On the one hand, there was trouble from his own subjects, and on the other, there were constant threats from the Muslims settled in the coastal areas of the country.[74] In fact, a formidable attack under Adirāsa Rāya of Kāyal Paṭṭanam, was repelled only with considerable difficulty. The Portuguese arrival in the country, at the close of his predecessor's reign, added further confusion to the political situation. In spite of these political troubles he had to face, Dharma Parākramabāhu did not completely neglect the maintenance of religious activities.

Queyroz, writing on Dharma Parākramabāhu, states: 'Their priests, called *changatheras (sanghatheras)*, picture this king as one so friendly to the poor and to the worship of Budun, that for this reason they gave him the name of Dharma, which means "Almsgiver".[75] This remark by Queyroz helps us understand the king's popularity among his subjects, including the Sangha. However, besides his acts of generosity his major religious undertaking reported is the restoration work he had carried out in the Kelaniya monastery, which was in a dilapidated condition at the time. The repairs were carried out at the direction of the king by the *gaṇanāyaka-thera* or the chief incumbent of the monastery and by the minister called Vijayakkōnāra.[76] After the completion of the work, Dharma Parākramabāhu directed that a paddy tax and a *fanam* for every ten coconut trees were to be paid towards the maintenance of the monastery. Moreover, he had the boundaries of the parish belonging to the monastery extended so as to include Vattala, Gōnahēna, and Diviyāmulla up to the Kelaṇi river.[77]

The successor of Dharma Parākramabāhu, Vijayabāhu VI, had to face growing tension in the political field. This was on the one hand, caused by the conflict between the Muslims and the Portuguese in Colombo. On the other hand, his position was challenged by his own sons on account of the succession to the throne. Despite political upheavals and confusion, Vijayabāhu VI was able to contribute towards the cause of religion in a limited way, and that only during the early part of his reign.

In the inscription at the Kappāgoḍa temple in the Kāgalla district, dated in the reign of Vijayabāhu VI, mention is made of a Pirivena attached to the monastery. For its restoration Vijayasiṅha Ekanāyaka Perumāl, the prime minister of the king, granted certain fields the revenue of which had to be used for this purpose.[78] Popular cults seem to have received his patronage, for mention is made in the *Kāgalla Vihāraya Sannasa* that the king dedicated lands to the *Moṭṭāpiṭiya dēvālaya* in the Kāgalla district.[79] In the *Devundara Dēvālaya Sannasa* mention is made of the dedication by the king of lands to the god Upulvan.[80] Like Bhuvanekabāhu VI, Vijayabāhu VI dedicated his *cāmara* 'whisk' and palanqain to the Maha Saman Dēvālaya of Ratnapura.[81]

While the Kōṭṭē kingdom suffered political upheavals and disturbances the kingdom of Kandy enjoyed a period of comparative peace and tranquillity under its founder Sēnāsammata Vikramabāhu. This enabled Vikramabāhu to turn his attention towards the promotion of Buddhism, which was much in decline. The *Cūlavaṃsa* enumerates a number of benefactions by this king towards the Sangha.[82] But a more comprehensive account of his religious activities is contained in the *Rājaratnākaraya* composed towards the end of his reign.[83] Among the various activities of Vikaramabāhu for the furtherance of Buddhism was the construction of religious edifices.

Vikramabāhu enshrined relics of the Buddha by founding a *dāgäba* near the city, built a great *vihāraya* with stone pillars by it, as well as a two-storeyed *uposatha* enclosure and the reference being to the *dāgäba* and the *pohoya- maluva* close to Malvatu Vihāraya of Kandy. Around the city in many places he had 86 monastic residences built so that 'such monks as who recommended for living soberly and piously be placed in the said houses'.[84] Among other good works, he constructed a new Mahā *vihāraya* (a great monastery) for the Great Elder, learned in the Tripiṭaka, who had come from abroad with 35 monks, viz. Dhammakitti, who reformed the Sangha and held an ordination in the Mahaväli-gaṅga: tradition has that he was of Pohoye Maluva of Kandy.[85] The *gedigē* at Ādāhana Maluva, Asgiriya, Kandy was built by Vikramabāhu at the site of cremation of his mother, enshrining the urn containing her ashes.[86] It is in the reign of Vikramabāhu that for the first time since the age of Parākramabāhu VI (1415- 1467) there is evidence for the copying of religious texts on a large scale. He is said to have had the sacred books copied on 30,000 palm leaves and for this purpose spent 60,000 gold pieces.[87]

Owing to the unsettled state of the country, it seems that no higher ordination ceremony had been held since the reign of Bhuvanekabāhu VI (1470-1478). Vikramabāhu now turned his attention towards the re-establishment of this very important ceremony which had been long discontinued. In the *udakukkhepa-sīmā* built on the Mahaväli-gaṅga he had the ceremony performed, presided over by the Elder Dhammakitti. At this ceremony no fewer than 350 novices received the higher ordination.[88]

As might have been expected, the Sangha had become corrupt during the disturbed times after the death of Parākramabāhu VI (1415- 1467). The *Rājaratnākaraya* states that this deterioration was more evident among the Gāmavāsi monks.[89] Taking into account this degeneration of the Sangha, Vikramabāhu assembled the monks belonging to both fraternities, Gāmavāsa and Vanavāsa, under the presidency of the Elder Dhammakitti. In this assembly diligent enquiries were made as to their character and those who were approved were promoted, whereas the others were accused of leaving unholy lives were disrobed and dismissed from the Sangha.[90]

Vikramabāhu's religious activities were not confined to his capital. The *Cūlavaṃsa* states that he went to Mahiyaṅgaṇa, and having seen the dilapidated condition of the *cetiya* there, had it repaired.[91] Considering the difficulties which pilgrims had to undergo in the ascent of the Samantakūṭa, he had bridges constructed to span the river, and had 765 steps built.[92] The nature and the extent of the benefactions of Vikramabāhu are clear evidence for the happy state of Buddhism in the Kandyan kingdom, and the Sangha owed much to his devotion during one of the darkest period of its history.

After its division in 1521, the kingdom of Kōṭṭē became a field of constant internal warfare. With the animosity of his brothers directed against him, the reign of Bhuvanekabāhu VII (1521-1551) could not have been peaceful. The Portuguese took the side of Bhuvanekabāhu VII against his brothers with the ulterior motive of making the king of Kōṭṭē entirely and absolutely dependent on them. These developments eventually led to a decline of Buddhism in the low-lands.

None of our sources mentions any religious activities of Bhuvanekabāhu VII. However, according to a palm-leaf manuscript seen by Bell at the Kodigamuva temple in Galaboḍa-pattuva (Kāgalla district), the said monastery appears to have been built by either Bhuvanekabāhu VI or Bhuvanekabāhu VII.[93] Judging from the state of the religious affairs mentioned in the manuscript and the political situation in the reign of Bhuvanekabāhu VII, it is more likely that the monastery in question was built in the former king's reign.

Although Bhuvanekabāhu VII lived as a Buddhist until his death, it would not be incorrect to consider his reign the beginning of serious decline of Buddhism. In order to protect his throne against his brother Māyādunne of Sītāvaka, this ruler relied upon the support of the Portuguese. As a manifestation of friendly relations towards the Portuguese, he had an effigy of his grandson Dharmapāla, the nominated heir to the throne of Kōṭṭē, crowned at the court of Portugal.[94] The ambassador selected for this historic purpose was Śrī Rādhārākṣa Paṇḍita, a *brahmin* minister of the king, whose name appears in the Portuguese documents as 'Panditar'.[95] One more request made by the ambassador on behalf of the king of Sri Lanka was that some missionaries might be sent to Sri Lanka for the purpose of converting the people.[96] He had brought with him letters addressed to the heads of the Franciscan Order to this effect. During the first four decades after the arrival of the Portuguese in Sri Lanka in 1505, a few conversions occurred but no regular mission was attempted. Rebeyro mentions a priest in Colombo in 1517,[97] and Queyroz mentions the presence of the Portuguese settlement rather than missionaries. Only towards the end of the reign of Bhuvanekabāhu VII was a real mission organized.

When at last Śrī Rādhārākṣa Paṇḍita came home six Franciscans, with Fr. João de Villa de Conde as their head, accompanied him. This group of Fransciscans were cordially received by the king. Furthermore, de Conde was entrusted with the education of Dharmapāla, the heir-apparent. The missionary activities in Sri Lanka began with these Franciscans who arrived in the country in 1543. Their success was rather meagre as the king adopted a neutral attitude.[99]

Several times Bhuvanekabāhu VII had given subsidies to the Protuguese for the maintenance of their chapel,[100] and Martin Affonzo de Souza, who was formerly at Kōṭṭē and later became governor of 'India', believed that this king would probably be converted to Christianity. Yet, benevolent as had been his reception of the missionaries, they came to be aware of an underlying attitude of diffidence in him which made their task delicate. Bhuvanekabāhu VII finally rejected an invitation to receive baptism and belied altogether the hopes he had aroused that he would renounce the beliefs of his ancestors.[101] It may be assumed that he dared not take such a step for the harm it would have caused to his political security, which was in constant danger because of his ambitious brother, Māyādunne of Sītāvaka. He was aware that his conversion to Christianity would make people disown him, and strengthen the hands of Māyādunne. It should be mentioned here that it was a traditional belief that no non-Buddhist should rule Sri Lanka.[102] This explains Bhuvanekabāhu's attitude towards the activities of the missionaries.

Although Bhuvanekabāhu VII (1521-1551) remained a Buddhist, his administrative and religious policy was regarded with contempt by posterity. Commenting on the reign of Bhuvanekabāhu VII, the author of the *Rājāvaliya* writes : 'It should be noted that King Bhuvanekabāhu was the cause of injustice which posterity had to suffer and that harm done to the cause of Buddhism after this was due to the action of this king'.[103]

The sympathy of Bhuvanekabāhu VII for the Portuguese and Catholics was not appreciated by most of his subjects, who longed for a national leader who would restore them to their former position. In Māyādunne of Sītāvaka they found a national leader, and Sītāvaka became the centre of national aspirations of the time. Māyādunne henceforth was the acknowledged champion of the cause of Buddhism in the low country.[104] His position was further enhanced by his possession of the Tooth Relic, the palladium of the kingdom. During the period of political confusion of Kōṭṭē, the Tooth Relic had been safely brought to Sītāvaka by Hiripitiye Nilame, the custodian of the Relic.[105] This reflected the keen wish of the people that the safety of the Relic should be guaranteed. When Hiripiṭiye Nilame safely arrived in Sītāvaka with the Relic, he handed it over to Māyādunne. It should be mentioned here that the possession of the Tooth Relic made its possessor the *de jure* ruler of the country.[106] Before he received the Relic, Māyādunne had already seen to the construction of a magnificent palace at Delgamuva where it was enshrined.[107] Except for the building the new Daḷadā Māligāva and his close relationship with the Sangha who were disappointed with Bhuvanekabāhu VII, Māyādunne could devote very little time to religious activities as this was a period of almost continuous warfare.

After the death of Bhuvanekabāhu VII (1521-1531) and the significant event of the baptism of Dharmapāla in 1557 A.D., the kingdom of Kōṭṭē ceased to be a Buddhist state. The *Rājāvaliya* informs us that on the eve of Dharmapāla's conversion, the Sangha of the city of Kōṭṭē fled either to Sītāvaka or to the Kandyan kingdom.[108] This reflects the unfortunate state of affairs that the Sangha had to face in the Kōṭṭē kingdom. With the enthusiasm of a new convert, Dharmapāla transferred to the Franciscans the Rajamaha Kelaṇi and Kitsirimevan Kelaṇi temples which face one another across the river at Kelaṇiya. Dharmapāla further donated the Tooth Relic temple at Kōṭṭē and all the temples of the Island, with their fields, gardens, rents and services which had been dedicated to their use, for the maintenance of the colleges which the Franciscans proposed to found in the country.[109] The policy of preventing religious worship other than that of the established religion, viz. Christianity, started in the days of Dharmapāla.[110] The major result of the application of this policy was the withdrawal of royal patronage from Buddhism.

The other disaster that befell Buddhism from the reign of Dharmapāla, was the destruction of Buddhist temples and places of worship. The Portuguese, who were the guardians of Dharmapāla, were instructed by the king of Portugal to 'discover all the idols by means of diligent offices, to reduce them to fragments, and utterly consume them'.[111] It has been observed by Abeyasinha that this policy was faithfully carried out by the Portuguese in Sri Lanka.[112] The temples at Navagamuva, Māpiṭigama, Vattala, Väligama, Devinuvara and Kelaṇiya were destroyed and some of them plundered.[113] This policy against Buddhism was carried out right through the period of the Portuguese domination in maritime Sri Lanka.[114]

However, Dharmapāla and the Portuguese could not expand this destructive policy into the interior on account of the strong resistance of the Sītāvaka kingdom. The successor of Māyādunne, Rājasiṅha I, was a great warrior and a strong ruler dreaded by the Portuguese and the king of Kōṭṭē. In the early part of his reign he was successful in carrying out the administrative and religious policy which had been adopted by his father, Māyādunne. Rājaṅsinha held the annual *daḷadā-perahära* or the procession of the Tooth Relic at the Maha Saman Dēvālaya of Ratnapura.[115] At the same time he is said to have continued the *baṇa-pirit-nilaya* or the function of reciting *pirit* and sermons by the Sangha in the said *dēvālaya.*[116] He is also said to have rebuilt the Dañduvälgama temple that had been destroyed by the Portuguese.[117] The *Alutnuvara Dēvālē Karavīma* mentions that he made some benefactions towards the Upulvan Dēvālaya at Alutunvara and the monastery attached to it.[118] He is extolled in the document as 'the defender of the religion and the world'.

The *Sävul-sandesaya* of Alagiyavanna, the famous poet at the court of Rājasiṅha I, demonstrates that the Tooth Relic temple at Delgamuva was in a flourishing state under the patronage of Rājasiṅha.[119] It further states that a prelate called Mahindālaṅkāra, who was renowned for his piety, lived at the Delgamuva monastery.[120] As for the composition of religious texts there was considerable activity in the reign of Rājasiṅha I. Since the days of Parākramabāhu VI (1415-1467) there had been little literary activity in the country. The only work of importance in the period between Parākramabāhu VI and Rājasiṅha I is the *Dahamsoñḍa-kava,*[121] a poetical work with a Buddhist story as its theme, the authorship of which is attributed to Dharmadhvaja Paṇḍita, generally believed to be

Alagiyavanna's father.[122] It is said that Alagiyavanna produced other works, viz. the *Kusajātakaya*[123], a Buddhist epic, and the *Subhāṣitaya* in the reign of Rājasiṁha I.[124] However, this happy state of Sinhalese culture during the reign of Rājasiṁha I did not last long.

In spite of the encouragement extended towards cultural activities in the early days of his reign, the *Cūlavaṃsa* has no word of praise for Rājasiṁha I, who is condemned as an apostate who destroyed the national religion. It is alleged in the chronicle that Rājasiṁha I killed his father and seized the throne.[125] After this terrible deed, it is alleged in the chronicle, that Rājasiṁha asked the Sangha whether there was a means of atoning for his sin of parricide. The Sangha are reported to have said that there was no way for him to free himself from the dire consequences of his misdeed as parricide is considered to be one of the five heinous crimes (*pañcānantariya-kamma*) in Buddhism.[126] According to the *Sulu-Rājāvaliya*, by this reply the Sangha brought great disaster on their heads.[127] Consequently Rājasiṁha embraced Śaivism, and made Ariṭṭakīvenḍu, a South Indian *brahmin*, his chaplain. Since then, it is alleged in the chronicles that Rājasiṁha followed a harmful and destructive policy towards Buddhism.

However, doubt can be cast upon the motive given in the *Cūlavaṃsa* for Rājasiṁha's hatred towards the Sangha, because the more contemporary records make no reference to his alleged parricide. The *Rājāvaliya*, written at a time much closer to the reign of Rājasiṁha, makes no reference to the alleged tragic death of Māyādunne, merely stating that 'king Māyādunne died after he had reigned 70 years'.[128] It also adds that during his life-time Māyādunne introduced his warrior son to the army and the people, and subsequently abdicated the throne in favour of Rājasiṁha.[129] On the other hand, the author of the *Rājāvaliya* did not fail to elaborate the destructive policy adopted by Rājasiṁha against the princes of Sītāvaka and Uḍaraṭa.[130] Furthermore, this work confirms the information of the *Cūlavaṃsa* on the relationship of Rājasiṁha and Ariṭṭa-kīvenḍu. It says that some fakirs (āñḍi) had come from the Solī country by about 1580 A.D., and one of them, Ariṭṭakīvenḍu Perumāl, became a favourite of Rājasiṁha, and consequently the king had given him the title *mānnapperuma mohoṭṭi* and appointed him commander-in-chief of the Sītāvaka army.[131]

The Portuguese historian Rebeyro, mentions Māyādunne as Rājasiṁha's father, but there is not a word of his alleged tragic death.[132] Another Portuguese historian Queyroz, gives a much more detailed account of the last days of Māyādunne. He says that as Māyādunne was not able to conduct the war against the Portuguese owing to his old age, in May 1578 A.D., with the full consent of his army, he renounced in Rājasiṁha's favour the realms of Sītāvaka and Kōṭṭē and the title of Emperor.[133] On another occasion, this writer records that after he had failed in the siege of Colombo in 1581, Rājasiṁha returned to Sītāvaka having received the news of the death of his father, Māyādunne, after a life of 85 years.[134] If Māyādunne had met with a tragic death as recorded in the *Cūlavaṃsa,* it would have been mentioned by this writer who was not favourable at all either to Māyādunne or to Rājasiṁha, and who says that Māyādunne 'lived for so long to persecute us'.[135] We have, therefore, to look elsewhere for the motive that prompted the allegation of the *Cūlavaṃsa* and the cause of alleged hatred of Rājasiṁha towards the Sangha.

From 1581 onward Rājasiṁha was heavily engaged in war against the Portuguese. During this critical period the Portuguese used every possible means to meet the growing danger of Rājasiṁha. At last they found an opportunity to create chaotic conditions in Sītāvaka by helping some of the princes conspiring against Rājasiṁha. It has been observed that some members of the Sangha, though they had always been favoured by Rājasiṁha and his father, actively participated in the plot.[136] It may be conjectured that some of them had family connexions with the princes who conspired against the king. Rājasiṁha inflicted terrible punishment on the guilty parties. Some of the princes were put to death and some others committed suicide. The king is said to have treated in the same manner the monks including the chief monk of Sītāvaka who took part in the conspiracy.[137] In spite of these severe punishments, one of the princes, Sotupāla Banḍāra, the prince of the Seven Kōralēs, succeeded in raising a revolt in his provinces, and sought the aid of the Portuguese.[138] But Rājasiṁha managed to crush the rebellion in time and beheaded whoever supported Sotupāla. He is said to have burnt down a number of villages in the Seven Kōralēs. Sotupāla fled to the Portuguese.

The *Mandārampura-puvata* tells us that another plot was hatched by some members of the Sangha of Uḍaraṭa at the same time.[139] The intention was to put on the throne of Uḍaraṭa Konappu Banḍāra, the son of Vīrasundara Banḍāra, of the Pērādeniya dynasty who was treacherously slain by Rājasiṁha I.[140] Konappu Banḍāra was in Colombo with the Portuguese at this time. This plot was also discovered in time and the guilty parties were harshly punished.

After these incidents Rājasiṁha became more and more tyrannical. In his animosity towards the Sangha after these conspiracies, it is alleged that he began to persecute monks. As mentioned earlier, the king is said to have abjured the Buddhist faith to become a follower of Śaivism. Many monks are said to have been put to the sword. The *Mandārampura-puvata* states that 121 (*häṭa-ăñdutu-onḍuvak*) monks of the Kandyan kingdom were put to the sword at the same place.[141] Rājasiṁha is said to have pulled down a large number of monasteries, and ordered that whatever books fell into his hands should be burnt.[142] Most of the monks who escaped death disrobed themselves and fled from the wrath of Rājasiṁha. The lands which had been endowed in ancient times for the maintenance of temples were taken away from them, and the king even entrusted the Samantakūṭa to the Śaiva priests.[143] According to these sources, the Sangha suffered both in the maritime provinces and the hill country. The king stationed Śaiva priests in different parts of the country.[143]

Now the Sangha, deprived of the royal patronage in the low country and in the hill country, and threatened with extinction, had to fight for their very existence. An inevitable result of this was that the majority of monks discarded their robes. Others entered the jungle and lived in disguise.[145] Some others again became laymen to look after the lands devoted to the monasteries and make a living.[146] In spite of his animosity towards the Sangha, the Tooth Relic, which had found a sanctury at Delgamuva, escaped Rājasiṁha's wrath,[147] apparently because he believed that its possessor was the rightful ruler of the Sinhalese kingdom. The *Mandārampura-puvata* states that at the moment of his death, Rājasiṁha begged the forgiveness of the Sangha, and again became a Buddhist.[148]

The foregoing pages show us that Buddhism, which had flourished in the reigns of Parākramabāhu VI of Kōṭṭē (1415-1467) and Vikramabāhu of Kandy (1472- 1510), collapsed within three decades at the end of the sixteenth century, especially in the low country and partly in the hill country as well. It is evident that the Sangha could not defend itself-largely because it relied upon the patronage of the Sinhalese rulers. This royal patronage in the past had been necessary in so internal a matter as the purification of the Order. So great a dependence on monarchy had deprived the Buddhists of any organization capable of independent action. As we have seen before, the kings who succeeded Parākramabāhu VI in Kōṭṭē were not distinguished for their patronage of the Sangha, and though these rulers followed the traditional religious observances and maintained the endowments of old, the relationship between the state and the Sangha began to decline during the half of a century which intervened the death of Parākramabāhu VI and the arrival of the Portuguese in 1505. This can be attributed to more than one reason.

The latter part of the fifteenth century and the whole of the sixteenth century are marked by political instability, chaos and constant warfare in the country. Preoccupied by these political troubles, the rulers of the country could not extend the necessary patronage to religious affairs. The growing influence of *brahmins* not only on the royal court but also on society of this time caused in some ways diminish the relationship between the state and the Sangha. The *Nikāyasaṅgrahaya* records that Vīrabāhu Ādipāda gave slaves, male and female, cattle, houses, elephants and villages to *brahmins*.[149] The latter seem to have come in increasing numbers from India to benefit from the liberality of the Sinhalese rulers of the day. This influx of *brahmins* to Sri Lanka from India no doubt was due to the fact that Muslim inroads deprived many of them of their livelihood.[150] A few of these *brahmins* were converted to Buddhism,[151] but most practised the forms of religion to which they were accustomed, and gained adherents from among the Buddhists.[152] The prestige of *brahmins* seems to have grown stronger in the course of time. It has been mentioned before that the historic mission to Portugal in 1541 was led by the *brahmin* prime minister of Bhuvanekabāhu VII, Śrī Rādhārākṣa Paṇḍita.[153] Ariṭṭakīvenḍu, the commander- in-chief and chaplain of Rājasiṅha, I, was a *brahmin.*[154] It is perhaps not too wide a guess to suggest that this growing influence of *brahmins* on the royal court weakened the relationship between the state and the Sangha after the reign of Parākramabāhu VI. This may be further supported by the fact that after Vīdāgama Maitreya in the reign of Bhuvanekabāhu VI we do not hear any member of the Sangha holding the title *rājaguru*, 'adviser to the king'.

Although the sixteenth century, saw the Buddhist Order at its lowest ebb, the beginning of its drift towards decline may be traced back to the fifteenth century. As we have seen earlier, after the reign of Vikramabāhu, none of our sources mentions the two fraternities, Vanavāsa and Gāmavāsa, which played an important part in the organization of the Sangha after its unification in the reign of Parākramabāhu I (1153-1186). Nor do they mention distinguished hierarchs, except Dhammakitti in the reign of Vikramabāhu. Alagiyavanna mentions two pious monks who lived in the realm of Rājasiṅha I,[155] but does not refer to either of the fraternities. Besides these two monks, the only one mentioned in our sources is Devanagala Ratanālaṅkāra, who played an active part in installing Vimaladharmasūriya I on the throne of Uḍaraṭa.[156] In short, no illustrious names adorn the record of the Sangha after the reign of Bhuvanekabāhu VI. The disappearance of the two fraternities was possibly a cause of the declining spirit of the Sangha.

Certain social factors prevailing in the country also contributed to the decline of the Sangha. As has been discussed in the preceding chapter, the caste system in the medieval society penetrated the Order, presumably after the Polonnaru period. We have seen a number of references made by some leading members of the Sangha to their affiliations to certain families some of which held influential positions in society and the political field as well. There is little doubt that these references show the class and caste- mindedness of these monks. One of these monks, in the thirteenth century, even expressed the wish to be re-born in a higher caste.[157] It has been shown above that from the fourteenth century onwards caste discrimination even affected ordination.[158] This was directly in opposition to the basic ideals of Buddhism and to the cosmopolitan character of the Sangha. Eventually this class and caste prejudice may have alienated the Sangha from a major part of society which consisted of numerous so-called lower castes. This is substantiated by the fact that the Catholic missionaries gained more results from their early activities on the seabord areas of the country which were populated by fishers and cinnamon peelers who lacked religious facilities at the time.[159]

Another measure of the Sangha detrimental to the interest of religion was the enthroning of those who approved of their policies. Although the Buddhist Order of Sri Lanka had played an important part in political affairs from very early-times the influence of the monks was not openly visible and generally remained on the background. The two centuries under discussion, however, witnessed a number of hierarchs who actively participated in politics. It was the Elder Vīdāgama I who installed Parākramabāhu VI on the throne of Kōṭṭē.[160] During the reign of this king Śrī Rāhula manifested a keen interest in politics by producing some of his literary works which directly dealt with political affairs of the country. After Parākramabāhu VI's death, as shown above, there were two factions of monks, one led by Śrī Rāhula and the other by Vīdāgama Maitreya, who tried to enthrone their favourites. Two years of this political struggle came to an end with the success of latter faction and the accession of Bhuvanekabāhu VI. That Śrī Rāhula was disappointed with this outcome is shown by his giving up public activities and leading a secluded life afterwards. Although Vīdāgama Maitreya and his followers were able to maintain religious activities unhindered in the reign of Bhuvanekabāhu VI, they do not seem to have gained the sympathy of the followers of Śrī Rāhula and his favourite Jayabāhu II. It will be seen later that Śrī Rāhula was the principal of Vijayabāhu Pirivena at Toṭagamuva, the most famous educational institution of the period.[161] It may be conjectured that Śrī Rāhula's departure led to the decline of this *pirivena* and the institutions affiliated to it, for nothing more is heard of these institutions in the reign of Bhuvanekabāhu VI. We have seen earlier how Rājasiṁha I adopted severe measures to crush the conspiracies against him in Sītāvaka and Uḍaraṭa in which some members of the Sangha were involved.

Political unrest and the lack of royal patronage to which the Sangha owed much in its organizational matters in the past may have led to disorganization of the Order. This disorganization would have caused the breakdown of monastic life. Without royal patronage the leaders of the Sangha might not have been able to prevent their ordinary members from neglecting the rules of discipline. As a consequence, slackness of discipline, including the pursuit of activities not sanctioned by their religion etc., became part of monastic life. We are informed by the *Nikāyasaṅgrahaya* about a number of attempts made by rulers in quick succession in the fourteenth century to arrest the degeneration of the Sangha.[162] While it is unfortunate that the work does not define the nature of degeneration, it states that in every attempt the monks who led unholy lives were expelled from the Sangha.[163] The only Formal Act of the Sangha concerning our period is the *Päpiliyāna Katikāvata* of Parākramabāhu VI.[164] But owing to its fragmentary nature the document does not yield satisfactory information. The remaining few injunctions of the *Katikāvata* bear great resemblance to those of the *Daṁbadeni Katikāvata*. For instance, one of these regulations stipulates that no monks should give away belongings of the monastic property to laymen in seeking their goodwill.[165] Another injunction lays down that it is unworthy for a monk to maintain close relationship with the laity in order to gain gifts from devotees.[166] It further stipulates that by doing so, they destroy both themselves and their associates. These injunctions may suggest that the close relationship maintained by monks with the laity, specially with their kinsmen, was one of the reasons of the degeneration of monastic life. This would have been expedited by the temporal-cum-spiritual succession of monastic property which had been gaining ground since the Daṁbadeni period. According to the *Pallkumbura Sannasa*, this practice developed in the sixteenth century to such an extent that the property of some monasteries became a part of the possessions of some families.[167]

The attempt made by Parākramabāhu VI to arrest the decline of the Sangha bore no lasting results. As has already been mentioned, by the end of the fifteenth century the state of the Sangha became so serious that Vikramabāhu of Kandy had to make another attempt to arrest the decline of the Sangha. According to the *Rājaratnākaraya*, the monks of the Gāmavāsa were so corrupted by this time that no one could prevent their decline.[168] We do not know how far Vikramabāhu succeeded in bringing this fraternity back to its former position. However, it may be presumed that as he was the ruler of the Kandyan kingdom his reforms would not have taken effect beyond the boundaries of his kingdom. Neither the Kōṭṭē nor the Sītāvaka rulers after Parākramabāhu VI are said to have made any attempt to arrest the degeneration of the Sangha. It is, therefore, apparent that the situation deteriorated throughout the sixteenth century in most parts of the country.

It was the misfortune of Buddhism that two rulers, Dharmapāla and Rājasiṁha I, both withdrew their patronage within about thirty years of one another, and became repressive towards the Sangha. As a result of Dharmapāla's religious policy the Sangha were deprived of not only a peaceful life in the maritime provinces but also lost a large number of monasteries which had been in a flourishing condition in the fifteenth century. The situation worsened when Rājasiṁha I adopted Saivism and expelled all the monks from his realm. This double misfortune had a disastrous effect on Buddhism all over the country, and the situation continued until the rise of a new dynasty under Vimaladharmasūriya I in Kandy at the close of the sixteenth century. It is said that this king was unable to assemble even four fully ordained monks from his realm. This situation prompted him to invite fully ordained monks from Arakan to restore the higher ordination. This may suggest that by the end of the sixteenth century the Buddhist Order was in a very difficult position.

## References

1. *Nks.*, p. 90.
2. See above, ch. II.
3. *Nks.*, p. 90; *Sdhrt.*, p. 294.
4. *Nks.*, p. 90; *Sdhrt.*, p. 294.
5. *ibid.*
6. *UCHC.*, p. 641.
7. *Tisara-sandeśaya*, ed. P. Wimaladhamma, Colombo, 1936, v. 44 ff.
8. *Nks.*, p. 93; *Sdhrt.*, p.294.
9. *Nks.*, pp. 93-94.
10. *Nks.*, p. 294.
11. N. Mudiyanse, *The Art and Arthitecture of the Gampola Period*, Colombo, p.46 ff., and 63 ff.
12. *Sdhrt.*, p.301.
13. H.W. Codrington, 'Gampola period of Ceylon History', *JCBRAS*, Vol. XXXII, No. 86, p.262.
14. *PS.*, p. 440.
15. Sdhrt., p. 301.
16. *EZ*, III, p. 45.
17. *EZ*, III, p. 45.
18. *Nks.*, p. 94.
19. *Rjv.*, p. 48; *JCBRAS*, XXII, No. 65, p. 312.
20. *Pañcikāpradīpaya*, v. i; *Pdst.*, v. 6.
21. *CALR*, II, part. I, p. 42.
22. *Rjv.*, p.46.
23. *JCBRAS*, XXII, No. 65, p. 15.
24. W. Geiger, *Culture of Ceylon in Medieval Times,*, Wiesbaden, 1960, p.214.
25. *Sdhrt.*, p. 297; *JCBRAS*, XXII, No. 65, p. 312.
26. *Sls.*, v. 16; *lims.*, v. 45; *Prs.*, vv. 39- 40; *Sdhrt.*, p.297.
27. *EZ.*, IV, pp. 16-17; *Cv.*, 91. 17.
28. *Sdhrt.*, p. 297; *Cv.*, 91. 17 ff.
29. *Sdhrt.*, p. 297.

30. *Sls.*, v. 60 ff.
31. *Sdhrt.*, p. 296.
32. *Sdhrt.*, p. 296.
33. *Sdhrt.*, p. 296; *Cv.*, 91. 24 f.
34. *Kts.*, p.40 ff.
35. See below, ch. V. p. 143 ff.
36. See below, ch. V. p. 142 ff.
37. *CCMT.*, p. 205.
38. *Cv.*, 54, 35.
39. *Cv.*, 84. 9.
40. The purpose of the *Sannasa* is to confirm the grant to Bodhiyānā (Bodhināyaka), a grandchild of Dharmālaṅkāra Paṇḍita. *EZ.*, V, p. 45.
41. *EZ.*, V, p. 45.
42. Eight syllables form one *pāda* (line); four *pādas* make one stanza; one stanza is called a *grantha*.. Thus, 32 syllables constitute one *grantha*. *Pali Sinhala Piritpota*, K. Pannasara, Kelaniya, 1963, p. 326.
43. *Kts.*, p. 42.
44. *Nks.*, p. 96.
45. *Sdhrt.*, p.503.
46. *Kts.*, p.42 f.
47. *Kts.* p. 32 f.
48. *Sdhrt.*, p.291.
49. *Cv.*, 60, 7.
50. *Cv.*, 78, 30.
51. *Cv.*, 81, 49 ff; 84. 37 ff; 87. 72 ff.
52. *Cv.*, 90. 39.
53. *Sdhrt.*, p. 297.
54. *Jkm.*, p. 7.
55. See below, ch. VI.
56. *Sls.* v. 102 ff.
57. M. Silva, Śrī Rāhula Saṅgharāja- tumā, Colombo, 1930, p.57 f; *Toṭagamuvē Vihāraya Pilibañda Purāṇa Itihāsa Kathāva, Anonymous*, Colombo, 1889, p.16 ff.
58. *Padasādhana-ṭīkā*, ed. Dhammananda and Vachissara, Colombo, 1908; *SSL.*, p. 142.
59. *IA*, p. 13 ff; *Ep. Bire*, III.
60. *Kks.*, v. 261 ff.
61. Sumanasuriya, *op. cit.*, p. 14.
62. See above, ch. II.

63. *Sls.*, v. 42 ff.
64. *SSL,*. p.142 ff.
65. *IA*, XXII, p. 13 ff; *Ep. Birm*, III, part. II, No. II, p. 220 ff.
66. In the fifteenth century, the Päpiliyāna document II of Parākramabāhu VI also refers to a coin called *massa*. Codrington observes that from 12 to 16 *massas* went to a *fanam*, another coin widely used in this period. The weight of a gold *fanam* is 5.8 grains. He mentions that the *massa* in this period was a copper coin. See, H. W. Codrington, *Ceylon Coins and Currency*, p. 80.
67. *Rjrt.*, p. 163.
68. *Lawrie, Gazeteer of the Central Province of Ceylon*, Colombo, 1896, II, p. 224.
69. *SSL.*, p. 144 ff.
70. *RKD.*, p. 28.
71. *CALR*, II, p. 38.
72. *GCPC.*, II, p. 33.
73. *RKD.*, p. 36.
74. *CPE.*, I, p. 63.
75. *Queyroz.*, I, p. 25.
76. *EZ*, III, p. 65.
77. *EZ*, III, p. 65.
78. *RKD.*, p. 87.
79. *RKD.*, p. 88.
80. *EZ*, III, p. 70; P. D. S. Weerasuriya, *Devündara Ithihāsaya*, p. 95.
81. *CALR*, II, part. I, p. 38.
82. *Cv.*, 92. 6 ff.
83. *Rjrt.*, p. 56.
84. *Rjrt.*, p. 56.
85. *EZ*, IV, p. 9.
86. *AAGP.*, p. 16.
87. *Rjrt.*, p. 56.
88. *Rjrt.*, p. 57; *Cv.*, 92. 25.
89. *Rjrt.*, p. 57.
90. *Rjrt.*, p. 57.
91. *Rjrt.*, p. 57; *Cv.*, 92. 16-17.
92. *Rjrt.*, p. 57; *Cv.*, 92. 18-20.
93. *RKD.*, p. 41.
94. *Queyroz.*, pp. 234-235.
95. *CPE.*, I, p. 85.
96. *Queyroz.*, p. 236.

97. *Rebeyro's Ceilao*, ed. P. E. Peiris, p. 8.
98. *Queyroz.*, p. 213.
99. Abeyasinha, *op.cit.* p. 192.
100. *Queyroz.*, p. 238.
101. Peiris-Fitzler, *Ceylon and Portugal,* (*Kings and Christians*) Leipzig, 1927, p. 11
102. *HBC.*, p. 63.
103. *Rjv.*, p. 56 ff.
104. *CPE.*, I, p. 135.
105. *Ethnology*, ed. P. E. P. Deraniyagala, Colombo, III, p. 136.
106. *CCMT.*, p. 214.
107. *Rjv.*, p. 60.
108. *Rjv.*, p. 58.
109. *Queyroz.*, p. 330.
110. Abeyasinha, *op. cit.* p. 208.
111. S. D Baily, *Ceylon*, 1852, London, p. 42.
112. Abeyasinha, *op. cit.* p. 207.
113. *Queyroz.*, pp. 441, 427 and 714.
114. Abeyasinha, p. 207.
115. K. Nanavimala, *Saparagamuvē Pāraṇi Liyavili*, p. 45.
116. ibid. p. 46.
117. *RKD.*, p. 33.
118. *ADK.*, folio. *ki.*
119. *Svls.*, v. 118 ff.
120. *Svls.*, v. 122.
121. *Sinhala Sāhitya Vaṃsaya*, p. 299.
122. ibid.
123. ibid., p. 300.
124. ibid., p. 303.
125. *Cv.*, 93, 6-8.
126. *Cv.*, 93. 6-8; *Mandārampura- puvata*, v. 63 ff.
127. *Sulu-Rājāvaliya*, ed. C. D. S. K. Jayawardhana, Colombo, 1914, p. 22.
128. *Rjv.*, p. 61.
129. *Rjv.*, p. 61.
130. *Rjv.*, p. 59.
131. *Rjv.*, p. 68.
132. *JCBRAS*, XVII, No. 56, p. 385.
133. *Queyroz.*, p. 431.
134. *Queyroz.*, p. 438.
135. *Queyroz.*, p. 323.

136. *Ceylon and the Portuguese*, p. 94.
137. ibid.
138. S. G. Perera, *A History of Ceylon*, (*The Portuguese and the Dutch Periods*), Colombo, 1948, p. 50.
139. *Mandārampura-puvata*, v. 62.
140. *Rjv.*, p. 65.
141. *Mandārampura-puvata*, v. 66 ff.
142. *Cv.*, 93. 10; *Mandārampura- puvata*, vv. 59-70.
143. *Seṅkaḍagala- śaila-sāsanavaṃsa*, Br. Mus. Ms. Or. 6606 ( 128), folio. *ja.*
144. *Sulu Rājāvaliya*, p. 22.
145. *EZ*, III, p. 127.
146. *SPL.*, p. 37 f.
147. *SPL.*, p. 36.
148. *Mandārampuara-puvata*, v. 135 ff.
149. *Nks.*, p. 94.
150. *UCHC.*, p. 767; R. C. Majumdar, *An Advanced History of India*, London, 1948, p. 305 ff.
151. See above, ch. I.
152. See below, ch. VII. p. 223.
153. See above, p. 120.
154. See above, p. 124-5.
155. *Sävul-sandeśaya*, vv. 122 and 171.
156. *Ḍevanagala Sannasa*, Br. Mus. Ms. Or. 6609 (113).
157. *Hatthavanagalla-vihāra-vaṃsa*, ed. Sri Silaskandha, 1909, Colombo, p. 46.
158. See above, ch. III.
159. *Rjv.*, p. 58; J. E. Tennent, *Christianity in Ceylon.*, London, 1856, p. 24; *CPE.*, p. 94; R. Boudens, *The Catholic Church in Ceylon under Dutch Rule*, Rome, 1957, p. 32 ff.
160. *Rjv.*, p. 48 ff.
161. See below, ch. V, pp. 227 ff.
162. *Nks.*, pp. 94-97.
163. *Nks.*, pp. 94, 96 and 97.
164. *Kts.*, p. 34 ff.
165. *Kts.*, p. 35.
166. *Kts.*, p. 35.
167. *EZ.*, III, p. 240 ff.
168. *Rjrt.*, p. 57.

## Chapter Five

# Monastic Education

The prosperous reign of Parākramabāhu VI, lasting over half a century, saw a number of educational institution' attached to Buddhist monasteries flourishing in different parts of the Island, and satisfying the needs of scholars, some of whom were attracted from foreign lands. The contemporary literary works, especially the *sandeśa* poems, give interesting descriptions of some of these leading institutions which appear to have reached the zenith of their glory during the first half of the fifteenth century. Inspired by the feelings of security and contentment, which they experienced in the reign of Parākramabāhu VI, the people again turned their attention to the cultivation of the finer arts, and especially the Sangha leisurely engaged in literary activities which resulted in a large number of literary works. The king's generous endowments towards shcolars and monastic institutions made his reign one of the most glorious epochs in the history of education in Sri Lanka.

The monastic educational institutions of this period were generally known as Pirivenas (Pali: *pariveṇa).* The word *pariveṇa* occurs from the earliest times, but it is difficult to detemine the time when the term came to be applied to an educational institution.

The term *piriveṇa* is now used in Sri Lanka solely to denote a monastic college where Buddhism and languages associated with Buddhism are taught as the principal subjects of study. But in the early Anurādhapura period the word *pariveṇa* denoted the living quarters of *bhikkhus.*[1] In the *Sāratthadīpanī* the tem is defined as one of the residences within a *vihāra* (complex of monastic establishments), each of which was surrounded by protective walls.[2] References to *pariveṇas* corresponding to this definition occur in a number of sources pertaining to the early period. In the *Mahāvaṃsa* the term *pariveṇa-panti* is used in the meaning of 'a building which contains living quarters or cells'.[3] In the *Cūlavaṃsa* the term usually denotes a cell or cells built within a *vihāra* by a king or another layman.[4] Geiger presumed that in such connexion *pāsāda* and *pariveṇa* may have been used as synonyms.[5] Childers, in his Pali Dictionary, only admits the meaning 'cell' for *pariveṇa*.[6] According to the *Nikāyasaṅgrahaya*, the Mahāvihāra at Anurādhapura had 364 *pariveṇas* and the Mahāvihāra in Rohaṇa, i.e. the Tissamahāvihāraya, had 363 *pariveṇas*.[7] However it seems that the term *pariveṇa* did not necessarily denote a 'cell'in the later Anurādhapura period as seen from frequent use in the chronicles as well as in the inscriptions.

In the seventh century, during the reign of Aggabodhi IV (667-683), *vihāras* and *pariveṇas* were built by the chiefs of districts *(maṇḍalikas)* in different parts of the kingdom.[8] Māna (eleventh century) is said to have erected for his elder brother Mānavamma, a splendid *pariveṇa* and made him the head of it.[9] Apparently, Mānavamma chose monastic life in order to devote himself to meditation and religious studies. We are not certain whether his chief incumbency of the *pariveṇa* should be interpreted as reffering to his being the head of a scholastic establishment of a large monastery. According to an inscription of Kassapa V (914-923), the *piriven laddan* of the Mahā Kapāra Pirivena were alloted one *amuṇa* of rice and four *akas* of gold at the end of each year for providing robes.[10] Here we receive information on *piriveṇas* within a large *pirivena*, probably a complex of monastic establishment. Hence it can be assumed that the term *pariveṇa* which originally meant a 'cell' had by this time also come to denote one of the 'colleges' of monks living in a large monastery. Yet we have no data that allow us to conclude that these colleges were educational institutions as in the later centuries.

In the Polonnaru period we find the term *pariveṇa* used to denote a group of buildings devoted to various monastic activities. The *Cūlavaṃsa* records that Parākramabāhu I (1153-1186) founded the Āḷāhaṇa- *pariveṇa* which was equipped with all the buildings generally attached to a *vihāra:* an image house, two *dāgäbas*, an *uposatha* house and several *pāsādas* with their appertainances, to the north of the Jetavana Vihāra and connected with it.[11] The description of this institution shows us that it was meant for the *bhikkhus* who were engaged in learning and literary pursuits. Nevertheless, this description does not help us to identify whether this instituion was a Pirivena where students learned as in the Kōṭṭē period.

During the Daṁbadeni period the term *pariveṇa* was commonly used to describe the residential quarters of monks who were known for their literary and educational activities. Devapatirāja, the prime minister of Parākramabāhu II (1236-1270), is said to have built for the Elder Anomadassi, who is well known for his contributions to the literature of the period, a *pariveṇa* at Attanagalla.[12] This minister is also credited with the founding of the Mayurapāda Pirivena at Vākirigala, in the Kāgalla District, where the Elder Buddhaputra, the author of the *Pūjāvaliya* lived.[13] It is not certain whether these residential quarters of scholary monks served also as educational institutions of any kind.

Although we do not have sufficient information about the gradual development of Pirivenas as educational institutions before the fifteenth century, it is quite clear that education and learning centred round the monasteries of the Sangha, by whose zealous and untiring efforts education and learning were maintained. Their main concern was the following of religion, and it was also considered their obligation to propagate the teachings of the Buddha. They taught their monastic pupils, each of whom had to attach himself to a preceptor at the time of his ordination.[14] Hence, from the earliest times the Dhamma must have been imparted to the monastic pupils only; but as time went by and the monks led a more settled life, the portals of the *vihāras* were thrown open to lay pupils as well. Thus the monastery which was the centre for all religious activities had also become the village school, and many of them later grew into famous centres of learning where distinguished scholars resided.

This growth of monastic education, which centred round the monasteries and took a new shape as *Pirivenas,* is best seen in the fifteenth century which witnessed the rise of a number of educational institutions in various parts of the country.

Although there is evidence of some monasteries in the capital, Kōṭṭē.[15] there is no mention of great seat of learning there, which could attract the attention of the writers at the time. The cloisters at Palābatgala of the Vanavāsi fraternity, too, were not known as a *Pirivena* of great learning. But it was the abode of the line of Dharmakīrti famous for their learning and scholastic achivements.[16]

Some of the seats of learning of this period had been in existence for some years before they became famous under the patronage of Parākramabāhu VI. Of these, the Padmāvati Pirivena at Kāragala was an outstanding educational institution in the fifteenth century. The message of Vīdāgama in the *Haṃsa-sandeśaya* was meant to be delivered to the Elder Vanaratana of Kāragala who was the principal of this institution.[17]

The building of Kāragala monastery is mentioned in the Kāragala inscription.[18] According to the document, the monastery was built in the Daṁbadeni period. It was well provided for by the state with the grant of large tracts of land for its maintenance.

Although the monastery at Kāragala was built before the reign of Parākramabāhu VI, it seems to have grown into an outstanding educational institution during the reign of that monarch. The *Haṃsa- sandeśaya,* written in the early years of his reign, describes in glowing terms this educational institution and its principal, the elder Vanaratana.[19] From the description it is clear that the Padmāvatī Pirivena was attached to the Padmāvatī Vihāraya at Kāragala.

The next important centre of education in this period was the Vijayabāhu Pirivena at Toṭagamuva the principal of which was the Elder Śrī Rāhula, the greatest scholar and poet of the period.

The Vijayabāhu Pirivena was attached to the monastery at Toṭagamuva, a village in the Southern Province of Sri Lanka.

This monastery was an institution with a long history, as it was first built in the Daṁbadeni period. Geiger identifies the builder of the monastery with Vijayabāhu IV (1270-1272), who had the epithet of Bōsat (Bodhisattva),[20] and is said to have built a *vihāra* at Vattala.

Although the description of religious works of Vijayabāhu IV in the *Cūlavaṃsa* gives no reference to his building a monastery at Toṭagamuva, in the chapter on Parākramabāhu IV (1302-1326), the chronicle states as follows:-

In the *vihāra* at Titthagāma where the big, long *pāsāda* forty-five cubits in size erected by the great Vijayabāhu had fallen into decay, King Parākramabāhu himself built a beautiful long *pāsāda* of thirty cubits in size, two storeys high, provided with lofty spires, glorious with bright-hued painting, and assigned them to the Venerable Great *thera* Kāyasatthi, who dwelt in the Vijayabāhu Pirivena. He also granted him a village, called Salaggāma, on the banks of the river forming the boundary (of the monastery) making it a possession of the *Pirivena*.[21]

This account of the chronicle does not help us to locate the Vijayabāhu Pirivena, where the beneficiary of the *pāsāda* lived, nor to identify the monarch. The account merely says that the lofty *pāsāda* renovated by Parākramabāhu IV was originally built by the great Vijayabāhu. Medhaṅkara, the author of the Pali poem *Jinacarita,* lived in the Pirivena erected by Vijayabāhu who was the 'pinnacle of the line of kings'.[22]

Some writers, on the basis of the epithets 'great' and 'pinnacle of the line of kings', are inclined to believe that the founder of the Vijayabāhu monastery at Toṭagamuva was Vijayabāhu I (1070-1110).[23] This seems most unlikely for this king is not credited with any kind of religious works in the Southern part of the island. On the other hand, the two epithets also suit Vijayabāhu IV, who lived not so long before the first recorded date of the Pirivena and was regarded as a very pious king. Moreover, in view of the fact that the attention paid by the kings of the Daṁbadeni dynasty to the Southern part of the country,[24] where Toṭagamuva was situated, it can be surmised that the founder of the Pirivena at that village was Vijayabāhu IV.

However, this monastery developed into a Pirivena in the reign of Parākramabāhu IV who ruled at Kuruṇāgala.

The hierarch of Galaturumula and the hierarch of Uturumula had held the post of principal of this institution after the Elder Kāyasatthi. They were succeeded by Śrī Rāhula in the fifteenth century, and it was during his time that the Vijayabāhu Pirivena achieved its highest fame.

Two contemporary works describe this institution. Of these, the *Kokila-sandeśaya* refers to this institution as the monastery at Toṭagamuva, and it describes the image house in detail.[25] But it does not describe a Pirivena or another educational institution at that place. The poem, however, mentions Śrī Rāhula as the head of the Vijayabāhu Pirivena.[26] It is the *Girā-sandeśaya* that gives a clear picture of the Vijayabāhu Pirivena in the fifteenth century.[27] According to the description given in this work, the Vijayabāhu Pirivena was the highest educational institution at that time.

The Śrīghanānanda Pirivena at Vīdāgama has been mentioned in the contemporary literature as another educational institution of the period.[28] Two well-known hierarchs of the fifteenth century hailed form Vīdāgama, a village about fifteen miles south of Kōṭṭē. The senior of the two, according to tradition, was the teacher of Śrī Rāhula, but was not known to have been an author. However this hierarch, according to the *Rājāvaliya*, exerted an outstanding influence on the political affairs of the country at the beginning of the fifteenth century.[29] As has been observed before, his great influence on the army and people of the country helped Parākramabāhu VI in his way to the throne.[30]

It was the junior Vīdāgama *thera* who had gained much fame as a scholar and author of this period. Both these monks resided at the Vīdāgama monastery in succession, and the junior may have been a pupil of the senior. The monastery at Vīdāgama was a long standing one and attached to this was the Pirivena built by Parākramabāhu IV of Kuruṇāgala.

The building of the Śrīghanānanda Pirivena by Parākramabāhu IV is recorded in the *Cūlavaṃsa* as follows:-

In fair Viddumagāma, not far from the town of Rayigama, he had a splendid *vihāra* built, connected with Śrīghanānanda

Pirivena, with a *bodhi*-tree and image house and assigned it to his teacher, the grand *thera* from the Coḷa country.[31]

It appears from the *Cūlavaṃsa* account that the *Pirivena* was already in existence by the time the Vīdāgama temple attached to it was built. However old the *Pirivena* may have been, it does not seem to have been well known as a seat of learning. Late in the fourteenth century, Kavīśvara in the *Mayūra- sandeśaya* gives a passing reference to this institution, and he makes special mention of the Buddha at Vīdāgama monastery.[32] Besides the *Mayūra-sandeśaya,* no contemporary work has tried to describe the Pirivena at Vīdāgama. Even Vīdāgama Maitreya, the author of several works of the period, does not refer to the *Pirivena* in the colophons to his books. In the *Haṃsa-sandeśaya,* he refers to himself as the incumbent of the lofty and lovely Vīdāgama monastery.[33] Even the *Kavlakuṇu-miṇimala,* another work of Vīdāgama Maitreya, the author merely says that he was residing at the Vīdāgama monastery.

Thus the Śrīghanānanda Pirivena, attached to the Vīdāgama monastery, does not appear to have been a great centre of learning that attracted the attention of scholars.

It is also not certain whether Vīdāgama Maitreya, the poet, was the principal of this Pirivena. What is apparent is that the Śrīghanānanda Pirivena was not a prominent seat of learning in this period, although Vīdāgama Maitreya was well known as a poet and scholar.

The author of the *Kokila-sandeśaya* refers to himself in the colophon of the poem as the principal of the Tilaka Pirivena.[34] He also says that he is the younger brother of the Great Elder residing at Mul Giri (mod. Mulkirigala) monastery near the famous Devinuvara.[35] Malalasekara, taking into account this reference, locates the Tilaka Pirivna at Mulkirigala.[36] However, it should be mentioned here that the author of the *Kokila-sandeśaya* starts describing the journey for the messenger with a long account of Devinuvara. Thus it is easy to surmise that the Tilaka Pirivena was nowhere else than at Devinuvara.

It is strange, however, that in the description of Devinuvara the author has given no account of the Tilaka Pirivena of which he was the principal. The *Cūlavaṃsa* gives an account of a monastery and a *Pirivena* said to have been built by Vīrabāhu' the nephew of Parākramabāhu II of Daṁbadniya, at Devinuvara.[37] It further states that as it was a place admired by the people and this Pirivena came to be known as Nandana Pirivena. Nevertheless, there is no evidence to identify the Nandana Pirivena in the thirteenth century as the Tilaka Pirivena in the fifteenth century.

It may be observed that there was no occassion for many contemporary authors of the *sandeśa* poems to describe the Tilaka Pirivena at Devinuvara, for the messengers of the *Girā-sandeśaya*, the *Haṃsa-sandeśaya* and the *Sälalihiṇi-sandeśaya* did not go as far as Devinuvara. Even in the *Parevi-sandeśaya*, where the messenger had to go to Devinuvara the author has not found it necessary to describe the Pirivena there.

The temple at Devinuvara is said to have been built by Parākramabāhu IV of Kuruṇāgala in the foutreenth century and is referred to in the *Cūlavaṃsa* as follows:-

In Devapura he built a long temple consisting of two storeys provided with four pairs of gate for the image of recumbent lion.[38] To this temple he assigned the grove-encircled village Ganṭhimāna (mod. Gäṭmānna) by name, which was proclaimed as the property of the Buddha".[39]

Thus, although there is no referrence to the building of a Pirivena there, the origin of the Tilaka Pirivena can be traced back to the fourteenth century. Like the Śrīghanānanda Pirivena at Vīdāgama the Tilaka Pirivena at Devinuvara, too, does not appear to have been a great centre of learning like the Padmāvati Pirivena or the Vijayabāhu Pirivena.

The youngest of the Pirivenas in the fifteenth century was the Sunetrādevi Pirivena at Päpiliyāna. the founder of the Pirivena was Parākramabāhu VI (1415-1407). Although the *Cūlavaṃsa* account of this king is rather brief, the fact of his building this Pirivena in memory of his mother, Sunetrādevi, is mentioned in the chronicle.[40] The Päpiliyāna documents I and II also give detailed accounts of the building of the Sunetrādevi Pirivena by the king.[41] According to the documents, the institution was ordered to be built by the king in memory of his mother on the Mädin full-moon day in the thirty-ninth year of his reign. Thus the building of the Pirivena seems to have taken place in 1415 A.D.

The king dedicated the monastery and Pirivena at Päpiliyāna to Maṅgala *thera* who was the chief disciple of the Great Elder Medhankara of Galaturumula, one of the foremost hierarchs of the period.

Apart from the Päpiliyāna documents, this institution has not been mentioned in detail as a great seat of learning even by the writers of the *sandeśa* poems who had the opportunity to do so. It seems that they have been content with the description of the *vihāra,* and not the Pirivena, though founded by Parākramabāhu VI, presumably because it was not such a great seat of learning as the Padmāvati Pirivena or the Vijayabāhu Pirivena.

In addition to the Pirivenas mentioned above, there were several Pirivenas occasionally referred to in our sources. Of these, the Laṅkā Senevirat Pirivena is mentioned in the *Vimuktisaṅgrahava* whose author seems to have been the principal of the institution.[42] In the *Padasādhana-ṭīkā* of Śrī Rāhula mention is made of a Pirivena called Saptaratna Pratirāja whose principal Dīpaṅkara requested Śrī Rāhula to compose this work.[43] The hero of the *Vṛttamālā* of Śrī Rāmacandra Bhārati was a monk called Rammuṅgoḍa Dīpaṅkara of the Śrīnivāsa Pirivena.[44] Another institution called the Pañca-pariveṇa (Sinh. Pas Pirivena) of which the principal was a monk named Maṅgala is mentioned in the Kalyāṇī inscriptions of Dhammaceti.[45] The *Aramkäle Sannasa* of Bhuvanekabāhu VI mentioned Niyadavanē Phussadeva Sumaṅgala , the chief disciple of Vīdāgama Maitreya, as the principal of the Dharmarāja Pirivena at Erabattoṭa, near Kōṭṭē.[46] There was another educational institution at Kelaṇiya called Rājaratna Pirivena.[47] In addition to the Sunetrādevi Pirivena, Parākramabāhu VI is said to have built the Mahapāya Pirivena at Ussāpiṭiya in the Kägalla district.[48] Beside these occasional references to those institutions, we have no detailed infomation about their history or functions.

As regards the education imparted at the Pirivenas the best details are given in two *sandeśa* poems of the period. Of these, the *Haṃsa-sandeśaya,* which describes the Padmāvatī Pirivena at

Kāragala, helps us to reconstruct a general picture of that institution during the first half of the fifteenth century.[49] A fairly detailed description of the Vijayabāhu Pirivena at Toṭagamuva is given in the *Girā-saṇdeśaya* whose author was either a pupil or a great admirer of Śrī Rāhula, the principal of that Pirivena. However, it is necessary to stress the different kinds of limitations of our sources for the study of these institutions; for instance, they do not give any information regarding the administration or the maintenance of the Pirivenas and, in such cases, we have to rely on the scanty information given in other sources such as the Päpiliyāna documents.

As has been discussed above, education at the monastic educational institutions of the country was generally confined to the monks. In describing the Padmāvatī Pirivena the *Haṃsa-sandeśaya* refers to monastic students only of that institution.[50] It may be argued that, as it was a centre of learning belonging to the Vanavāsi fraternity, the Padmāvatī Pirivena did not accomodate lay students. But this argument cannot be justified, for when we examine the curriculm of the Pirivena we can find secular subjects such as astrology, poetics and drama being taught there although they were condemned by the *Dambadeni Katikāvata* as "forbidden branches of knowledge".[51] The *Girā-sandeśaya* mentions monastic students as well as lay students in the Vijayabāhu Pirivena at Toṭagamuva.[52] Among the lay students of this Pirivena there were *brahmin* youths who learned the four Vedas as well as Buddhism.[53] Some of these *brahmin* youths like Śrī Rāmacandra Bhārati the author of the *Bhaktiśataka* and several other Sanskrit works, were of Indian origin and may have directly come from India for the purpose of receiving instruction under Śrī Rāhula. The higher standard of religious education found at the Pirivenas of the Kōṭṭē period attracted students even from South East Asia, for we are informed in the *Jinakālamāli* that one of the main objects of the mission of the South East Asian monks who came to Sri Lanka in 1425 A.D., was to learn the Tripiṭaka under the guidance of the Sīhaḷa-mahātheras.[54] The text adds that these monks spent several months learning the Sinhalese script and the style of reciting the text in Sri Lanka with the correct vocal intonation under Vanaratana of the Padmāvatī Pirivena at Kāragala and later received the higher ordination.

As for the monastic students of the Pirivenas there were two main groups of them. The first was that of the *sāmaṇeras*, who studied the texts that were meant for their period of novices,[55] the other that of the *upasampannas* 'higher ordained monks', who were divided into several grades according to their age and education.[56]

In general, the curricula of the Pirivenas were confined to learning the Tripiṭaka; i.e. Sutta: Vinaya and Abhidhamma. In this connection the *Haṃsa-sandeśaya* describes a graduated course of studies for the monastic students of the Padmāvatī Pirivena. The *sāmaṇera* students of that Pirivena were engaged in learning the *Heraṇasika* (Pali. *Sāmaṇerasikkhā*) or the code of disciplinary rules laid down for the monks who were preparing for higher ordination.[57] According to *vinaya* rules a novice should be placed in charge of two superiors qualified by learning, character, and standing, who were called *ācariya* and *upajjhāya*. It is difficult to determine their precise functions from the texts, such as the *Mahāvagga*.[58] The distinction seems to be that the *upajjhāya* was the higher authotiry entrusted with the duty of instructing the novice in the sacred texts and doctrines, while the *ācariya* assumed responsibility for his conduct, and was thus called also *kammācariya*. The *upajjhāya* is to be at least ten years and the *ācariya* at least six years after their higher ordination.[59]

It is stated in the *Dambadeni Katikāvata* that the *sāmaṇeras* should live during their training period with their *upajjhāyas*, and during that period the *upajjhāyas* should take full responsibility for their novices and teach them the *Heranasika*, and train them as stated therein.[60] This rule applies to both fraternities, the Vanavāsa and the Gāmavāsa. The *Girā-sandeśaya* states that in the Vijayabāhu Pirivena, the *sāmaṇeras* studied *viyaraṇa* (grammar) in addition to the *Heraṇasika*.[61]

The subsequent stages of a *bhikkhu's* education at the Pirivenas mainly concerned the study of the texts written on various parts of the Tripiṭaka. The *Haṃsa-sandeśaya* states that the student monks who had already completed the period of *sāmaṇera* training and had just obtained the higher ordination studied the *Mulsika* and *Sikavalañda*.[62]

The *Mulsika*, (Pali. *Mūlasikkhā*), a short work on *vinaya* rules, is said to have been written in the early Anurādhapura period. Being a short summary of *vinaya* rules, it was meant to be learnt by heart by the new entrants to higher ordination. This work is alluded to by name in the Polonnaru and Dam̆badeni *Katikāvatas*.[63]

The other work, the *Sikavalañda*, by an unknown author who also wrote a commentary on it called *Sikavalañda- vinisa*, is a code of monastic rules drawn up for the guidance of monks.[64] The *Sikavalañda* contains quotations from the *Samantapāsādikā*, the commentary of the *Vinaya Piṭaka*. The purpose of teaching the *Mulsika* and the *Sikavalañda* to the *bhikkhu* students of the *Pirivenas* was to give them a thorough grasp of the rules of monastic life.

The monks who had already studied the fundamentals of the monastic regulation engaged themselves in studying the *Nisabaṇa*.[65] This *Nisabaṇa* was meant for monks of the lowest grade after admission to full membership of the Sangha and thus known as *navakas*.[66] In pursuing the course of the *Nisabaṇa*, they should learn by heart *(vācuggata)* two *Mātikās* [67] and four *bhāṇavāras*.[68] From the *suttantas* for the purpose of preaching on *uposatha* days, some important *suttas* like *Andhakavinda, Mahā Rāhulovāda* and *Ambaṭṭha* for the purpose of talking to those who visited the monastery, three *anumodanās* for the purpose of giving benedictory talks on special occasions,[69] particulars about certain fundamental *vinayakammas* such as *uposatha* and *pavāraṇa*, and also one topic of meditation (*kammaṭṭhāna*).[70] According to the *Samantapāsādikā* all this *nisabaṇa* he should learn; and then he is qualified to go about freely (*cātuddiso*) and to live independently of his *ācariya* (*attano issariyena vasitum*).[71] The *Dambadeni Katikāvata* includes the *Khuddasikkhā* and the *Dhātupāṭha* in the course of *nisabaṇa*.[72] The period of learning for the *navakas* was five years, at the end of which, according to the *Katikāvata* they should be sent to the *nāyaka* or the *mahāsāmi* of the time.[73] If the *mahāsāmi* consented to the admittance of the *navaka* into the next grade, thereafter he should be called *nissayamuccanaka,* and allowed to study a higher course of the Dhamma.[74]

The course of study for the *nissayamuccanaka* is called the *terabaṇa.*[75] The *terabaṇa* consisted of the two *Vibhaṅgas* of the Vinaya, the *Pācittiyapāli* and the *Pārājikapāli,*[76] in addition to the knowledge *of vinayakammas*. When the *nissayamuccanakas* had completed the study of the prescribed texts by heart, and had proved their good conduct as *upasampannas* or higher ordained monks, it is stated in the *Dambadeni Katikāvata* that they should be given the *therasammuti* or the recognition as *theras* by the Sangha.[77] The duration of this course of study was five years.

The monks who had completed the period of ten years after their higher ordination and had successfuly learnt the prescribed texts for that period were allowed to study the Tripiṭaka itself. In the Vijayabāhu Pirivena there was a group of monks who studied the *Suttapiṭaka* and a second group of monks who were engaged in learning the *Vinayapiṭaka* while a third group concentrated their attention on the Abhidhammapiṭaka[78] These three group of monks are in the Samantapāsādikā called *bhikkhunovādakas* or advisors to *bhikkhus.*[79] According to this work, a *bhikkhuṇovādaka* monk should learn the three Piṭakas with their commentaries, failing which he should master the commentary to one of the four *nikāyas.*[80] That would enable him to explain the other *nikāyas*. Among the seven Adhidhamma texts,[81] he would master the commentaries to four, because that would enable him to explain the rest. The *Daṁbadeni Katikāvata* also refers to the *bhikkhuṇovādaka* monks[82] but does not give any details regarding their course of study. We are not certain whether all the texts prescribed in the *Samantapāsādikā* were studied by the *thera* monks in the Pirivenas in the Kōṭṭē period.

The next stage of monastic education may be described as the period of specialisation. The senior monks of the Pirivenas who had successfuly completed the study of the *thera* period concentrated on acquiring a specialised knowledge of one of the Three Piṭakas. Of those monks, the first group studied the *Abhidhammapiṭaka* with its commentaries and sub- commentaries.[83] The others who preferred to specialise in the *Suttapiṭaka* learned it with its commentaries and sub- commentaries, while the third group specialised in the *Vinayapiṭaka.*[84] No mention is made of the monks who studied the Tripiṭaka as a whole. However, we have references to some distinguished monks of the period who acquired a complete knowledge of the Tripiṭaka. The principal of the Padmāvatī Pirivena, the Elder Vanaratana, was a monk who had a deep knowledge of the Tripiṭaka.[85] Śrī Rāhula gained the title *tripiṭaka-vāgīśvarācārya* due to his mastery of the Canon.[86] Vīdāgama Maitreya and the principal of the Tilaka Pirivena at Devinuvara also held the title *tripiṭaka- vāgīśvarācārya*[87]. The foregoing account may make it apparent that the *bhikkhu* education in the fifteenth century was a well-planned scheme with the main object of providing extensive religious knowledge to the members of the Sangha.

The curricula of the Pirivenas in the Kōṭṭē period were not confined to the training of monks or to the teaching of the Dhamma, for we have information regarding various other subjects that were taught in these institutions. There were students in the Vijayabāhu Pirivena who studied languages such as Pali, Sanskrit, Sinhalese and Tamil.[88] That Pali was a subject of learning is also made clear by the study of the Tripiṭaka the language of which is Pali. Śrī Rāhula is well known for his two contributions to the study of Pali grammar, the *Moggallāna-pañcikā-pradīpaya* and the *Buddhippasādanītīkā,* also called *Padasādhana-tīkā.* The first of these, the *Pañcika-pradīpaya* is one of the most comprehensive works on Pali grammar in Sri Lanka or anywhere else.[89] It is written partly in Pali and partly in Sinhalese and is a commentary to the *Pañcikā* written by Moggallāna, the well known Pali grammarian. Śrī Rāhul'a other grammatical work, the *Buddhippasādanī-tīkā* is, as its second name implies, a commentary on Piyadassi's *Padasādhana.*[90] These works may imply the enthusiasm for the learning of the Pali language in the Kōṭṭē period. Furthermore, it can be assumed from these works that Śrī Rāhula and his students followed the Moggallāna School of Pali Grammar, one of the two major Schools of Pali grammar. The *Haṃsa-sandeśaya* refers to the study, by the students of the Padmāvatī Pirivena at Kāragala, of the *Kaccāyana* and its commentary the *Nyāsa-ṭīkā,* two works belonging to the other School of Pali grammar called Kaccāyana.[91] There is no doubt that the Vanavāsi fraternity led by Vanaratana followed the Kaccāyana School, while the Gāmavāsi fraternity led by Śrī Rāhula followed the Moggallāna School of Pali grammar.

Learning of the Sanskrit language side by side with Pali prevailed in the Buddhist monasteries of Sri Lanka from very early times. The frequent contacts with South India and the large influx of *brahmins* into Sri Lanka from the Polonnaru period would have encouraged the cultivation of Sanskrit learning throughout in the succeeding centuries. The influence of Sanskrit on the literature of medieval Sri Lanka, both Pali and Sinhalese, is clearly evident. The influence which Sanskrit learning exerted on the political and social spheres may be judged from the statements in the chronicles with regard to the education of princes like Parākrambāhu and the references therein to authorities like Kautilya and Manu.[92] This great enthusiasm for Sanskrit learning continued throughout the fifteenth century. Among other subjects, Sanskrit held a very important place in the curricula of the Pirivenas in this period. Among the students of the Vijayabāhu Pirivena there were a number of *brahmin* youths who studied the Sanskrit language.[93] It is interesting to note here that none of our sources refers to *bhikkhu* students learning Sanskrit in the Pirivenas. Although an argument from silence is generally unreliable, one may consider whether in this case it may imply that Sanskrit study was discouraged for *bhikkhu* students. However, most of the scholarly monks of the period were well known for their Sanskrit knowledge as well. Śrī Rāhula enjoyed the honorary title *saḍbhāṣā-parameśvara,* the master of six languages, which, according to tradition, were Sanskrit, Prākrit. Māgadhi, i.e. Pali, Sauraseni, Apabhraṃsa and Paiśācī.[94] It seems somewhat strange that Tamil, which was very popular among the Sinhalese scholars at this time, was not included in the list of six languages. It may have been excluded because of the fact that this language was never regarded as an Aryan language whereas the languages included in the list belonged to that category. In addition, the six languages in the list were frequently used in Sanskrit dramas, which were taught in the Pirivenas in this time, and Tamil did not have a place in this field too. Śrī Rāhula's mastery of Sanskrit is well reflected in his literary works.[95] Vanaratana of Kāragala was also famous for his mastery of Sanskrit.[96] The Sinhalese poets of the period, most of whom were undoubtedly monks, have not only been largely influenced by Sanskrit works but have often borrowed ideas and imagery from them as well.[97] The *sandeśa* poems, written in imitation of Kālidāsa's *Meghadūta*, show to what extent Sanskrit knowledge was widespread in this time[98] It may be assumed that the famous *brahmin* scholar, Śrī Rāmacandra Bhārati, who learnt Buddhism under Śrī Rāhula, was a teacher of Sanskrit at the Vijayabāhu Pirivena. He composed the Sanskrit *śataka* poem, the *Bhakti-śataka*, in honour of the Buddha.[99] His other work, the *Vṛttamālā*, a biography of Rammuṅgoḍa Dīpaṅkara, is composed with the additional intention of giving examples of some popular Sanskrit metres found in the *Vṛttaratnākara*.[100] Wijesekara observes that the majority of *śataka* poems extant in Sri Lanka were written in the Kōṭṭē period.[101]

The scholarly monks of this period often manifested a great aptitude for studying and mastering foreign languages, even those which had little or no bearing on their religion or mother tongue. Of the Indian languages, Tamil took a prominent place in the syllabus of the Pirivenas of this period. Both the Padmāvatī Pirivena and the Vijayabāhu Pirivena had facilities to teach their students the Tamil language.[102] Apart from the Tamil population in the northern part of the country, there was a considerable Tamil element in the Sinhalese areas in this period. The influence of this element can be well seen from the Sinhala-Tamil intermarriages, particularly in the upper strata of society of the time. Parākramabāhu VI chose a Tamil prince Nannūrutunayyār as the husband for his daughter, Lokanāthā.[103] This princess, after her marriage with Nannūrutunayyār, used the Tamil form of her name, Ulakuḍ-ayadēvī.[104] Besides Nannūrutunayyār, there were several princes like Sapumal (Tamil. Sembagapperumāl), the conqueror of the Jaffna kingdom, and his brother Ambulugala in the retinue of Parākramabāhu VI.[105]

The *Oruvala Sannasa* gives a clear indication of the influence of the Tamil *brahmins* on the court of Kōṭṭē.[106] This situation may have rendered Tamil an important language in the educational institutions of the period. The *Girā-sandeśaya,* tells us that in the Vijayabāhu Pirivena dramas written in Tamil were studied.[107] The author of the *Kokila-sandeśaya,* who was the principal of the Tilaka Pirivena at Devinuvara, is said to have been able to give sermons through the media of Tamil and Sinhalese.[108] Alagiyavanna, in his *Subhāṣitaya,* states that this text was composed with the object of elucidating the teachings of the Elders for the benefit of the common people who could not understand the standard languages such as Tamil, Sanskrit and Pali.[109] These instances may clarify for us the position the Tamil language held in the curricula of the Pirivenas of the Kōṭṭē period.

Subjects like prosody *(chandas),* ornaments of speech *(alaṅkāra),* logic *(tarka),* astrology *(nakṣatra),* and medicine *(vaidyaśāstra)* seem to have been taught in the Pirivenas.[110] Though the students of the Padmāvatī Pirivena studied these subjects, it is stated in the *Haṃsa-sandeśaya* that the principal of that institution, Vanaratana, rejected them as 'forbidden branches of knowledge' not to be studied by monks.[111] This would imply that only lay students of that Pirivena learnt those subjects. The *Dambadeni Katikāvata* clearly mentions these subjects as forbidden branches of knowledge, and advises monks not to learn them or teach others.[112] Nevertheless, the literature of this period makes it clear that there were a large number of monks like Śrī Rāhula who were well acquainted with subjects like prosody, ornaments of speech and drama *(kavnaḷu- satara).*

The *Girā-sandeśaya* refers only to the lay students who studied medicine at the Vijayabāhu Pirivena.[113] However, Buddhist monks were not prohibited from studying medicine and even attending on the sick.[114] But this was for special purposes, and the relevant *vinaya* rules clearly stipulate that the monk should not practise medicine for mere gain. In keeping with this injunction the *Dambadeni Katikāvata* says that it is wrong for a monk to give medical aid to people other than those belonging to the five categories mentioned in the *vinaya.*[115] It should be mentioned here that some schools of Buddhism even encouraged the monks to learn medicine. According to Asaṅga, the exponent of the Yogācāra School of Buddhism, the art of healing was one of the subjects in which the noble ones had to train themselves for the benefit of others.[116] Precisely, the same view of Asaṅga is echoed in the *Girā-sandeśaya,* for its author says that the physicians used to study medicine at the Vijayabāhu Pirivena conscious of the fact that like Dhamma, which is the panacea for the ills of existence, medicine too exists for the well-being of the mankind.[117] It was when monks practised medicine for the purpose of gain that the *Dambadeni Katikāvata* decries them as being engaged in the pursuit of a *garhita-vidyā* or 'a forbidden branch of knowledge', and there is no doubt that the permission to practise medicine without infringement of the rules of Buddhism led to considerable abuse of this concession.

From the *Girā-sandeśaya* we notice that some students of the Vijayabāhu Pirivena engaged themselves in learning astrological calculation as set out in the *Sūryasiddhānta.*[118] The principal of that Pirivena had much enthusiasm for astrology as is evident from his two *sandeśa* poems, the *Parevi-sandeśaya* and the *Säḷalihiṇi-sandeśaya.*[119]

While the Padmāvatī Pirivena forbade its students to study politics *(arthaśāstra),* the students of the Vijayabāhu Pirivena were taught that subject.[120] With their knowledge of Sanskrit, the students of the Vijayabāhu Pirivena would have had access to such works as Kauṭilya's *Arthaśāstra* and the *Mānavadharmaśāstra,* for the principal of the above mentioned institution displays his mastery in these works in his *mahākāvya,* the *Kāvyaśekharaya.*[121].

The students of the Vijayabāhu Pirivena were allowed to learn not only Buddhism but also other religions *(samayāntara)* as well.[122] It has been mentioned that some of these students studied the Four Vedas; i.e. Ṛk, Sāma, Yajur and Atharvan.[123] In addition to that, they were taught the eighteen Purāṇas and the two Mahākāvyas: *Rāmāyaṇa* and *Mahābhārata.*[124] It is stated in the *Haṃsa- sandeśaya* that the principal of the Padmāvatī

Pirivena looked down on the Vedas, Purāṇas and Mahākāvyas as frivolous.[125] Vīdāgama Maitreya, in his *Buduguṇālaṅkāraya*, despised these works as falsifications composed by *brahmins* for the sole purpose of gain.[126] Nevertheless, the enthusiasm of Śrī Rāhula and his followers for Hindu literature is well reflected in the *Girā-sandeśaya*, for it not only eulogize the *thera* as an expert on the subjects[127] but also gives an account of public enthusiasm for Hindu mythology.[128] It may be safely concluded that at least some aspects of Hinduism were taught in the Pirivenas of the Kōṭṭē period. Apart from that, we do not know what other religions were taught in the Pirivenas.

The foregoing remarks would make it clear that the Pirivenas in the Kōṭṭē period provided their students with a wide range of subjects. It may further indicate that the Padmāvatī Pirivena at Kāragala, being the main centre of the Vanavāsi fraternity, had some restrictions regarding its curriculum, while the Vijayabābu Pirivena at Toṭagamuva, the great centre of learning of the Gāmavāsi fraternity, allowed its students to study a large number of subjects without any reservation.

From what has been discussed about the graduated system of education in the Pirivenas we may assume that there were tests conducted for students to this effect. But it is unfortunate that we have no information whatsoever on this aspect of monastic education of the Kōṭṭē period. However, according to the *Dam̆badeni Katikāvata* there were several type of tests in that period conducted for student monks to test their memory power, the power of comprehension of texts and intelligence.[129] Memory power was partly tested by asking students to recite by memory what they had to learn by heart.[130] The *Girā-sandeśaya* refers to a group of *bhikkhu* students of the Vijayabāhu Pirivena, who committed grammar *(viyaraṇa)* to memory *(vanapot)*.[131] The expression *vanapot asvā* (having recited by memory) in the *Dam̆badeni Katikāvata* shows the method of testing memory power, and on the basis of that it may be conjectured that the students of the Vijayabāhu Pirivena prepared for this test by committing grammar to memory. The second method of test *parīkṣā-gena* mentioned in the *Dam̆badeni Katikāvata* seems to represent the testing of comprehension of the contents of books, and intelligence.[132] The *Katikāvata* says that the student may be able to answer questions asked by way of comparison and contrast from the beginning to the end of the text. Thus, in accordance with this rule some students of the Vijayabāhu Pirivena studied the *Sikavalañda* by way of examining it from the beginning to the end.[133] It may be surmised that this necessiated a clear mind, an ability to organize ideas, memory power and intelligence to show one's own competence. Information given in the *Daṁbadeni Katikāvata* regarding tests conducted for *bhikkhu* students may be applied to the general scheme of education in the monastic institutions of the Kōṭṭē period.

As for the methods of teaching that may have been applied during this period it would seem that the usual traditional pattern was followed. The teacher recited the texts and it was the duty of the student to listen to him carefully and learn the text from the mouth of the teacher. In the case of the student monk he resided in the monastery with the teacher himself. The day was spent in following the various duties of a *bhikkhu* apart from learning. These duties are enumerated in the *Heraṇasika*.[134] Spiritual and moral training, too, formed a part of the early training of the novice. The teacher was waited upon by the pupil as a form of duty. Both the duties of serving the elder and studying formed an important part of the life of a student. Each day was devoted to revision of earlier work, explanations and discussions, questions and answers[135] which perhaps formed the general pattern of education during this time.[136]

It may be assumed that the medium of instruction in the Pirivenas was mainly Sinhalese, for the majority of students spoke that language. Nevertheless, Pali and perhaps also Sanskrit may have served as media when occasion demanded. We have seen earlier that some students of the Padmāvatī Pirivena came from South East Asia and some students of the Vijayabāhu Pirivena came from India.[137] It is likely that the Buddhist monks from foreign countries who came to learn in these institutions used Pali as medium of instruction. This is substantiated by the fact that the author of the *Dāṭhāvaṃsa* says that his object of translating the story of the Tooth Relic, which was in Sinhalese, into Pali is to make it accessible to readers of other countries.[138] Hence, it is probable that the South East Asian monks who came to study the Tripiṭaka under Vanaratana of Kāragala used Pali as their medium of instruction because it was the international language in the Theravāda world.

It is possible that Sanskrit was a medium of instruction at least in a limited circle. The influx of *brahmins* to Sri Lanka and the spread of their culture became intensified in the medieval period,[139] especially in the Kōṭṭē period. The *Girā-sandeśaya* mentions *brahmin* youths studying the Vedas among other subjects in the Vijayabāhu Pirivena.[140] We have seen earlier that *Rāmacandra Bhārati* came to the same Pirivena as a student. Hence it is possible in case of *brahmin* students the medium of instruction was Sanskrit.

Information procured by our sources is hardly sufficient to ascertain the part played by libraries as a means of education. According to the *Cūlavaṃsa*, Bhuvanekabāhu III (1272-1284) had the whole Tripiṭaka copied by scribes and had the texts preserved here and there in the *vihāras* of Laṅka thereby causing the dissemination of the sacred texts.[141] Parākramabāhu IV (1302-1326), having translated Pali *jātakas* into Sinhalese distributed them throughout Laṅka, possibly preserved in the *vihāras*.[142] The copying of books in the Sunetrādevi Pirivena at Päpiliyāna is recorded in the Päpiliyāna document No.I.[143] Senāsammata Vikramabāhu of Kandy is said to have spent a large amount of money for the copying of sacred texts.[144] Apart from the Sunetrādevi Pirivena there must have been other places where books were copied and preserved. Subhūti, in his *Nāmamāla*, has drawn up a list of 53 grammatical works, some of which are no longer extant, quoted by Śrī Rāhula in his compilation of the *Pañcikāpradīpaya*.[145] This enables us to have some idea of the vast amount of books the library of the Vijayabāhu Pirivena had for one subject. Hence, it is probable that the libraries of the Pirivenas contained large collections of books on the religion as well as other subjects.

The chief benefactors of Pirivenas were the kings, and endowments made by them were perhaps more than sufficient for the maintenance of these establishments. These endowments took several forms. As mentioned earlier, in some cases the king made grants of land, fields or villages.[146] In other cases, deposits of paddy or other grains and money kept in trust,[147] or "even levying of taxes and collection of fines"[148] were the endowments made to these institutions by kings. A typical case was that of Parākramabāhu VI, who built the Sunetrādevi Pirivena at Päpiliyāna and granted to it numerous lands and fields for the maintenance of the institution.[149]

The same king granted several lands including the villages of Mahagoḍa and Valpiṭiya to Śrī Rāhula, the principal of the Vijayabāhu Pirivena,[150] probably for the maintenance of the institution. The Kāragala inscription II records the grant by this king of land and fields towards Vanaratana, the principal of the Padmāvatī Pirivena.[151] The *Aramkälē Sannasa* of Bhuvanekabāhu VI enumerates the grant of land and fields to Vīdāgama Maitreya and his chief disciple, Niyañdavane Phussadeva Sumaṅgala, the principal of the Dharmarāja Pirivena at Erabattoṭa.[152]

We are not quite certain whether the student in the monastic education system paid fee to the teacher or institution. It seems most likely that the education provided by the Pirivenas was free, both for members of the Sangha and the laity who may have come there for their studies. Monk's maintenance, lodgings and other facilities were provided free. Their only obligation to the institution and to the teacher seems to have been the performance of duties which were part of monastic life,[153] and did not amount to the payment of compensation for what they had received by way of instruction, finding lodgings etc. Dhammavisuddhi has drawn attention to a rule of the *Daṁbadeni Katikāvata* which tends to suggest that some monks made it a practice to receive rewards from laymen for instruction imparted to their children.[154] But the condemnation of the practice in the *Katikāvata* may suggest that such practices were not legal and probably crept into the Sangha where there were no proper arrangements; therefore one may not tend to regard this as a part of the monastic education system under review. Nevertheless, the fact that the *Katikāvata* condemns these practices seems to suggest that it occurred regularly. We do not know how far the *Katikāvata* was successful in banning such practices. In view of the fact that the *Päpiliyāna Katikāvata* also condemns these illegal practices may lead one to assume that the regular occurrence of such practices, though always condemned by *Katikāvatas*, continued to prevail. However, as we do not have evidence to suggest that such illegal practices were followed in the organized institutions such as Pirivenas, on the whole it may be correct to say that the education imparted by the Pirivenas was free. And the only form of payment that was made was that the student generally served the teacher, and the laity maintained the teacher by their generous gifts of *dāna* and other requisites.

As mentioned earlier, the Pirivenas reached their highest development in the fifteenth century under the patronage of Parākramabāhu VI. This monarch who ruled the country for a great part of the fifteenth century, not only extended his patronage to scholars and educational establishments but give them every encouragement. Some of the contemporary poets who sang his praise compared him with King Bhoja, the patron of learning in ancient India.[155] It is evident from the contemporary works that there were a large number of writers and poets who were encouraged by the king, and took pleasure in composing poetry at a poets' hall *kavikāra-maḍauva)*.[156] The abounding interest in learning shown by the king is best evident from his composing the *Ruvanmala*, a lexicon for poets.[157] Besides the king, there were other members of the royal household who evinced a patronising interest in learning. For, it was Ulakuḍayadevi, the younger daughter of the king, who requested Śrī Rāhula to compose a *jātaka* story in verse.[158] Thus the only Sinhalese epic of the period, the *Kāvyaśekharaya* was the result of the request made by the princess. Among the non-Sinhalese writers who made contributions to Sinhalese literature during this period was Nannūrutunayyār, the son-in-law of the king, who composed a lexicon, *Nāmamālāva*.[159] It was at the request of this prince that Śrī Rāhula composed his *Sälalihiṇi-sandeśaya*.[160] Patronage of learning was extended by other chiefs of the period as well. For it was a retired chief minister, Salāvata Jayapāla, who requested Vättāve to versify another *jātaka* story, resulting in the *Guttila-kāvyaya.*[161] These instances may indicate not only the patronage extended by the nobility of the country towards learning but the high standard of learning prevailing in the upper strata of society as well.

It seems that after the reign of Parākramabāhu VI the Pirivenas suffered a general decline. This can be attributed to more than one reason. As has been discussed before, after the death of Parākramabāhu VI the peace and prosperity witnessed in his reign gave way to political unrest and disunity in the country. One of the most conspicuous results of the political struggle between Jayabāhu II and Bhuvanekabāhu VI, which lasted for three years was the disunity not only in the country but among the Sangha as well. Political disunity dragged the country towards internecine warfare which came to its climax after the arrival of the Portuguese in 1505, and lasted for the whole of the sixteenth century. There is tittle doubt that this state of affairs would have had disastrous effects on the Pirivenas almost all of which were situated in the south-western and southern part of the country which became the battle field for well over three centuries.

It is noteworthy that the only Pirivena mentioned in our sources after the death of Parākramabāhu VI is the Dharmarāja Pirivena at Erabattoṭa, the principal of which was Niyañdavane Phussadeva Sumaṅgala, the chief disciple of Vīdāgama Maitreya.[162] Śrī Rāhula's departure from public life would also have had damaging effects on the Pirivena education system, most probably on the disappearance of the Vijayabāhu Pirivena, one of the most outstanding institutions of the period. After Vanaratana, the Padmāvatī Pirivena also cannot be traced in our sources for unknown reasons.

It is apparent that, engaged in continued political struggles, the Sinhalese rulers could no longer extend their patronage towards the Pirivenas. Since royalty were no longer the patrons of the Pirivenas, these had to look after themselves. As a result, these establishments did not remain competent in the filed of education, and were gradually, relegated to a subordinate position as temple schools which were noticed by Queyroz in the seventeenth century.[163] and the Colebrooke Commissioners in the nineteenth century.[164]

## References


1. *HBC.*, 132.
2. *Sāratthadīpanī*, ed. T.Davarakkhita, Colombo, 1914, p.510.
3. *Mv.*, 35.57; 36.10.
4. *Cv.*, 45.29; 48.135.
5. *CCMT.*, p. 193
6. R.C. Childers, A Dictionary of the Pali Language, London, 1875, *sv.*
7. *Nks.*, p.7; see also, *Sdhrt.*, pp.135 , 334, 335, 343, 345,; *HBC.*, p.132; *EZ*, III, pp.223, a.1
8. *Cv.*, 46.31.
9. *CV..*, 46, 31.
10. *EZ.*, I, p.45.
11. *Cv.*, 78.48 ff.
12. *Cv.*, 86.37-38.
13. *Pjv.*, p.41.
14. *Kts.*, p.9.
15. *Grs.*, vv. 54.57; *Kks.*, vv. 116, 120; *Rjv*, pp.48,54.
16. *Sdhrt.*, p.294.
17. *Hms.*, v.200.
18. *JCBRAS.*, XXXII, No.86, pp.298-304.
19. *Hms.*, 189 ff.
20. *Cv.*, tr.p.203,n.3.
21. *Cv.*, 90.88 ff.
22. *Jinacarita*, (PTSJ), ed.T.W.Rhys Davies, London,1896, p.31.
23. *Kotte Yugaye Siṅhala Sāhityaya*, p.87, Dhammavisuddhi, op.cit., p.251.,1937.p.14 ff.
24. *UCHC.*, p.718 ff.
25. *Kks.*, v.77.
26. *Kks*, v.81.
27. *Grs*, vv. 214 ff.
28. *Myrs.*, v.71.
29. *Rjv.*, p.48.
30. ibid.

31. *Cv.*, 90.98 ff.
32. *Myrs.*, v.27.
33. *Hms.*, v.201 ff.
34. *Kks.*, v.291.
35. *Kks.*, v.291.
36. *PLS.*, P.248.
37. *Cv.*, 83.50.
38. *Cv.*, 90.94 ff.
39. *Cv.*, 91.24 ff.
40. *Kts.*, p.40 ff.
41. *Kts.*, p.41.
42. *Vmkts.*, p.215.
43. *Pdst.*, vv.1-2.
44. *Vṛttamālā*, *Br.MUSMs.*Or. 6611 (189), folio, *Ki*,
45. *Ep.Birm*, III, No. II, p.249.
46. *Ssl.*, p.144.
47. *SSS.*, p.180
48. *Rkd.*, p.91.
49. *Hms.*, vv.169 ff.
50. *Hms.*, vv.169 ff.
51. *Kts.*, p.15.
52. *Grs.*, vv.219 ff.
53. *Grs.*, 223.
54. *Jkm.*, p.93.
55. *Grs.*, v.222; *Hms.*, v.109.
56. *Grs.*, v.219 ff; *Hms.*, v.170.l
57. *Sāmanera-Baṇadahampota*, ed.G.Seelaratana, Panadura, 1937.p.14 ff.
58. *Mahāvagga*, I.25.33
59. ibid. V.4.2.
60. *Kts.*, p.9 ff.
61. *Grs.*, v.222.
62. *Hms.*, v.169.
63. E.Muller, *Ancient Inscriptions of Ceylon*, No.137, p.11; *Kts.*, p.2 and 10.
64. *Sikhāvalaňda*, ed. D.B.Jayatilaka, Kelaniya, 1945, preface, p.ii.
65. *Hms.*, v.172.
66. *Kts.*, p.10.
67. i.e. *bhikkhu-bhikkuṇī mātikā*, generally known as the *Pātimokkha*
68. i.e. the four *bhāṇavāras* of the *paritta*.
69. The occasions for the *anumodanā* are *saṅgha-bhatta* (alms-giving), *maṅgala* (an auspicious occasion like occupying a new house

or a wedding) and *avamangala* (a funeral or a *mataka-dāna*, alms-giving for the dead.).

70. *Samantapāsāsādikā*, ed. J. Takakusu and Nakoto Nagai, Oxford University Press, 1934, IV, p.788 ff.
71. ibid.
72. *Kts.* p.11.
73. *Kts.*, p.12.
74. *Kts.*, p.12; *Smp.*, p.577.
75. *Hms.*, v.173; *Kts.*, p.11.
76. i.e. the two Vinaya texts known as *Pārājikā* and *Pācittiya.*
77. *Kts.*, p.11.
78. *Grs.*, vv.219-221.
79. Smp., p.577.
80. Four Major Collections of the *Suttapiṭaka* known as *Dīgha, Majjhima, Saṃyutta,* and *Anguttara.*
81. Seven *pakaraṇas (compositions) of the Abbhammapiṭaka* known as; *Dhammasanganī, Vibhanga, Dhātupāṭha, Puggalapññatti, Kathāvatthu, Yamaka and Paṭṭhāna.* See, *Pali Sāhityaya*, p.128.
82. *KTS*, p. 11.
83. *Hms.*, v.174.
84. *Hms.*, vv.175. and 176; *Grs.*, vv. 229.
85. *Hms.*, v.184 ff.
86. *Sls.*, v.108; *Grs.*, v.231 ff; *Kvsk.*, v.11; *TB.*, p. 155.
87. *Kks.*, v. 291; SSL., p. 43.
88. *Grs.*, v.226 ff.
89. *PLC.*, p. 186.
90. *PS.*, p. 523.
91. *Hms.*, v.171; *PLC.*, p.87.
92. *Cv.*, 64. 2ff.
93. *Grs.*, v. 223.
94. D. Pannasara, *The Sanskrit Literature of Ceylon*, Colombo, 54, p.7.
95. *Kvsk.*, preface, pix ff; R. Tennakon. Srī Rāhula Kṛti, Colombo, 1956, p. 23.
96. *Hms.*, v. 187 ff.
97. Pannasara, *op. cit.*, p. 117.
98. *SSS.*, p. 10 ff.
99. *Bhakti-śataka*, ed. Ratnakara, Colombo, 1939.
100. *Verttamālā* ed. W. Dipankara, Pandura, 1918.
101. N.de S. Wijesekara, 'Sanskrit Civilization among the Ancient Sinhalese' *CHJ.*, I, 1951, No. I, p. 29.

102. *Hms.*, v. 178; *Grs.* v.227.
103. See above, Ch. I,
104. C.E. Godakumbure, *Sinhalese Literature*, p. 152.
105. See, above, ch. II.
106. *EZ.*, III, p. 64 ff.
107. *Grs.*, v. 227.
108. *Kks.*, v. 286.
109. *Subhāṣitaya*, v. 3.
110. *Hms.*, v. 188; *Grs.* v.235 ff.
111. *Hms.*, v.190 ff.
112. *kāvya-nāṭakādi-garhita-vidyā tamā nūgatayutu, anunut nūgānviyayutu.* (Do not learn or cause others to learn such forbidden arts as those of poetry and drama) Kts. p. 12.
113. *Grs.* v. 225.
114. *Mahāvagga*, 1 (bhesajjakkhandaka), pp. 199-152.
115. *Kts.*, p. 12.
116. *Mahāyānsūtrālaṅkāra*, ed. Sylvan Levi, 1907, p. 70.
117. *Grs.*, v.225.
118. *Grs.*, v.224.
119. *Prs.*, v.43 f; *Sls.*, v.15 ff.
120. *Grs.*, v. 226.
121. *Kvsk.*, preface, p. 22 and cantos, 14 and 18.
122. *Grs.*, v.238.
123. *Grs.*, v.227.
124. *Grs.*, v.227.
125. *Hms.*, 189 and 241.
126. *Bdgnl.*, v. 134 ff.
127. *Grs.*, v.241 ff.
128. *Grs.*, v. 114 ff.
129. *Kts.*, p.11.
130. ibid.
131. *Grs.*, v.222.
132. *Kts.*, p. 11.
133. *ibid*
134. *Sāmaṇera Banadahampota*, p. 9 ff.
135. *Grs.*, vv.219, 220 and 223.
136. A.A. Altekar, Education in Ancient India, Benares, 1934, p. 112; R.K. Mookerji, *Ancient Indian Education*, London, 1947, p. 327.
137. See above. p. 148 ff.
138. *Dāthāvaṃsa*, v.10.
139. UCHC., p. 767.

140. *Grs.* v. 223.
141. *Cv.*, 90.37-37.
142. *Cv.*,90.84.
143. *Kts.*, p. 41 ff.
144. *Rjrt.*, p.57.
145. B. Subhuti, *Nāmamālā*, Colombo, 1876, p. 2 ff.
146. See above, ch. IV.
147. *HBC.*, p. 141.
148. *HBC.*, p. 141.
149. *Kts.*, p.41 ff.
150. *Grs.*, v.234.
151. *JCBRAS.*, XXXII, No. 86, p. 86, p. 298 ff.
152. *SSL.*, p. 42 f.
153. *Cullavagga*, VI, 21. 1-2; *Sikhavalañada*, p. 32 ff; S. Dutt. *Early Buddhist Monachism, London, 1924, p. 177 ff.*
154. Dhammavisuddhi, *op. cit.* p.309.
155. *Pärakumbāsirita*, v. 16.
156. *KYSS.*, p.1.
157. *Ruvanmala*, ed. G. Silananda, Kandy, 1934.
158. *Kvsk.*, vv. 14-22.
159. *Nāmamālāva*, ed. w.ed Alwis, Colombo, 1914.
160. *Sls.*, v.96.
161. *Guttila-kāvyaya*, v.7.
162. *SSL.*, p. 43.
163. *Queroz* p. 281.
164. *Colebrooke-Cameron Papers*, ed. G.C. Mendis, 1956, p.84; According to the statistic which were provided for the Commission by the Collector of Colombo, there were ninetyfour Buddhist schools in the year of 1827. This is no doubt an indication of classes conducted by the Buddhist monks in their temples. See, R. Ruberu, *Education in Colonial Ceylon*, Colombo, 1962, p. 241.

# Chapter Six

## Relations With Other Buddhist Countries

The prestige and reputation of the Sangha of Sri Lanka were so high during the fifteenth century that other Buddhist countries regarded the Kōṭṭē kingdom as the centre of Theravāda Buddhism, particularly as the place where the living tradition of the ancient Mahāvihāra of Anurādhapura was maintained. By this time Buddhism had virtually diappeared from India, its land of origin, especially owing to the Muslim invasions. The holy places in that country were no longer accessible to Buddhists of the other countries. This situation which had been rapidly developing since the tenth, and especially the twelfth century A.D. resulted in Sri Lanka becoming the holy land of Buddhists where relics, images and the scriptures were preserved with great veneration. A visit to the Island, and the gaining of admission to the Order there were a mark of distinction for a foreign monk even in the fourteenth century.[1]

The supremacy given to Sri Lanka in religious affairs appears from a large number of visits by foreign Buddhists, especially monks, throughout the thirteenth, fourteenth and fifteenth centuries. The purpose of these visits varied from a mere pilgrimage to seeking ordination, training under the Sīhaḷa Sangha or learning the Scriptures under the reputed *mahātheras* of the Mahāvihāra fraternity.[2] This close contact, which Sri Lanka maintained with other Buddhist countries, is reflected in historical documents and monuments of those countries. As has been mentioned before, it is strange that the Sri Lankan chronicles do not even make a passing reference to these missions.

By this time, as the Indian Buddhist centres had completely disappeared, the Sinhalese Sangha had its foreign relations with their counterparts in South East Asia. It has been observed that Sri Lanka's cultural relations with South East Asia go back as early as to the Anurādhapura period. Pierre Dupont, having examined two Buddha images from Java and another from Celebes, has pointed to the influence of Sinhalese sculptural traditions in these works.[3] He dates the image from Celebes to the second or third century and the two images from Java to the sixth or seventh century. Mirella Levi D' Ancona, too, though disagreeing with the dating of these images, accepts the possibility of their origin in Sri Lanka.[4] George Coēdēs had also accepted that some of the sculptural works from South East Asia, grouped under the Amarāvatī School, could have come from Sri Lanka.[5] Devaprasad Gosh, in a discussion on an image of Avalokiteśvara found at Bingin in the Plaembang district in Sumatra, has suggested the possibility that the inspiration for the work came from Sri Lanka, comparing it with a statue of the same *bodhisattva* at Situlpavva, and ascribed it to about the seventh century.[6]

An important fragmentary inscription from the Ratubaka Plateau in Central Java would take Sri Lanka's religious contacts with that island to at least the end of the eighth century. De Casparis has drawn attention to this interesting record, in the light of which he has suggested that, Sri Lanka, too, played a part in the 'Indianisation' of South East Asia.[7] This inscription attests to the existence of an 'Abhayagiri Vihāra of the Sinhalese ascetics in the province.

**Commenting on this record De Casparis observes :-**

"The most important detail is the name of the foundation, viz. the Abhayagiri Vihāra. The name at once suggests that of the famous monastery at Anurādhapura and the addition "of the Sinhalese" proves that this is not just a coincidence. In fact the foundation is a second Abhayagiri Vihāra; either a more or less exact replica of the Sri Lankan monastery or, more probably, a building which had enough in common with it- in form or spirit or both to deserve the same name. Further excavations on the Ratubaka Plateau may yield materials capable of giving an impression of this interesting building. In the present stage of research there is, however, one important conclusion that may be drawn from the inscription: the existence of cultural relations between Java and Sri Lanka in the Sailendra period."[8]

Of all South East Asian countries Sri Lanka's relations with Burma were the closest. With the decline of Buddhism in India, Sri Lankan Buddhists turned more and more to Burma and the vice versa. We learn from the *Cūlavaṃsa* that Vijayabāhu I (1070-1111) sent envoys to the king of Burma (Rāmañña), Anuruddha (1044-1077), requesting him to send competent *bhikkhus* to re-establish the higher ordination in Sri Lanka, which had been in abeyance during the Coḷa occupation (1017- 1070) of the greater part of the Island.[9] This request was duly acceded to and the higher ordination of the country was re-established as a result. From this time the relationship between the two countries, which had momentous consequences for Buddhism in Burma, seems to have continued for several centuries. If the *Jinakālamālī* is to be trusted, Anuruddha received texts of the Tripiṭaka from Sri Lanka in the early years of his reign.[10]

But this seems most unlikely because Sri Lanka was not in a position to help other countries in any case until 1070 which marked the re-establishment of Sinhalese power. But, as Luce has suggested, it seems likely that Anuruddha obtained the copies of the Pali Canon from Sri Lanka by about 1075, when Mon monks were busy in Sri Lanka helping the Sinhalese to revive Buddhism in the island.[11] If so, the main flood of the Pali Canon only reached Pagan in the closing years of Anuruddha's reign.

Luce demonstrates that the real changeover of the Pagan court from Tāntric Mahāyāna to Theravāda took place in Kyanzittha's reign rather than Anurudda's.[12] In fact, during and after the reign of Kyanzittha religious life of Pagan underwent strong Sinhalese influence as is revealed by ephigraphical sources. According to some sources, Kyanzittha took much care to "collect and purify the Tripiṭaka, which had become obscure and corrupt."[13] They not only confirm the fact that Kyanzittha, early in his reign, instituted a large-scale study and revision of the Tripiṭaka, but also that this new recension based on the orthodox Sinhalese Mahāvihāra of Anuruddha's youth and lodged it finally in the Theravāda fold.[14] This is hailed as Kyanzittha's more lasting contribution to his country's history.

Kyanzittha, at the beginning of his reign, had *jātaka* stories, which were used in Pagan, revised following the Sinhalese tradition.[15] The influence of Sinhalese Buddhism on Pagan can even be seen in the temple paintings and sculptures. In contrast to the Brahmanic paintings in the early temples, (e.g. Nanpoya), temples dating from Kyanzittha's reign, (e.g.Pāhtothāmya c. 1080), began to be decorated with Buddhist paintings. Luce, commenting on these paintings, observes: "Here paintings depict the life of the Buddha, boldly painted; rule after rule of the *vinaya, sutta* after *sutta* of the *Dīgha* and *Majjhima Nikāyas*, each with a written gloss to identify it, all with names and details following the Sinhalese Canon.[16] The process of the Sinhalese influence grows and extends, both in painting and sculpture, throughout Kyanzittha's reign, and reaches its climax in the year after his death, i.e. 1113, in the Myinkaba Kubyauk-gyi temple of his son Rājakumāra.[17] Rājakumāra's aim, it appears, was to depict on its walls the whole history of the world as known to the Buddhists, and told it in the Sinhalese chronicles, followed by the *Dīpavaṃsa, Mahāvaṃsa,* and *Cūlavaṃsa,* right down to his own day.[18]

The cultural contact between Sri Lanka and Burma continued uninterrupted throughout the medieval period except in the short interval when Parākramabāhu I (1153- 1186) led an expedition to Lower Burma.[19] In spite of this political conflict between Sri Lanka and Burma at this particular time, the strong religious bond which existed between them remained unimpared. This can be seen even in the events which followed immediately after the war, for the people of Burma are said to have made an appeal to the monks of Sri Lanka to bring about a settlement with Parākramabāhu I.[20] The successor of this king, Vijayabāhu II (1186-1187), is said to have sent a letter written in the Māgadhī (Pali) language to the king of Arimaddana and thus revived the friendly relations which existed in the days of his great grandfather, Vijayabāhu I.[21] Nissaṅkamalla (1187-1196) in his inscriptions claims to have entered into friendly relations with Aramaṇa.[22]

The most spectacular result of the relationship between Sri Lanka and Burma was the establishment of a sect known as the Sīhaḷa Sangha in Burma. The founder of this sect was, according to the Kalyānī inscriptions, a monk called Chapaṭa who came to Sri Lanka with his teacher, Uttarājīva *mahāthera*, and several other Burmese monks in the reign of Parākramabāhu I.[23] Chapaṭa received his ordination in Sri Lanka and stayed in the Island for ten years, mastering the Tripiṭaka and the Aṭṭhakathās. On his return to Burma, he took with him four other monks from Sri Lanka who were also well versed in the scriptures.[24] After their arrival in Burma, Chapaṭa and his colleagues began to perform ecclesiastical acts separate from other Burmese monks, and thus the Sinhalese Church or the Sīhaḷa Sangha, as it is called in the *Sāsanavaṃsa*, came to be established in Burma.[25] According to the Kalyāni inscriptions, this event took place in 1181-1182 A.D.

A Pagan inscription attributed to 1260 A.D. records that a Sīhaḷa-*thera* by name Ānanda reformed the Pagan Sangha on the strict model of the Sri Lankan Mahāvihāra, and he was strongly supported by a personage called Jayavaddhana, the nephew of Queen Vataṃsikā.[26] The evidence about Vataṃsikā is not conclusive. Luce has suggested that there may have been marriages between Burmese kings and Sinhalese princesses in the latter part of the Pagan period, and Vataṃsikā might have been one of these princesses.[27] He also assumes that with Sinhalese queens and ministers came the Sinhalese monks who became increasingly influential in the latter part of the Pagan period.[28] As archaeological evidence tend to suggest, these emissaries and missionaries were followed by the Sinhalese style of Pagoda building, with the large cubic *harmikā* revived, and left its mark at Pagan.[29]

Binnya U (1353-1385), king of Pegu, sent a mission to Sri Lanka to obtain relics to be enshrined in a *stūpa* which he built.[30] The *Sāsanavaṃsa* records that two monks from Sri Lanka, Siri Dhammālaṅkāra and Sīhaḷa Mahāsāmi landed at Kusīma in 1429, bringing relics from Sri Lanka.[31] The then king of Pegu,

Binnya Ram, refused to allow them to settle down in his dominions, and the monks proceeded to Sirikkhetta where the king of Ava, Mriññana (Mohnyinthado) (1427-1440), gave them a splendid reception. The Sri Lankan monks settled in Mrammā (Burma proper), and the spread of religion in that country is ascribed to them.[32] The *Jinakālamālī* states that there were several Mon monks among the foreign monks who received their higher ordination at the Kalyāni *udakukkhepa-sīmā* in 1426.[33] One of Mohnyinthado's successors, Narapati (1443- 1469), was also a good patron of religion and is said to have appointed a certain *mahāsāmi-thera* as his *ācariya*. This *mahāsāmi*, according to the *Sāsanavaṃsa*, went to Sri Lanka and studied the Tripiṭaka under the reputed Sinhalese monks at the time and thus came to belong to the Later Order, i.e. the Sīhaḷa Sangha in Burma.[34]

Another Burmese monk named Chapaṭa, was in Sri Lanka about this time. In his commentary to the *Abhidhammatthasaṅgaha* he claims to have purified the Sāsana in Sri Lanka with the help of Parākramabāhu VI, established a duly constituted boundary *(sīmā)* at Jayavaddhanapura, and trained pupils in the Vinaya and Abhidhamma.[35] We have no reference to this purification of the Sangha in Sri Lankan sources. On this basis, Paranavitana is of the opinion that there is no reason to assume that the country at this time was in need of a Burmese expert to put its house in order.[36]

It is true that none of our sources refers to a purge of the Sangha which would have taken place in the reign of Parākramabāhu VI. But this does not exclude the possibility that the king took necessary steps to arrest the degeneration of the Sangha which had continued through decades before his reign. For, the *Päpiliyāna Katikāvata* makes it clear that some regulations were drawn to this effect.[37] The preamble to the *Katikāvata* states that it was promulgated on the advice of Maṅgala *mahaterasāmi* of the Päpiliyana monastery.[38] It adds that all the *gana-detu- teras* (leaders of the *gaṇas)* were also consulted in drawing the regulations. There is evidence to speculate that there was a considerable number of Burmese monks in Sri Lanka at this time, for king Narapati of Ava is said to have bought a piece of land in Kōṭṭē, apparently to erect a monastery for the support of the Burmese clergy residing in Sri Lanka or visiting the Island from time to time.[39] Hence it may be surmised that as he was in Sri Lanka at this time, and seems to have been an elderly and well versed monk, Chapaṭa must also have been consulted on this important occasion.

King Narapati, in spite of political troubles, continued to maintain relations with Sri Lanka. He is said to have sent offerings of gold and gems to the sacred Tooth Relic, then in Kōṭṭē.[40] The successor of this king, Thihathura (1469- 1481), whose reign marked a brief interval of relative calm in Ava[41] continued religious contact with Sri Lanka. The king and his queen made their hair into a broom, studded its handle with gems, and sent it to sweep the floor of the Tooth Relic temple of Kōṭṭē.[42] His envoys brought dresses of Chinese silk to be presented to the Sinhalese monarch.

Under king Dhammaceti (1472-1496) Southern Burma (Pegu) witnessed a fresh religious revival.During the centuries that preceded his reign the country was subjected to a great deal of political disturbance and Buddhist practices seem to have been neglected as a result.[43] Dhammaceti, who had been a monk before his accession to the throne, had a great zeal for the propagation and reform of the religion. The first point which caught his eye in the Sangha was the various contending sects into which the Order had become divided, and the bitter rivalry among the different sects.[44] The next point was probably the laxity in the rules of discipline among the monks of various sects. The only remedy to these unsettled affairs of the Sangha lay in bringing all the sects together under one ecclesiastical authority through one standard and absolute *upasampadā* ordination.[45] As a monk Dhammaceti has had a training under the Sīhaḷa Sangha in Burma. As a result of that he held fast to orthodox views regarding the affairs of the Sangha. Moreover, numerous pilgrimages and missions of Burmese monks to the Mahāvihāra of Sri Lanka during the last three centuries had built up a tradition in Burma which held that the religion in its pure and unsullied form existed there alone.[46] When, therefore, Dhammaceti thought of effecting reforms in the Order, he had naturally his face turned towards Sri Lanka.

Having consulted the leading monks of various sects, Dhammaceti finally decided to send envoys to Sri Lanka in quest of higher ordination. His resolution towards this end is recorded in the Kalyānī Inscriptions as follows:-

> Reverend Sirs, the *upasampadā* ordination of the monks of the Mon country now appears to us be invalid.....From the establishment of the religion in the island of Sri Lanka up to the present day, there has been existing in that island an exceedingly pure sect of monks, who were the spiritual successors of the monks of the Mahāvihāra, a Chapter, who are pure and free from censure and reproach; receive at their hands the *upasampadā* ordination in the *udakukkhepa-sīmā* consecrated on the Kalyānī river.....and if you make this form of *upasampadā* ordination the seed of the religion, as it were, plant it (after you return here from that island), and cause it to sprout forth by conferring such ordination on men of good family in this Mon country....Reverend Sirs, by your going to the island of Sri Lanka, much merit and great advantage will accure you.[47]

In accordance with Dhammaceti's request 22 Mon Monks and their disciples embarked on two ships for Sri Lanka on 9 January, 1476 A.D.[48] To represent the king were accompanied by two ministers, Citradūta and Rāmadūta. Citradūta's ship arrived in Sri Lanka in February 1476, handicapped by adverse winds and adverse circumstances, Rāmadūta's ship arrived in the Island a few months later, in June 1470.[49]

At the time of the arrival of this foreign religious mission there was a wide-spread rebellion in the country against the then king, Bhuvanekabāhu VI.[50] The Kalayānī inscriptions inform us that the brother of the king (Ambulugala Raja) was ordered to go by sea to the port of Väligama to engage in operations against the rebels under the leadership of Garavi-*amātya*, who occupied the coastal region between Kōṭṭē and Väligama where the Mon mission landed.[51] The inscriptions allude to the fact that the mission had to break their journey to Kōṭṭē and stay several months at Väligama, owing to the risk involved in the journey; for the rebels were maltreating the supporters of the king during this time. The mission was thus forced to remain at Väligama for over three months until the rebellion was suppressed.

When the mission arrived at Kōṭṭē, Bhuvanekabāhu VI (1470-1478) directed the clergy of the Mahāvihāra to make necessary arrangements for the ordination of the 22 Mon monks with their 22 disciples. The Chapter of the Sangha for this ceremony was summoned by Vīdāgama Maitreya at the request of the king. "In conformity with the custom followed by the Sīnhaḷa *mahātheras* of old, whenever monks from foreign countries were ordained, the 44 Mon monks were first made to don the garments of laymen, and then admitted to the Order as *Sāmaṇeras*" through the act of Vanaratana *mahāthera* who presented them with Yellow robes, and accepted their profession of faith in the Three Refuges.[52] It then took four days to confer the higher ordination on all the 44 Mon monks, the last day being allotted to the 22 younger monks. On the first day Dhammakitti *mahāthera* and Pañcapariveṇavāsi Maṅgala *thera* were the *upajjhāya* and *ācariya* respectively. On the second and third days Vanaratana and Maṅgala acted as *upajjhāya* and *ācariya* respectively, while on the last day Maṅgala and Sīhaḷa-rāja-yuvarājācariya *mahāthera* were the *upajjhāya* and *ācariya* respectively.

It should be noted here that, as mentioned before, most probably owing to the animosity between the king and himself for political reasons, the Primate of the time, Śrī Rāhula, seems not to have taken part in the higher ordination ceremony. The Kalyānī inscriptions mention him as a virtuous monk and as the present *Saṅgharāja* and the principal of the Vijayabāhu Pirivena.[53] Vanaratana *mahāthera* referred to in the inscriptions was no doubt a personage other than Vanaratana of Kāragala, for the inscriptions mention the latter as 'the late *saṅgharāja*[54] Dhammakitti *mahāthera* of the inscriptions can be identified with the Elder Dhammakitti mentioned in the *Kokila-sandeśaya*, who was the incumbent of the Pohoyage Vihāraya at Kōṭṭē.[55]

Pañcaparivenavāsi Maṅgala *thera* of the inscriptions seems to have been Maṅgala of the Sunetrādevi Pirivena at Päpiliyāna, who held the incumbency of a number of religious institutions in the reign of Parākramabāhu VI.[56] It is extremely difficult to identify the monk referred to in the inscriptions as Sīhla-rāja-yuvarājācariya *mahāthera,* for none of the indigenous sources mentions a hierarch of the time having held this high sounding title.

After their arrival in Burma the newly ordained monks carried out mass higher ordination ceremonies in that country. Several hundred Mon monks received the *upasampadā* of the Sinhalese form. Through this process of valid higher oridnation, Dhammaceti was able to purge the Order in his realm of all impurities and corruption that had crept into it. He helped the Sīhaḷa Sangha become supreme and officially recognized Order in the land.[57] Dhammaceti's reformation is an important event in the history of Buddhism in Burma. After his reformation the Mramma Sangha, the older school that maintained the religion in the country presumably from the time when Sona and Uttara introduced the religion, became less important, and the Sīhaḷa Sangha, which had been introduced to that country by Chapaṭa in the twelfth century, and re-established by the monks who had a new *upasampadā* at the *udakukhepa- sīmā* at Kalyānī in Sri Lanka became the most powerful and influential school of the Sangha in Burma.[58]

One of the South East Asian countries with which Sri Lanka had very close contact during the medieval period was Thailand which became an independant kingdom from about the thirteenth century.[59] When they first appear in history, the Thai people had already embraced Theravāda. Until very recently it was thought that Buddhism did not enter the Mekong delta until the sixth century. But the discovery at Oc Eo, the port of Fu-nan, of many rings inscribed with short texts in Brahmi script has led to the belief that Buddhism became popular in ancient Fu-nan from the second century.[60] It has been observed that the Buddhism in Fu-nan was Hīnayāna, but used the Sanskrit canon.[61] Archaeological evidence testify to the prevalence of Hīnayāna in ancient Dvāravatī, whose culture came to embrace large areas of modern Thailand, from the sixth century.[62] It is conjectured that the Thai people embraced the Buddhist faith either from the Mon people to the west of Thailand or from the kingdom of Śrī Dharmarāja (mod.Ligor) in the Malay peninsula in both of which territories Theravāda was flourishing.[63]

The *Jinakālamālī*, a Pali chronicle which belongs to the sixteenth century, relates a story concerning a king named Rocarāja of Sukhodaya, according to which Thailand first came into contact with Sri Lanka, possibly in the thirteenth century.[64] This contact was said to have based on a belief of the existence of a miraculous Buddha image possessed by Sinhalese kings. One may find many difficulties in giving credence to this story. Jayawickrama has drawn attention to the chronological difficulties arising from this story and some other events related in the *Jinakālamālī*[65]. Apart from chronological difficulties, King Rocarāja of the story of the *Jinakālamālī* cannot be identified in any other source. The work relates that when a handsome young man (unnamed) of Gogāma was wandering in a forest a divine damsel who was taken up by his physical charm desired sexual intercourse with him, which eventually took place. As a result, a son was born who grew up to become a powerful and handsome young man. People who were impressed by these qualities consecrated him as their king and he came to be known as Rocarāja.[66] It is apparent from this story that Rocarāja does not appear to have been a historical figure.

It has been observed that during the reign of Jayavarman VIII (1243-1295) of Cambodia the Thais gained control over most of what is today the kingdom of Thailand.[67] A big step in this direction was taken when a Thai chieftain who had married daughter of Jayavarman VII defeated the Khmer governor of the Upper Menam valley and established the kingdom of Sukhodaya. In the light of these observations it may be concluded that the story in the *Jinakālamālī* is a mere legend explaining the establishment of Theravāda in Thailand, together with local stories about a Sīṅhaḷa *paṭimā*.

Sources dating from the fourteenth century onwards testify to the enthusiasm of the kings of Sukhodaya in establishing the ecclesiastical institutions in Thailand on the Sinhalese model.

Some inscriptions from Sukhodaya refer to the Sinhalese form of Buddhism in that country in the fourteenth century.[68] In the reign of Lo Thai (?1317-1347) of Sukhodaya relations between Sri Lanka and Thailand became much closer.[69] To this king, who held the title of Dharmarāja, we owe the construction of many Buddhapādas, or replicas of the foot-print of the Buddha, said to have been made in imitation of that worshipped in Sri Lanka on the summit of Samantakūṭa.[70] In his reign a Thai prince assumed the yellow robe and made a journey to India and Sri Lanka, from which countries he claims to have brought back miraculous relics.[71] This prince, who bore the title of Mahāthera Śrī Śīddhārāja Cūlāmaṇī Śrī Ratanālaṅkāra, after this journey, was responsible for important works of enlargement and restoration of Wat Mahatat of Sukhodaya. Commenting on the art of these buildings Le May observes: "These labours were executed in part by workers brought from Ceylon; here is valuable indication of the possible origins of the Sinhalese influence that has been detected in the art of Sukhothai."[72]

The successor of Lo Thai, Lu thai, who ascended the throne of Sukhodaya in 1347,[73] continued to maintain the religious ties with Sri Lanka. One of his inscriptions, which gives him the title of Śrī Sūryavaṃsa Rāma Mahādharma Rājādhirāja, furnishes a long account of the reception accorded to a hierarch from Sri Lanka invited to Thailand to reorganize the religious institutions there.[74]

The author of the *Saddhammasaṅgaha* was a monk from Thailand who came to Sri Lanka and studied under Dhammakitti *mahāsāmi* of Gaḍalādeniya.[75] The *Cāmadevivaṃsa*, one of the chronicles of Chieng Mai, records that on the eve of the construction of Vat Mahavan and Ratana Chedi certain monks from Sri Lanka came with sacred relics and these relics were enshrined in the *cetiyas*[76] The founder of Haripuñjaya in the Meping valley, Mang Rai, is said to have received relics from Sri Lanka[77] It is reported that these relics were brought to him by a group of Sinhalese monks from Sri Lanka.[78] The king, who had a great devotion for the relics, enshrined them in Vat Kan Thom which he built in his capital Chieng Mai. These instances may help us to understand the close relationship between Sri Lanka and Thailand in the thirteenth and fourteenth centuries.

The most singnificant religious mission from Thailand to Sri Lanka took place in the reign of Parākramabāhu VI (1415-1467). The *Jinakālamālī* gives a detailed account of this mission in its chapter entitled *Sīhaḷasāsanāgamanam.*[79] According to the chronicle this mission was led by the Elders called Mahā Dhammagambhīra and Mahā Medhaṅkara. The main purpose of the mission was to acquire a complete knowledge of the religion and higher ordination from the Sangha of Sri Lanka which were in a flourishing condition there. The two Elders were accompanied by a number of Mon, Cambodian and Thai monks, and arrived in Sri Lanka in 1968 B.E., i.e. 1425 A.D., the tenth regnal year of Parākramabāhu VI.[80] The foreign monks, having arrived in Sri Lanka, went to Vanaratana *mahāsāmi,* the then hierarch of the Buddhist Church of the country. They paid their respects to the *mahāsāmi* and pleased him with agreeable speech, and resided with him. Under the guidance of the *mahāsāmi* the foreign monks learned the scriptures preserved in the country and the correct manner of reciting and chanting these texts, requested ordination, being desirous of attaining the supreme goal[81]

The higher ordination ceremony of the foreign monks took place under the auspices of the king at Yāpāpaṭṭana, on the Kelani-river. The scene of the ceremony, Yapapaṭṭana, cannot be identified. This is definitely not Jaffna, the Yāpāpaṭuna of the Sinhalese literary works of this period, because that city is nowhere near the Kelaṇi river and besides, Jaffna was brought under the control of the Sinhalese kingdom only during the latter part of Parākramabāhu VI's reign, i.e. 1450 A.D.[82] At present there is no locality bearing the name of Yāpāpaṭuna in or near Kelaṇiya. There are two *sannasas* of the Kōṭṭē period in which the name "Yāpāpaṭuna" occurs. One of these is dated on the 7th day of the dark half of Vesak in the third year of Sirisañgabo Siri Sakalakalā Sarvajña Paṇḍita Bhuvanekabāhu Chakravarti, i.e. Bhuvanekabāhu VI, and registers a grant by the king then residing at Yāpāpaṭuna to Vīdāgama Maitreya Mahanetpāmula *mahāsthavira* and his pupilary successors.[83]

The second document already referred to in this study, also belongs to the reign of Bhuvanekabāhu VI who, having heard a sermon from Vīdāgama Maitreya at Yāpāpaṭuna, made a grant to him and his pupil Niyaṅdavane Phussadeva Sumaṅgala. The last document definitely states that the Yāpāpaṭuna mentioned therein was in Pihiṭi (ancient Rajaraṭa) kingdom. There is, therefore, no reason to conclude that the Yāpāpaṭuna of these documents was the place of that name at Kelaṇiya. On the contrary, in these cases Yāpāpaṭuna no doubt indicates Jaffna.

The higher ordination ceremony was presided over by Vanarataṅa *mahāsāmi* of Kāragala.[84] He was the *kammācariya* of the novices. The *mahāsāmi* was assisted by the Elder Dhammācariya as the *upajjhāya* of the ceremony.

The foreign monks, after arriving in Sri Lanka, worshipped the Tooth Relic, the Foot Print on the Samantakūṭa and the sixteen great places of worship, and having taken leave of the *ācariya* and *upajjhāya* set out to return to their homelands. On their return they persuaded two Sinhalese monks, Mahā Vikkamabāhu and Mahā Uttamapañña, to accompany them so that they might hold office as *ācariya* and *upajjhāya* at future higher ordinations.[85]

This historic mission had far reaching results in South East Asian countries, especially in Thailand and Laos. The monks of this mission all along their way, even in mid-ocean right up to the time they took up their residence at Vat Phra Daeng Luang in Chieng Mai in 1430 A.D., conferred the higher ordination on distinguished monks of Ayudhyā, Śrī Sajjanālaya and Sukhodaya.[86] The first higher ordination conducted on a grand scale was held on the Mae Vang river at Lamp'un (Haripuñjaya) in 1433 A.D.[87] The monks of the mission returned to Lamp'un in the same year and, commencing with the second act of higher ordination there, they next conferred the higher ordination on many monks at various neighbouring cities until the Sīhaḷa fraternity grew in number and influence.[88] The Sīhaḷa Sangha, thus introduced to Thailand and Laos, continued to enjoy royal favour, and played a great part in the religious history of both countries. At Chieng Mai in Thailand there was a monastery called Sīhaḷārāma (now known as Vat Phra Sing), and under the guidance of the Sīhaḷa Sangha Thai kings of Yonakaraṭṭha (Laos) built many sacred edifices, some of which still exist.[89] The Sīhaḷa fraternity of *bhikkhus* also introuced to Thailand and Laos a higher standard of Pali scholarship than that which was prevailing there before, and the author of the *Jinakālamāli*, to whom we are indebted for much of the information given regarding this religious intercourse, was himself a member of this Sīhaḷa fraternity.[90]

Even after this mission the relations between Sri Lanka and Thailand continued for some time. In 1455 A.D., at the request of the members of the Sīhaḷa Sangha, a seedling grown from a seed from the southern branch of the Mahābodhi at Anurādhapura was planted by King Tilakarāja (Tilok) (1448-1488) at the premises of Vat Bodhārāma Mahāvihāra at Nibbīsapura (Chieng Mai).[91] This is said to have taken place in 1455 and followed by a higher ordination ceremony.[92] The relic which has brought from Sri Lanka by Mahā Dhammagambhīra was deposited in 1478 A.D. in a shrine called Rājakūṭa (Phra Chedi Luang) in the same city.[93] A Buddha image named Ratanapaṭimā was also installed in this shrine in the reign of Tilakarāja. The *Jinakālamālī*, which gives the history of image in its chapter entitled *Ratanapaṭimāya-āgamanam*, relates that this was originally fashioned by King Milinda according to the advice of Nāgasena *thera* and after some time was brought to Sri Lanka.[94] King Anuruddha of Arimaddana (Pagan) is said to have taken it from Sri Lanka to Burma. In turn, the Ratanapaṭima was taken to various cities in Cambodia and Thailand , until it found its final resting place at Chieng Mai, in the reign of Tilakarāja.[95] This statue is reckoned as the most important image in Thailand and it now reposes in the Chapel Royal of the Cakkri Grand Palace in Bangkok.[96] Tilakaraja, who had done a great service for the propagation of the Sīhaḷa Sangha in Thailand and entered the Order for a time, died in 1488, and was succeeded by his son Boromarāja III.[97] From this time for about three hundred years we have no record of religious relationship between Sri Lanka and Thailand till the reign of Kīrti Śrī Rājasiṁha (1747-1780) of Sri Lanka. However, it is possible that Thailand maintained its relations with Sri Lanka throughout the period.

Apart from the countries treated above, the other South East Asian Theravāda country with which Sri Lanka maintained cultural contact was Cambodia, which was originally a vassal kingdom of Fu-nan.[98]. Cambodia began to feel the influence of Sinhalese Mahāvihāra, which was introduced into Burma by at the end of the twelfth century by Mon monks,[99] in the first part of the thirteenth century. Commenting on this great change Çoedēs writes: "From the day when the sovereign ceased to be Śiva descended to earth, or the living Buddha, as Jayavarman VII had been, the royal dynasty failed any longer to inspire the people with the religious respect which enabled it to accomplish great enterprises. Under the threat of the anarchical spirit of Sinhalese Buddhism his prestige diminished, his temporal power crumbled away, and the god- king was thrown down from his alter."[100] Theravāda had become the predominant religion of the people of Angkor by the end of Jayavarman's reign (1243-1295).[101]

It is recorded in the *Cūlavaṃsa* that the king of Rāmañña seized a princess that Parākramabāhu I sent to Kamboja. He is also said to have apprehended and imprisoned some Sinhalese envoys on the charge that they were taking a letter to the king of Kamboja.[102] Kamboja occurs together with Aramaṇa in a number of inscriptions of Nissaṅkamalla.[103] These references point to the exisence of continued relationship between Cambodia and Sri Lanka in the Polonnaru period.

From this time until the beginning of the fifteenth century our sources are silent regarding the religious contact between Sri Lanka and Combodia. We have seen earlier that, according to the *Jinakālamāli*, a certain *ratana-paṭimā* which is said to have been imported to Burma by Anuruddha of Pagan was taken to various cities in Cambodida in its roving period.[104] We have no evidence to ascertain the impact of this *patimā* on the religious life of Cambodia. It has been mentioned earlier that there were several Cambodian monks in the mission of Mahā Dharmma-gambhīra and Mahā Medhaṅkara who came to Sri Lanka in the reign of Parākramabāhu VI with the intention of receiving the

Mahāvihāra higher ordination.[105] There is no doubt that these monks played a prominent part in the propagation of Theravāda in their homeland. After this mission we have no records of the presence of Cambodian monks in Sri Lanka or the Sinhalese monks in Cambodia for several centuries, but it may be assumed, as in the case of other South East Asian countries, that Cambodia maintained its relationship with Sri Lanka throughout the medieval period.

The foregoing pages make it clear that the Mahāvihāra of Sri Lanka played a prominent role in the propagation of Theravāda in Mainland South East Asia all along the medieval period. In spite of their country's political disturbances and upheavals, the Sinhalese monks were always enthusiastic in helping their counterparts in those countries. This influence of the Sinhalese Buddhism resulted in causing very significant changes in the culture, particularly in the religious life of the peoples of that part of the world

## References

1. *UCHC.*, P.753.
2. ibid
3. Pierre Dupont, 'Les Buddha dits d'Amaravati en Asie du Sud-Est, *BEFEO*, XLIX, 1959, pp.632-636.
4. Mirella Levi D'Ancona, 'Amaravati, Ceylon and three imported images'*The Art Bulletin*, XXXIV, No.I, 1952, pp.125-127.
5. G. Coèdes, *The Indianized States of Southeast Asia*, Honalulu, 1968. pp.18, 54.
6. D. Gosh, 'Two Bodhisattva Images from Ceylon and Śrī Vijaya; Jnl. of the Gtr. *Ind. Soc.*, IV,1937, pp.125- 127.
7. J.G.de Casparis, 'New evidence on Cultural Relations between Java and Ceylon in Ancient Times', *Felicitation Volume presented to Prof. G.Coèdes on his 75th birth day' Artius Asiae*, XXIV,1964, pp.241- 248.
8. ibid.
9. *Cv.*, 50.17 ff; *UCHC.*, P.563 f.

10. *Jkm.*, p.100.
11. G.H.Luce, 'Mons of the Pagan Dynasty', '*JBRAS*, XXXVI, pt. I. August, 1953, pp.1-9.
12. G.H.Luce, *Old Burma-Early Pagan*, New York, 1969, Vol. 61.
13. ibid.
14. ibid.
15. ibid. p.62.
16. ibid.
17. ibid.
18. ibid.
19. *Cv.*, 76. 10-35; See also, *UCHC.*, P.473.
20. *Cv.*, 76.10 ff.
21. *Cv.*, 80.6.
22. *Ez.*, II, Nos.17,26,27.
23. *IA.*, XXII,P.151 ff; *Ep.Birm*, III, pt.II p.200f.
24. IA., XXII, p.29; *The Glass Palace Chronicle of the Kings of Burma*, Tr. Pe Maung Tin and G.H.Luce, Oxford, 1923, p.142 ff.
25. *Sav.*, p.65 ff.
26. Luce, *Old Burma-Early Pagan*, p. 127.
27. ibid.
28. ibid.
29. G.E.Harvey, *History of Burma*, p.28.
30. ibid.
31. *Ssv.*, p.29.
32. *Ssv.*, p.29.
33. *Jkm.*, p.91 ff.
34. *Ssv.*, p.95.
35. *PS.*, P.33.
36. *UCHC.*, P.755.
37. *Kts.*, p.32.
38. ibid.
39. op. cit. p. 100.
40. ibid.
41. D.G.E. Hall, *History of South-East Asia*, New York, 1970, p. 164.
42. ibid.
43. ibid., p. 100.
44. ibid., p. 101.
45. N.R.Ray, *Theravāda Buddhism in Burma*, Calcutta, 1946, p.183.
46. ibid.
47. *IA.*, XXII, p.15 ff; *Ep.Birm.*, III, pt.II, p.220 ff.
48. ibid.

49. ibid.
50. See above, Ch.II.
51. IA., XXII, p.158.
52. ibid; *Ep.Birm.* III pt. II, p.220 ff.
53. *pubbakāle Rāhulabhad nāmakam, idāni Vijayabāhu Saṅgharājānam, IA,* XXII, p.239.
54. *Vanaratananāmakaṃ porāṅamahāsaṅgharājānam, IA.,* XXII, p.239.
55. See above Ch.III,
56. Ray, *op.cit.* p.191.
57. ibid.
58. ibid.
59. Coedēs, *op.cit.* p.218.
60. L.Malleret, *L'Archaeologie du Delta du Mekong,* Paris, 1962, III, p.311.
61. H.G.Quaritch Wales, *Dvāravatti,* (The Earliest Kingdom of Siam, 6th to 11th century), London, 1969, p.3.
62. ibid. p.52 f.
63. Coedès, *op.cit.* p.218.
64. *Jkm.,* p.86 ff.
65. *Epochs of the Conqueror,* p.xi ff.
66. *Jkm.,* p.87 f.
67. Hall, *op.cit.* p.123.
68. G.Coedès, *Receuil des inscriptions du Siam,* Bangkok, 1924-29, p.89 ff and pp. 127-129.
69. *ISSA.,* p.220.
70. Re..des ins..du Siam, pp.89-90; *ISSA.,* p.356,
71. ISSA., P.356.
72. Reginald Le May, *A Concise History of Buddhist Art in Siam, Cambridge, 1938, p.114 f.*
73. *Issa.,* p.219.
74. G.Coedes, 'Documents sur la dynastie de Sukhodaya', *BEFEO.* XVII, NO.2, P.4 ff.
75. *PS.,* p.383 ff; S. Paranavitana, 'Religious Intercourse between Ceylon and Siam in the 13th-15th Centuries', *JCBRAS.,* XXXII, 1932, pp.190-213.
76. *Annals du Siam,* III Volume, (*Chronique de La:pun, Histoire de la Dynastie de la Dynastie Chamat'evi,*), tr. M.Camille Notton, Paris, 1930, p.55.
77. *Annals du Siam,* III Volume, *Chronique de Xieng Mai*), tr.M.Camille Notton, Paris, 1923, p.52.
78. ibid.

79. Jkm., p.91 ff; G.Coedès, 'Documents sur L'Histoire Politique et religieuse du Laos occidental,' *BEFEO*, XXV, 1925, PP.4-12.
80. *Jkm.*, p.93.
81. ibid.
82. Somaratna, *op.cit.p.201 ff.*
83. *JCBRAS.*, XXXII, No.85, p.209.
84. *SSL.*,p.144.
85. *Jkm.*, p.93.
86. ibid.
87. ibid.
88. ibid.
89. EC., p.XXV.
90. *JCBRAS.*, XXXII, No.85, p.209.
91. *EC.*, p.XXV.
92. Jkm., p.98; se also,M.Camille Notton, *Annals du Siam*, (Chronique de Xieng Mai), Voice II: p.115.
93. ibid.
94. *jkm.*, p.99.
95. ibid.p.111.
96. *EC.*, p.xxvi.
97. Hall, *op.cit.* p.94.
98. *ISSA*, p.65.
99. See above, p.399. 98. G.Coedès, *Pour miex Compredre Angkor*, Paris, 1947, p.66.
100. Hall, op.cit. p.125.
102. *CV.*, 76,21-23 and 55.
103. *EZ.*, II,p.151.
104. *Jkm.*, p.100 ff.
105. See. above, p. 177.

## Chapter Seven

# Cults, Rituals, Ceremonies and Festivals

Although cults, rituals, ceremonies and festivals are not strictly in keeping with the spirit of Buddhism, they are natural and inevitable developments, bound to come when the teachings of the Buddha had developed into a popular religion. Even during the early years of its history, Buddhism came to terms with popular cults such as the worship of *yakkhas* and *nāgas* and the worship of Brahmanical gods. Buddhist texts merely claim that the *yakkhas, nāgas,* and *devas* accepted the supremacy of the Buddha.[1] Its early developments in Sri Lanka Buddhism absorbed various cults, rituals and ceremonies that had been practised in the country and were not directly in conflict with the fundamental teachings of the Buddha. This popular aspect of Buddhism in Sri Lanka developed into a system capable of serving the varied religious needs of society. The following pages will be devoted to a survey of this aspect of the religious history of the country during the two centuries under review.

Among the religious cults in medieval Sri Lanka that of Tooth Relic held the most important place. Although the history of this relic goes back to the fourth century A.D.,[2] it gained in importance most probably because of the idea emerging in later centuries, that its possession conferred on a prince the legitimate right to the sovereignty of the country.[3] This belief seems to have become established during the Polonnaru period, and thus the Tooth Relic became the palladium of the kingdom from that period onwards.[4] The utmost care with which the Sinhalese kings protected the Tooth Relic is evident from the fact that they always kept the relic in a shrine very close to the royal palace and guarded it day and night. The belief in the supreme position of the Tooth Relic became more firmly established from the twelfth century onwards. By the close of the thirteenth century, Parākramabāhu IV not only built a magnificent shrine to house it but also promulgated an ordinance to regulate the ritual and public ceremonies in its honour.[5] This ordinance, with a detailed history of the Tooth Relic attached to it, is still preserved in the *Daḷadāsirita,* from which we can learn how elaborate the ritual of this Royal Palladium was, and how magnificent the public celebrations in its honour were.[6]

As has been mentioned earlier, in the disastrous times that preceded the reign of Parākramabāhu VI (1415-1467), the Tooth Relic shared all the vicissitudes of the Sinhalese kingdom, and it was often necessary to protect the Relic against foreign invaders and usurpers of the throne. When Parākramabāhu VI became king of kīng of Kōṭṭē, one of his earliest public activities was the building of a palace for the Relic. The *Saddarmaratnākaraya* states that the king had a magnificent three-storeyed building (*tunmahal- pahaya*) erected for the Tooth Relic adjacent to his own palace.[7] It is to be noted here that the Alms Bowl Relic, which was always kept with the Tooth Relic for centuries, is not mentioned in the sources of this period. The last known reference to it is in the reign of Parākramabāhu IV.[8] After this time, this relic seems to have disappeared from the scene, and we are not informed by our sources when and for what reason this happened.

Every poet of the day who described the city of Kōṭṭē mentioned the Daḷadā Māligāva (the palace of the Tooth Relic) which was looked after with much care by the king himself.[9] The *Girā-sandeśaya* states that Parākramabāhu IV held annual festivals in honour of the Tooth Relic.[10] This is corroborated by the account of the *Saddharmaratnākaraya,* where a rather detailed description of the offerings made by the king to the Tooth Relic is given. The account of the chronicle follows:-

> This Lord of the Land (Parākramabāhu VI) built for the Tooth Relic of the great sage a beautiful three-storeyed

> temple, delightful to behold. And he made a casket of gold, inlaid with precious stones shining with divers rays; and this again also he enclosed in another golden casket made for this purpose. Moreover, he made a great and excellent casket gilt with gold of the first and most beautiful lid; ... and he deposited the Tooth Relic within the four caskets.

The work adds that the king held daily ceremonies and annual festivals in honour of the Relic but gives no details of these ceremonies and festivals. It can be surmised that these ceremonies and festivals were carried out in accordance with the rules and regulations laid down in the *Daḷadāsirita*.

It seems that until the last part of the reign of Bhuvanekabāhu VII (1521-1551) the Tooth Relic was enshrined in the temple of Kōṭṭē. By about 1543, presumably on the eve of Dharmapāla's conversion to Christianity, the relic seems to have been taken out of Kōṭṭē by its custodian, Hiripitiye Nilame, who entrusted it to Māyādunne.[11] It has been said that people were concerned with the safety of the relic in Kōṭṭē because of the growing influence of Catholic missionaries on the court of Kōṭṭē, and therefore took the relic out of the Kōṭṭē kingdom.[12] Whatever the historicity of this tradition may be, the possession of the relic, the palladium of the kingdom, enhanced the political position of Māyādunne; thereafter he seems to have used the title *tri-siṅhalādhīśvara,* the lord of Tri Siṅhala.[13] At Delgamuva Māyādunne built a new palace for the relic. There it was enshrined and worshipped with annual festivals.[14] Māyādunne's successor, Rājasiṅha I, in spite of bitter clashes with the Sangha, is reported to have held annual Tooth Relic festivals at the Maha Saman Dēvālaya of Ratnapura.[15] This may suggest that Rājasiṅha I co-ordinated the annual festival in honour of Maha Saman with that of the Tooth Relic. However, our sources give no more details regarding this festival.

The Samantakūṭa or Samanoḷa (otherwise called the Adam's Peak), where the Buddha was said to have left his Footprint on the surface of a rock, became a favourite place of pilgrimage in medieval Sri Lanka. The popularity of the cult of Footprint and pilgrimages made for its worship are attested in the sources dealing with the preceding centuries. According to the *Mahāvaṃsa*, the Buddha, on his third visit to Lankā, went to the Samantakūṭa and left his Footprint there.[16] But, apart from this reference, neither the chronicle, nor any other indigenous source bears any reference to this mountain or the Footprint until the reign of Vijayabāhu I in the eleventh century. Nevertheless, there is evidence in Buddhist writings outside Sri Lanka that the Footprint on the Samantakūṭa was held in high veneration by the faithful even before the eleventh century.[17] The *Cūlavamsa* and the Aṁbagamuva inscription of Vijayabāhu I (1070-1111) record that the king himself ascended the mountain, worshipped the Footprint, and, having realized the difficulties undergone by pilgrims on their way to sacred spot, undertook numerous developments there and dedicated a village called Gilīmalaya to provide for their needs.[18] The fact that local sources refer to the cult of Footprint and pilgrimages to the Samantakūṭa only from the time of Vijayabāhu I shows a revival of the cult of the Footprint at that time. From then it seems that the significance of Samantakūṭa continued to grow as appears from its patronage by Sinhalese rulers of the succeeding centuries. Thus, Nissaṅkamalla (1187-1196),[19] Parākramabāhu II (1230-1270)[20] and Vijayabāhu IV (1270-1272)[21] are all recorded to have ascended the sacred mountain and, after having worshipped the Footprint with great devotion, made offerings and dedicated numerous villages to it in honour of the Buddha. The increasing importance which was being attached to the cult of Footprint on the Samantakūṭa by the Sinhalese Buddhists in the medieval period appears from the composition by a monk called Vedeha of a Pali poem named *Samantakūṭavaṇṇanā* to elucidate its history and importance.[22]

Although it was not situated on any of their routes, most of the *sandeśa* poets of the Kōṭṭē period did not omit passing reference to the Samantakūṭa and the Footprint there.[23] No mention is made of Parākramabāhu VI or any other king of Kōṭṭē having undertaken repairs or made pilgrimages to the sacred spot. However, Sēnāsammata Vikramabāhu, who ruled the highlands of Sri Lanka with Kandy as capital in the latter part of the fifteenth century, is recorded to have visited sacred mountain, conducted elaborate festivals and made valuable offerings to the Footprint.[24] It seems that by this time the Samantakūṭa had become a wealthy religious institution owing to numerous land grants made by kings at various times, and the income accruing from the offerings presented by numerous pilgrims. It is recorded that Rājasiṇha I, who is alleged to have renounced Buddhism and embraced Hinduism, deprived the Sangha of the Footprint and its revenues, which he subsequently granted to the priests of the religion of which he became a convert.[25]

The Footprint on the Samantakūṭa was held in the highest veneration by not only the Sinhalese Buddhists but those of other countries as well. Medhaṅkara, one of the leaders of a mission of Cambodian and Thai monks who received higher ordination at Kelaṇiya in 1425 and, on their return to their lands, established fraternities known as the Sīhaḷa Sangha, set up, in a shrine at Sukhodaya, a representation of the Buddha's foot which, according to the inscription engraved on the stone, 'exactly resembled the monument of the Precious Foot which was manifested on the summit of the Samantakūṭa, the jewelled crown of the Island of Laṅkā."[26] The members of the religious mission which was dispatched to Sri Lanka by Dhammaceti of Pegu to introduce the Sīhaḷa Sangha to that country and arrived in Sri Lanka during the reign of Bhuvanekabāhu VI (1469-1476) also went on a pilgrimage to the sacred mountain.[27] The trillingual inscription of Galle gives a long list of valuable offerings sent in 1410 by the first Ming Emperor, Yung-lo, through the envoys Cheng-ho and Wang-chieng-Lien to "the shrine of the Buddhist temples on the mountain of Sri Lanka". by which, according to Paranavitana, most probably was meant Laṅkāparvata (Samantakūṭa).[28]

The cult of the Footprint was so famous in the outside world that most of the foreign travellers and writers who refer to Sri Lanka in their works give at least a passing reference to the Samantakūṭa or Adam's Peak. Among the medieval European travellers, Marco Polo and Marignolli mention Adam's Peak as one of the marvels of Sri Lanka and give quaint accounts of it, naturally laying more emphasis on the Muslim traditions than on those of the Buddhists.[29] Portuguese historians, Joao Ribeiro and Fernão Queyroz have given accounts of Adam's Peak.[30] When the Portuguese got hold of the districts at the foot of the southern Peak in the seventeenth century they consecrated the mountain to Saint Eusebius.[31]

The cult of images in Sri Lanka can be traced back to early times. Although references to Buddha images before fourth century A.D. are not numerous in the chronicles we have a large number of references in the *Mahāvaṃsa* and elsewhere to it from that time.[32] The popularity of the image cult appears from the large number of image houses (*paṭimāghara*) ecreted everywhere in the island, especially at Anurādhapura and Polonnaruva. The outstanding architectural monuments after the Polonnaru period are those of Gaḍalādeṅiya and Laṅkātilaka, built in the fourteenth century.[33]

Among the specifically mentioned image houses of this period those of the Kelaṇi Vihāraya are significant. The *Säḷalihiṇi-sandeśaya* gives a vivd description of the Kelaṇi Vihāraya and its image houses. According to this work, a visitor to this place first sees the huge image house known as Laṅkātilaka, which resembles its namesakes at Polonnaruva and Gampola.[34] The author describes the image house next in importance as the Saḷapiḷimageya, and says that the colour of the image therein resembles that of the sea created by Sakka when the god caused the ocean to over flow.[35] Verse 62 of the poem is devoted to the description of the reclining Buddha image of golden colour on the right of the former image house.[36] There was another Buddha image under the hood of a cobra (*nāmeṇevigeya*) depicting the Buddha when he was sheltered from the heavy rains by the hood and coils of the *Nāga* Mucalinda.[37] The Buddha image under the Bo-tree is described as depicting the Buddha in a concentrated posture with all the thirty-two auspicious marks.[38] Departing from the southern gate of the temple the messenger bird is asked to listen to the beating of drums and to worship the two *tivaṅka* (Sht. *tribhanga*) images in the Tivaṅkapiḷimageya provided with all the auspicious marks.[39] There was another image house called Telakaṭārageya, founded on the spot, according to tradition, where an Arhat was placed in a heated-oil couldren by king Kälaṇitissa.[40]

The rituals concerning all sacred objects, especially images, were partly based on the idea that they should be treated like living persons. Probably because of this idea it became common to designate some special images with special personal names like Upasumbha and Abhiṣeka.[41] Some of these names, such as Tivaṅka, were based on distinctive sculptural features of the images.

As the images were treated as living persons, they were bathed, dressed and served with food. In the Anurādhapura period there seems to have been a particular kind of ceremony known as *abhiṣeka* (sprinkling Buddha images with holy water)[42] Details of this ceremony are not available. However, the *Saddharmaratnākaraya* of the fifteenth century gives detailed account of rites performed at Dhanyakaṭaka in South India by the author's teacher's teacher(*prācārya*) Sīlavamsa Dharmakīrti a century earlier.[43] According to this work, the stone image in the temple at Dhanyakaṭaka was daily bathed. The marble image was covered with a layer of scented paste two inches thick. Sevvandiya flowers[44] were fixed on the paste so that the image looked like a figure made of flowers. The following day it was bathed first in perfumed water, then in sesame oil and finally in milk. Then it was rubbed with unguents and finally bathed in clear water.[45] It may be presumed that similar ceremonies were held on special occasions and for special images. The rituals here described for Amarāvatī images conforms to the Hindu practice. It is possible that in this period the Buddhism still remaining in Amarāvatī Province was strongly influenced by Hinduism. Although the monk who conducted the ceremony was a Sinhalese, we are not certain whether similar ceromonies were popular among the Sinhalese Buddhists of this period.

Although after the arrival of Mahinda the people of Sri Lanka embraced Buddhism, their ancient beliefs in gods and demons did not disappear.[46] As mentioned earlier, gods and demons are realities in the Buddhist cosmology. However, the deities who became most popular in Sinhalese Buddhism were not those mentioned in the scriptures but those who had their origin either in pre-Buddhist Sri Lanka or in the Mahāyāna or Hindu pantheons. The Tamil invasions which occurred from time to time led to the introduction into Sri Lanka of the cults of South Indian gods which, by the beginning of the Polonnaru period, had become very popular among the Sinhalese. Although the Indian invasions and the marriages between Tamil princesses and Sinhalese kings in medieval Sri Lanka gave Hindu gods an established position in the beliefs of the people, it was only in the Gampola period that the Hindu gods found their abodes in the same building with the Buddha.[47] We have seen earlier that in the Kōṭṭē period Buddhist monks came to worship these gods.[48] Among the gods that were held in high veneration there were some Mahāyānic *bodhisattvas* too.

The *bodhisattva* cult, a common feature of Mahāyāna, seems to have been very popular in medieval Sri Lanka, especially as regards the worship of Nātha or Avalokiteśvara. We have seen before that the belief that kings of Sri Lanka had to be *bodhisattvas* is attested since the later Anurādhapura period. It has also been observed that the only *bodhisattva*, apart from the Buddha himself before attaining Enlightenment, known to early Theravāda was Metteyya or Maitreya.[49] The popularity of the cult of this *bodhisattva* in the Anurādhapura period is evident from certain inscriptions which contain the warning that those violating the regulations laid down therein would not be able to raise their hands in adoration even if the Maitreya Buddha were to pass by their doors.[50] The *Cūlavamsa* says that Mahāvihāra monks were so impressed by Buddhaghosa's intelligence that they believed he was none but Metteyya.[51]

The belief in Metteyya as the future Buddha, first expressed in the *Cakkavatti-sīhanāda Sutta* in the *Dīgha Nikāya,*[52] is elaborated in the Pali *Anāgatavaṃsa.*[53] It was subsequently incorporated into well known Sinhalese works such as the *Pūjāvaliya*, the *Saddharmālaṅkāraya* and the *Saddharmaratnākaraya*[54] The Päpiliyāna inscription of Parākramabāhu VI mentions the image of Maitreya alongside with that of Nātha.[55] Although it seems that, in this period, Nātha occupied a higher place as a *bodhisattva* than Maitreya, the common aspiration of the faithful to see

Maitreya when he would become the Buddha in future enchanced the position of this *bodhisattva* among the Sangha as well as the laity.

The cult of Avalokiteśvara seems to have been very popular in Sri Lanka during the fifteenth century for, as Paranavitana has observed,[56] almost all the refernces to this god found in Sinhalese writings date back to the reign of Parākramabāhu VI. Nevertheless the prevalence of the cult of Nātha in Sri Lanka from the Anurādhapura period has been discussed in detail by a number of writers.[57]

The popularity of the cult in the fifteenth century can be well seen from the number of Nātha images in different *vihāras* and *dēvālayas* in different parts of the country at this time. The author of the *Kokila- sandeśaya* requests the messenger, when he passes Mātara to Mihiripänna, to rest at the temple of Nātha by the seashore at Tummōdara.[58] The best known and probably the principal centre of the cult of Nātha in the fifteenth century was at Toṭagamuva (near Hikkaduva in the Galle district) which was at the time the greatest centre of learning in Sri Lanka and presided over by the Elder Śrī Rāhula. The *Tisara-sandeśaya* mentions another abode of Nātha which was at Doravaka in the Kāgalle district.[59] In the north of the Island, at Jāvaka-kōṭṭē, close to the Jaffna peninsula, there was another magnificent temple dedicated to the cult of Nātha.[60] Although the *Kokila- sandeśaya* mentions that this temple was lofty and the (image of the) *bodhisattva* (Natiňdu) in it was pure and comparable to the colour of the peak of mount Kailāsa, it is not mentioned in any other contemporary work, and is not traceable nowadays.

The *Girāsandeśaya* contains numerous references to the cult of Nātha. The message of this poem is addressed to Śrī Rāhula requesting him to pray the god to protect Laṅkā and its ruler Parākramabāhu VI.[61] In the message the god is referred to as possessing divine eyes and as one who is compassionate.[62] The prayer is that all dangers, including those from enemies, poision, disease and evil spirits, may be removed and that victory and prosperity to the king and the country be increased. By such an action, the poet says, the qualities of the *bodhisattva* would be made known to the world.[63] It is interesting to note that the *bodhisattva* eulogized as the protector of the Buddhist Church of Sri Lanka till the passing away of 5,000 years from the date of the death of the Buddha,[64] for this task was popularly entrusted to Upulvan[65]

At the beginning of the *sandeśaya* the poet compares the Toṭagamuva temple to the city of Kubera (Alaka), shining in white colour.[66] The comparison is made because Nātha is also white in colour and rays emanating from his body are as white as those of the moon.

In verse 230 the author requests the messenger to behold Lord Nātha (Natiñdu), 'who is beautiful, who is famous in the world and who continually fulfils the functions of a *bodhisattva* with the aim of bringing to Nirvāṇa all sentient beings who are merged in the great ocean of *saṃsāra*.[67] As this description follows immdeately that of the Buddha images of the temple it is probable that the reference to an image of the *bodhisattva* which would have been placed in a chamber adjacent to principal shrine or in itself. The *Kokila- sandeśaya* also mentions the image of Nātha of the Toṭagamuva temple as having been erected in close proximity to the image of the Buddha, which gives the inference that the *bodhisattva* image was placed in principal shrine room itself. Here the author requests the messenger to worship the god in order to make his journey successful.[68]

Stanzas 234 and 235 of the *Gira-sandesupaya* show that Nātha had, in this period, begun to be worshipped as a deity who grants boons to supplicants.[69] The *Tisara-sandeśaya* describes Nātha, whose image was in the shrine of the Buddha itself at Doravaka temple. The description is mainly concerned with the glorification of the physical beauty of the *bodhisattva* and it shows that this image of him was also white in colour (as that of Toṭagamuva) and had a *jaṭāmukuṭa*.[70]

Śrī Rāhula seems to have been a great devotee of Nātha. In his *Parevi- sandeśaya*, the Elder refers to Nātha at Toṭagamuva temple as *divayurusiya*, 'kinsman of the Sun', an epithet also applied to the Buddha.[71] In his *Kāvyaśekharaya*, Śrī Rāhula says that the glory and fame of Nātha, who is to become a Buddha, is comparable to that of the sun and the moon respectively.[72]

The most interesting reference to Nātha in the fifteenth-century literature is found in the *Vṛttaratnākara-pañcikā* of Śrī Rāmacandra Bhārathi.[70] As has been suggested before, this scholar would have been a teacher of the Vijayabāhu Pirivena, and, therefore, it is most likely that he also became a great devotee of this god as his teacher Śrī Rāhula was. The eulogy of the god in the *Vṛttaratnākarapañcikā* has been quoted by Paranavitana, who gives the following translation:-

"May Avalokiteśvara, the Refuge of the Virtuous and the Ocean of Compassion, remove my suffering-he who endeavours day and night, to deliver beings plunged in the midst of the great sea of *saṃsāra*.

May this Avalokiteśvara, who has compassion for the lowly and poor folk, protector thee- Avalokiteśvara by whose lustre, equal to the radiance appeard like the Ocean of Milk.

I now worship Avalokiteśvara, the Lord of Prosperity, who is as beautiful as the autumnal moon or the jasmine flower, or snew, or the garland of pearls, or the lance, or quiksilver, who holds in his hands a rosary and a jewel lotus, who wishes well to the whole world, who has, as his crown, a figure of the conqueror, i.c. Buddha, who is the foremost teacher, and who is adorned with ornaments like the *Jaṭāmukuṭa* etc.

The all knowing and the incomparable Lord Avalokiteśvara, assuming that this action affords protection to the world, daily removes fear; having known that he is compassionate towards the lowly and the poor, I go for refuge to that Lord, who is the abode of my rejoicing, and who is indeed the foremost among *bodhisattvas*. May you and all people who desire heaven and final beautiude go at once for the accomplishment of your aims to that teacher. May it be well!"

The description of the *bodhisattva* is of special significance because it is one of the few instances where Nātha is mentioned by his best known name Avalokiteśvara[74] in a Sri Lankan document, as in most inscriptions and literary works he is referred to by the South Indian name Nātha.[75] It is interesting to note that this description is found at a time in Sri Lanka when Mahāyāna all but disappeared from the Indian subcontinent.

It is interesting to add that Nātha images at Toṭagamuva are mentioned with those of Tārā, who is, according to Tantric texts, the consort of Avalokiteśvara.[76] The *Tisara-sandeśaya* mentions the image of Tārā by the side of Nātha, and the author requests the messenger to worship this goddess too before he leaves the temple.[77] In his description of Tārā' the author says' that the goddess dispelled the forces of evil in *saṃsāra* and that she is like a divine tree that grants happiness and prosperity.

Nātha at Toṭagamuva seems to have been popularly worshipped even in the sixteenth century and afterwards. A poem called *Nātha-devi-puvata,* attributed to the sixteenth century,[78] has Nātha at Toṭagamuva as its theme. The poet invokes the god to descend to a flower throne from Tusita heaven, and he is referred to as the patron of Toṭagamuva and help of the help-seeker, and a rider on the goose.[79] The *Vadan- kavipota,* a short trac (used as a text in temple schools), which is attributed to the late Kandyan period,[80] also mentions Nātha at Toṭagamuva. Stanza 70 of the poem is translated as follows:

> O Nātha! King of Gods, thou who abidest,
> meditating on the Dhamma in the temple of
> Toṭagamuva in the low country, who, in the
> countless *koṭis* of aeons past, hast set thy
> mind on the Buddhahood and hast received the
> prediction from former Buddhas, who hast destroyed
> passions and art andowed with miraculous powers
> and who dost lengthen the life of those devoted,
> to thee, I bow down with the two hands placed
> on my brow. May thou grant me wisdom.[81]

From what has been observed above it can be assumed that the cult of Nātha was very popular in medieval Sri Lanka, especially in the fifteenth century. The main centre of the cult was for centuries at Toṭagamuva, and not only the laity but also the most prominent monks of the period such as Śrī Rāhula were great devotees of the deity.

The four deities, namely Upulvan, Saman, Vibhīṣaṇa and Skanda (Skandakumāra), are described in the inscriptions and the literature of the period as the protectors of the Island. The belief of four guardian deities can be traced back to the fourteenth century, for the first time, the Laṅkātilaka inscription of Bhuvanekabāhu IV (1341-1351) names these deities as the guardians of Laṅkā.[82]

Of these, Upulvan seems to have been the most popular god of this time. His popularity is proved by the fact that the majority of the *sandeśa* poems written in this period, namely *Mayūra, Kokila, Parevi,* and *Tisara,* are addressed to him. The functions that this god was requested to carry out in this period were manifold, but he was specifically expected to grant political favours to supplicants. Upulvan's position in this period was enhanced by the belief that he was the god whom Sakka (king of gods) entrusted with the protection of Laṅkā.

The *Parevī-sandeśaya* mentions Upulvan as protecting Buddhism in Sri Lanka following the words of the Buddha just before his Nirvāṇa.[83] The origin of the belief that Upulvan was entrusted with the protection of Laṅkā can be traced back to the early Anurādhapura period. According to the *Mahāvaṃsa* the Buddha, when he was entering into Nirvāṇa, ordered the king of gods, Sakka, to protect Laṅkā, the future home of the true doctrine, and Sakka handed over the guardianship of Sri Lanka to Upulvan (Uppalavaṇṇa).[84] The *Saddharmālaṃkāraya,* a fourteenth-century Sinhalese prose work, records that Vijaya was protected by Upulvan who had orders from Sakka to guard the island of Laṅkā in accordance with the wishes of the Buddha.[85] The *Mayūra-sandeśaya* also refers to this traditional story of Sakka's order to Upulvan to be the guardian of the island.[86] How Uppalavaṇṇa came to assume this responsibility, and the efficient manner in which he carried out his first assignment in the capacity of the protector of Sri Lanka, almost immediately after he had received instructions to that effect from high quarters, is narrated in some detail in the *Mahāvaṃsa.*[87] However, as has been observed by Paranavitana,[88] it is not known whether Upulvan was, in fact, invoked for the protection of Sri Lanka during the period which followed the safe arrival of Vijaya of Laṅkā, for the preserved historical writings, Pali as well as Sinhalese, contain no reference to this god after his first appearance, until we come to events dealing with the thirteenth century.

Upulvan figures in the *Culavaṃsa* for the first time when Vīrabāhu, the nephew and Comander-in-Chief of Parākramabāhu II (1230-1272), having gained victory over Caṇdrabhānu, went to Devapura (mod. Devinuvara) to make offerings to him.[89] The *Cūlavaṃsa* again informs us that the shrine of Upulvan at Devapura was repaired by Parākramabāhu II. The account of the chronicle follows :- Then when the monarch learned that in the sacred town of Devanagara which was a mine of meritorious work, the shrine long since erected to the Lotus-hue God, the king of gods, had now fallen into decay, he betook himself to the superb town and rebuilding the dwelling of the king of the gods, like to the heavenly mansion of the king of gods, he made of it an abode all riches.....Hereupon he determined to celebrate every year in the town, as Äsaḷa festival for the god.[90]

This reference to the god is ample evidence to show that the cult of Upulvan gained new impetus in the reign of Parākramabāhu II. The *Alutnuvara Dēvāle Karavīma,* a seventeenth century Sinhalese work, gives a vivid description of Parākramabāhu II's connexion with the shrine of Upulvan at Devinuvara. According to the work, when Parākramabāhu was afflicted by an incurable disease, it was to Upulvan that the prime minister of the king, Devapatirāja, was sent in supplication.[91] It was of Äsaḷa Full Moon Day that the minister prayed the deity on behalf of his master; this coincided with the annual Äsaḷa festival of the *dēvālaya*. The document adds that the god was so manifested himself in the night in the guise of a *brahmin* attired in white robes, but with no beneficent effect on the king, for what the deity could do was only to assert that it was useless trying to cure him. However, the disappointment caused by this divine revelation seems not to have ended the devotion of the king to the god, for, according to the document, the king honoured his pledge made before by the grant of some productive lands to the shrine of Upulvan at Devinuvara.

Almost all the sources which refer to the cult of Upulvan are unanimous in confirming that the centre of the cult in the medieval period was at Devinuvara. The *Cūlavaṃsa* records that the shrine of Upulvan at Devinuvara, originally built by Dāpulusen (Dāṭhāpabhuti) in the sixth century A.D., was restored by order of Parākramabāhu II, who also celebrated the Äsaḷa festival of that deity.[92] The *Pärakumbāsirita*, a fifteenth-century panegyrical poem on Parākramabāhu VI, informs us that King Dāpulusen built the shrine of Upulvan at Devinuvara after having seen the great king of gods, Upulvan, emerging from the ocean in order to protect Laṅkā as instructed by the Buddha.[93] Another reference to this traditional story of the arrival of Upulvan in Sri Lanka is found in the *Parevi-sandeśaya* where the author describes Magulvälla, a spot not far from Devinuvara by the sea-shore, which the author says appears like a carpet laid by Dame Earth to welcome Upul, the king of gods, when he came from the sea.[94]

Paranavitana, who previously identified Upulvan with Avalokiteśvara, the Mahāyāna *bodhisattva*, is now of the opinion that he was no other than Varuṇa, a god of the Vedic pantheon.[95] In his identification Upulvan with Varuṇa this scholar gives much credence to the traditional story mentioned in the *Pärakumbāsirita* and the *Parevi- sandeśaya* that the god arrived in Sri Lanka from the sea, for Varuṇa also evolved into a sea god in post-Vedic times.[96] In the *Parevi-sandeśaya* the bird is asked to arrive at the shrine of Upulvan at Devinuvara at dusk when the beginning of ritual dance of the nautch girls was fixed.[97] The Upulvan shrine is referred to as Raja-ge, 'the king's house'.[98] In the *Mayūra-sandeśaya* the messenger is given directions, first to pay homage at the various places of worship in the *vihāra* and then to proceed to the shrine of Upulvan through Māvatmaḍuva, seeing the town on the way.[99] In the *Kokila-sandeśaya* the itinerary starts from Devinuvara; here the poet begins with conventional descriptions of the town, and conducts the messenger to the shrine of Upulvan.[100] Devinuvara was one of the busiest ports in medieval Sri Lanka.[101]

The *dēvālaya* of Upulvan at this city was situated on a cape protruding into the ocean.[102] Judging from the references made in the *sandeśa* poems and epigraphic sources, it can be assumed that Devinuvara was at the height of its fame in the fifteenth century. The Galle Trilingual inscription records that envoys from distant China came bearing gifts from the Son of Heaven (Chinese Emperor Yung- lo) to the Lord Tenavarai (Devinuvara)- as the god is named in the Tamil part of epigraph recording this event.[103] The *Parevi-sandeśaya* bears testimony to the fact that some merchant princes from India, who had probably settled down at Devinuvara, built shrines for the gods of their own faith.[104] Ibn Batūtā says that during his time a thousand *brahmins* served in the shrine of Upulvan at Devinuvara.[105] The ancient shrine of Devinuvara was destroyed by Thome de Souza in 1588 A.D.[106] Queyroz, referring to the sack of Devinuvara by Souza, records that it was the worship of Viṣṇu which received a fatal blow at de Souza's hands.[107] Apart from the famous abode of Upulvan at Devinuvara, there was another *dēvālaya* dedicated to the cult of this god in medieval Sri Lanka. This second centre of the cult of Upulvan which became very famous later, was established by Parākramabāhu IV at Alutnuvara in the Satara Kōralē in the Kāgalla District.[108] The *Alutnuvara Dēvāle Karavīma* enumerates land and other endowments made to this new shrine of Upulvan by the Sinhalese kings up to the beginning of the seventeenth century.[109]

Upulvan is now identified in Sri Lanka with Viṣṇu, and images of this form of Viṣṇu are seen side by side with those of the Buddha in temples. But this identification is not more than three or four centuries old, for it is apparent from the references made to Upulvan in the fifteenth century and before that he was held to be distinct from Viṣṇu. Paranavitana points to the fact that the Laṅkātilaka inscription of Bhuvanekabāhu IV of the fourteenth century among the images set up in that temple Viṣṇu is mentioned together with gods like Brahma and Sakka, but Upulvan as a distinct deity in a class which includes guardian deities of Laṅkā.[110] That Upulvan was distinct from Viṣṇu at this period can also be proved from the references to him in the *Kokila-sandeśaya* and the *Tisara-snądeśaya*.

The *Kokila-sandeśaya,* while extolling Upulvan, states that he is comparable to Viṣṇu in divine powers.[111] Mudaliyar Gunawardhana, who first pointed out the difference between Upulvan and Viṣṇu, argues that if Upulvan were no other but Viṣṇu, this statement would mean that he is comparable to himself, which conveys no sense.[112] He further points out that the statement would have been meaningful if the poet had stated that there was none to compare Upulvan with except himself; but he had not said so, and the statement implies that Upulvan and Viṣṇu are two different deities.[113] Jayatilaka accepted this view and furnished additional evidence in support of it. The *Tisara-sandeśaya* describes Upulvan as a god with whom goddesses Siri (the goddess of prosperity) and Sarasavi (the goddess of wisdom) remain contentedly.[114] Siri (Skt. Śrī) is regarded as the consort of Viṣṇu and Sarasavi (Skt. Sarasvatī) is that of Brahma. The author writes, unlike Viṣṇu who was overcome with grief over this affair and consequently became dark of complexion, Brahma made a virtue of necessity and practised *brahmacaryā* (celibacy) thus escaping the bitter fate of Viṣṇu.[115] Jayatilaka points out that if Upulvan was believed to be identical with Viṣṇu, this verse would be meaningless.[116] For, there is no reason why he should grieve when his own spouse remained with him. It is apparent that to the poet of the *Tisara-sandeśaya* Upulvan was a god distinct from and greater than Viṣṇu. Paranavitana assumes that this also must have been the accepted view among the people, for otherwise his contemporaries would have condemned his poem as containing absurdities.[116] These observations show that up to the time of the *Kokila-sandeśaya,* i.e. to the end of the fifteenth century, Upulvan was a god quite distinct from Viṣṇu.

The *brahmin* influence which became stronger in the Kōṭṭē period and afterwards, seems to have been the major reason for identifying Upulvan with Viṣṇu. We have seen earlier that Ibn Baṭūṭā noticed thousands of *brahmins* serving in the shrine of Upulvan at Devinuvara. The *Parevi-sandeśaya* also bears evidence to the *brahmin* influence at Devinuvara in the fifteenth century.[118] The *Alutnuvara Dēvāle Karavīma* records that the *brahmins* versed in Vaiṣṇava lore were invited from Rāmeśvaram to fashion an image of the Devinuvara god.[119] It was, according to this work, just after the red sandal- wood image of Viṣṇu had been washed ashore in the reign of Dāpulusen that these experts were brought from Rāmeśvaram. Paranavitana has suggested that this more recent document may ascribe to an earlier period an event which took place at a time when the votaries of Upulvan were beginning to lose faith in their traditions about the god, probably because of the influence of *brahmins* whose position in the society became stronger in the fifteenth century.[120] In that case, it is not unreasonable to assume that Upulvan was relegated to the background almost to the point of neglect, and Viṣṇu was enthroned as the god of Devinuvara. The prevalence in the sixteenth and seventeenth centuries of the belief that the god of Devinuvara was Viṣṇu is substantiated by the reference by Queyroz, who records that it was the worship of Viṣṇu at Devinuvara which received a fatal blow at de Souza's hands.[121] The identification of Upulan with Viṣṇu became fully accepted in the Kandyan period when Viṣṇu worship spread far and wide in Sri Lanka.[122]

As mentioned before, according to the *Mahāvaṃsa*, Upulvan was entrusted by Sakka to guard Laṅkā on the eve of the Buddha's passing away.[123] This traditional belief, which seems to have acquired a new impetus in the medieval period, would have inspired the Sinhalese kings and people to seek protection from him when the country faced political troubles. We have seen earlier that Vīrabāhu, nephew and the commander-in-chief of Parākramabāhu II, having gained victory over Candrabhānu, went to Devinuvara to make offerings to Upulvan.[124] It can be conjectured that Vīrabāhu invoked the blessings of the god for victory on the eve or before the campaign against the enemy and made offerings afterwards to show his gratitude. In the *Tisara-sandeśaya* Upulvan is requested to strengthen the political power of Parākramabāhu Äpā of Dädigama by weakening his enemies; these being Parākramabāhu VI and his well wishers.[125] Śrī Rāhula, in his *Parevi-sandeśaya*, invokes the blessings of Upulvan for the protection of the king (Parākramabāhu VI), the sub-king and the four-fold army.[126] The main object of this *sandeśaya* was to request the god to give a suitable husband to Candrāvatī, the elder daughter of Parākramabāhu VI, who could provide the king with worthy successor to that prince.[127] According to the *Haṃsa-sandeśaya,* the deities such as Upulvan, Saman, Savat (Skanda) and Vibhīṣaṇa are enjoined to bestow on Parākramabāhu VI a long reign devoid of troubles and the establishment of the sole sovereignty in the entire country.[128] The author of the *Kokila-sandeśaya* requests Upulvan to consolidate the political power of Parākramabāhu VI in Yāpāpaṭuna, which had recently been added to the Sinhalese kingdom after several centuries of Tamil rule.[129] According to the *Haṃsa-sandeśaya,* the deities such as Upulvan, Saman, Savat (Skanda) and Vibhīṣaṇa are enjoined to bestow on Parākramabāhu VI a long reign devoid of troubles and the establishment of the sole sovereignty in the entire country.[128] The author of the *Kokila-sandeśaya* requests Upulvan to consolidate the political power of Parākramabāhu VI in Yāpāpaṭuna, which had recently been added to the Sinhalese kingdom after several centuries of Tamil rule.[129]

The *Kokila-sandeśaya* and the *Mayūra-sandeśaya* refer to Upulvan as Kihirāli Upulvan probably in keeping with the traditional story of his image being made of *kaduru*-wood (red Sandal- wood).[130] An eigth-century inscription recently discovered at Devinuvara mentions the place as Kihirāli.[131] Paranavitana suggests that the legend of the red Sandal-wood image came into being at a time when Kihirāli as the name of Devinuvara had already become obsolete.[132] The *Kokila-sandeśaya* describes the god as having defeated with his arrows the forces of Māra, who threatened the Buddha before his enlightenment.[133] This seems an invention of the author of the *sandeśaya,* for there is no reference to a god who would have stood by the Buddha on this occasion.[134] The *Parevi-sandeśaya* contains a number of verses describing the beauty and majesty of Upulvan.[135] This work mentions his consort as Sañdavan and his son as Dhanu.[136]

According to the *Mahāvaṃsa,* the Samantakūṭa (otherwise called Sumanakūṭa), where the Buddha was supposed to have left his Footprint, is thus called because the Peak was regarded as the abode of a *devarāja* (king of gods) called Sumana.[137] This god first figures in the chronicle in the account of the supposed first visit of the Buddha to Sri Lanka, where the chronicle itself refers to him as Mahā Sumana of the Sumanakūta.[138] According to the *Samantakūṭa-vaṇṇanā*, it was at the special invitation of this god that the Buddha went to the Samantakūṭa on his third visit to Sri Lanka and made the Peak a sacred place by having left the impression of his foot thereon.[139] Paranavitana, who previously held the view that the god Sumana of Sumanakūṭa was none but the Mahāyāna *bodhisattva* Samantabhadra, expressed the opinion that Sumana had evolved from Yama of the Vedic pantheon.[140] It is noteworthy that, as in the case of Upulvan, this god also seems to have been relegated to the background for centuries after his initial appearance in the chronicle. For, neither the literature nor the epigraphic evidence belonging to the period preceding the thriteenth century make any mention of him.[141] It was in the reign of Parākramabāhu II that Sumana came to the scene again when the *Cūlavaṃsa* states that Devapatirāja, the chief minister of the king, went to Gañgasiripura (Gampola) on his way to Sumanakūṭa and fashioned an image of Sumanadeva with all the fair holding signs and decked it out with ornaments of gold and jewels.[142] The chronicle adds that this image was taken in procession to the Sumanakūṭa and installed in the courtyard of the *cetiya* of the Footprint there.[143] Since this time onwards the cult of Sumana seems to have occupied a significant position among the deities of Sri Lanka.

The *Haṃsa-sandeśaya* mentions the deity as Saman Bosat (Saman *bodhisattva*) and as one of the four guardian deities of Laṅkā to whom the *parittas* were recited and merit was given.[144] Alagiyavanna, towards the close of the sixteenth century, wrote the *Sävul- sandeśaya* in the form of a message sent through a cock to the god Sumana at Saparapura (mod. Ratnapura), requesting him to protect and grant victory to the poet's patron Rājasiṅha I of Sītāvaka,[144] who was engaged in war with the Portuguese at the time. The *Maha Saman Dēvālaya Sannasa* of Parākramabāhu VI gives a long account of land grants made to and services set out in the *dēvālaya* of Ratnapura.[145]

The principal centre of the cult of Sumana during this period seems to have been in Ratnapura, less than nine miles in a direct line from the foot of the Samantakūṭa. It seems probable that with the increasing popularity of the cult of Footprint the cult of Sumana became grew because from very early times the belief gained the ground that Sumana made the Sumanakūṭa his abode.[146] This belief seems to have become much more stronger owing to the supposition that to make the precipitious climb to the top of the mountain even the strongest required divine assistance. The *Sävul- sandeśaya* refers to in two places to the quality of mercy, compassion or pity (*kuḷuṇu karuṇā*) with which Sumana is endowed. Verse 188 of the poem says :-

> The pair of long blue eyes of the divine king
> of Sumana, which shine like priceless *indranīla*
> gems and *indīvara* flowers (blue water-lillies),
> are verily two beautiful fishes which move about
> in the river of his compassion extended equality
> towards all beings at all times.[147]
> Verse 193 describes the god's chest in these words :-
> The wide and broad expanse of the chest of this
> Lord of Suras, in which there are lines of hair
> in the manner of dark mass around which hoever
> bees in the shape of rays from the eyes of
> celestial nymphs, is a captivating lake filled
> to overflowing with the cool water of
> compassion.[148]

The emphasis made in these verses on compassion of the god may be taken as more than mere conventional rhetoric when one considers the shouts of *karuṇavai* (be merciful) of the pilgrims who make their yearly pilgrimage to *Samantakūṭa*. It is therefore natural that Sumana is regarded as merciful to the pilgrims going to his abode, especially as he is supposed to have been entrusted with the protection of the sacred Footprint. In return for the protection given and mercy extended by the god every pilgrim makes it a point to request the god to share in the merit that he has earned by climbing the Peak and worshipping the Buddha represented by his Footprint, for according to Buddhist belief the power of gods to do good is enhanced by such partaking of the merit earned by human beings, and also the gods may long for the bliss of Nirvāṇa.

Apart from his being the guardian deity of the Samantakūṭa, there seems to have been another reason that led to the popularity of Sumana in the medieval period. As mentioned above, after his first appearance in the *Mahāvaṃsa,* this god first figures in historical records in the Daṁbadeni period. The *Samansirita,*[149] an unpublished document attributed to the sixteenth century, records that the Maha Saman Dēvālaya of Ratnapura was erected in the reign of Parākramabāhu II in fulfilment of a vow made by his minister, the *brahmin* Āryakāmadeva, when he engaged in the mining of gems in the Sabaragamuva district on the direction of the king.[150] The document adds that the minister was not successful in his first attempt; the second attempt, however, proved successful, he would erect a *dēvālaya* in memory of the god. The historicity of Āryakāmadeva is attested by the *Maha Saman Dēvālaya Sannasa* of Parākrmabāhu VI, too.[151] Hence the reason given in the *Samansirita* for the establishment of a *dēvālaya* may suggest that extensive gem mining carried out in the district surrounding Samantakūṭa would also have led to the popularity of this god in the medieval period, for even nowadays the fortune-seekers who risk their lives in search of gems never omit to make a vow to this deity at the beginning of their efforts.

The *Samansirita* maintains that having erected the building of the *dēvālaya,* Parākramabāhu II himself carried the image of Saman within the precincts and installed it in the shrine.[152] The grant of villages of Sabaragamuva, Ratnapura, Veralupē and the appointment of some officers and attendants to maintain the cult of the god are enumerated in the document. The account given in the *Samansirita* concerning the establishment of the Maha Saman Dēvālaya of Ratnapura is substantiated by the information found in the *Maha Saman Dēvālaya Sannasa* of Parākramabāhu VI.[153] The object of the *Sannasa* was to confirm the land grants made by the previous kings and to record services reinstituted by Parākramabāhu VI at whose initiative the whole superstructure of the institution's services took a new shape.

The *Maha Saman Dēvālaya Sannasa* enumerates 26 villages including Sabaragamuva, Ratnapura and Veralupē dedicated to the institution from time to time by the Sinhalese kings from the reign of Parākramabāhu II.[154] The donations by kings to the *dēvālaya* included gold, silver, pearls, precious stones, elephants, horses, oxen, buffaloes, slaves etc. After the long account of these endownments, the document declares numerous appointments made by Parākramabāhu VI for the maitenance of the institution and its property. It is stated that Nīla Perumāl, a *brahmin* and the grandson of Āryakāmadeva who established the *dēvālaya* in the reign of Parākramabāhu II, had been appointed to improve the *dēvālaya* and *vihāraya* attached to it; he had the title Banḍāranāyaka conferred on him and the office of Basnāyaka (chief administrative officer of the *dēvālaya*) to be continued uninterruptedly in the line of his children, grandchildren etc. Another appointment made by the king was that of a *mukaveṭṭi*, whose functions or position are not defined in the document, but according to the *Haṃsa-sandeśaya,* the duties of the *mukaveṭṭi* were largely secretarial and the keeping of accounts and records.[155] The holder of the office was Maliya Perumāl, another *brahmin.* The king also enacted regulations to the appointment of sixteen servitors (*tevakāra; sevakāra, tevakāra*), including the Kapuvā, and to the supply of a garment made of gold studded with gems and made at a cost of 1,000 *karṣāpapas,* issued from the Royal treasury and given by kings, royal ministers etc. He, moreover, conferred the title of *kapuvādeva* on the Kapuvā who holds the gem-set crown and other ornaments in the presence of the image of the god. The king also appointed musicians of five kinds of musical instruments (*pañcatūrya*), musicians for performing services connected with dancing, vocal and instrumental music, and dancing girls. The remaining appointments made by the king concerning the administration of the *dēvālaya* were Ratnāyaka (chief charioteer), Raṭanāyaka (District Headman in charge of the civil and judicial administration of the villages belonging to the institution), Mudalnāyaka (Treasurer), and Vannaku (Valuer).

Another important aspect of the information given in the *Maha Saman Dēvālaya Sannasa* is that concerning the administration of the Buddhist monastery attached to the *dēvālaya*. It has been mentioned before that during the Gampola period the images of Hindu and local gods were placed for the first time in the Buddhist shrine rooms outside the sanctum between the inner and outer walls of the building of Laṅkātilaka temple and in the fifteenth century the practice had grown to such an extent that *dēvālayas* like the Maha Saman Dēvālaya of Ratnapura contained Buddhist monasteries as their appendages.[156] It is stated in the *sannasa* that a considerable amount of income accruing to the *dēvālaya* was appropriated, according to custom, for the daily maintenance of the three *bodhis* of this *vihāraya*.[157] There should be, according to the document, three monks in the monastery to look after the day-to-day needs of the place, and the head of these monks should be called *gaṇanāyaka*.[158] The *gaṇanāyaka* should be a monk well acquainted with the whole of Buddhist doctrine and discipline (*dharma-vinaya*), holy, and observant of religious precepts. Maṅgala *terasāmi* who had completed his course of study of *terabaṇa*[159] under Galaturumula Medhaṅkara *mahaterasāmi* of the Pāpiliyāna monastery, was appointed to this office. The second monk in importance of the monastery was given the title *vidānasāmi* whose duty was to attend to day-to-day services of the temple. It is stipulated that the *gaṇa* of the monastery should include a third monk who also should be pious and observant in religious precepts. The duty of the *gaṇa* in regard to the *dēvālaya* was to recite *pirit* in front of the deity and preach *baṇa* to the people who came to the *dēvālaya* in seeking the help of the god. With the view to a regular supply of the four priestly requisites (*sivpasaya*) of the monks, Parākramabāhu VI granted Menēripitiya, Uḍuvātänna, Gāṭangama and other villages with fields, gardens, oxen, buffaloes, attendants etc. to the monastery.

It is stated in the *sannasa* that there was an annual procession called *äsaḷa perahāra* at the *dēvālaya* in memory of Saman.[160] We have seen earlier that Rājasiṅha I made arrangements to hold this *äsaḷa perahāra* uninteruptedly, which he incorporated into the annual Tooth Relic festival.[161]

The *sannasa* mentions two other divinities, i.e. Bisō Deviyan and Kumāra Deviyan, associated with Saman.[162] In the *Sävul-sandeśaya*, the messenger, after his petition to the god, is enjoined to pay homage to the Consort (Bisō) of the deity, and inform her also of the business on which he had come.[163] The goddess is merely referred to as the deity who is the queen, (Bisō Devisañda), no personal name is given. Nor has either in the *sannasa* or in the *sandeśaya*, any individual trait of the goddess been mentioned. The next deity, named Kumāra Devi in the *sannasa*, and Kumāra Deviñdu in the *sandeśaya*,[164] also seems to have received the homage of those seeking success and protection.

It is noteworthy that in the *Säḷalihiṇi-sandeśaya*, like the *Sävul-sandeśaya*, homage is in the form of a message to be delivered to a god, in this case Vibhīṣaṇa, who was also with his consort, and the prince, i.e. the son of king of the gods.[165] It may therefore be concluded that during this period, a Trinity consisting of the principal deity, his consort and his son was worshipped in shrines dedicated to gods. Paranavitana has suggested that as there is no reference to a son of Sumana in the earlier texts where Sumana is mentioned, Kumāra Deviñdu was mentioned in the *Sävul-sandeśaya* and the *Maha Saman Dēvālaya Sannasa* merely to satisfy the demands of this Trinity scheme, particularly as neither of the documents refers to any individual characteristics of this deity.[166]

The *Sävul-sandeśaya* mentions with Saman yet another god, called Sapu, associated at the Maha Saman Dēvālaya in the sixteenth century.[167] The description of the god does not mention any individual features of the god, for the eulogy could be applied to any other divinity. No god of this name is worshipped today at the Saman Dēvālaya or any other shrine in the country. Nor is any reference to a god named Sapu found any other Sinhalese writing.

The third of the four guardian deities, Vibhīṣaṇa, seems to have been an indigeneous god who became popular about our period or a little earlier. According to the *Rāmāyaṇa*, Vibhīṣaṇa was the younger brother of Rāvaṇa, the legendary Rākṣasa king of Laṅkā.[168] Vibhīṣaṇa was said to have defected to Rāma's camp in the epic war between Rāma and Rāvaṇa and helped Rāma to defeat and kill his brother. As a compensation, he was enthroned as the king of Laṅkā by Rāma. Legend has it that Vibhīṣaṇa's seat of power was at Kelaṇiya.[169]

It is not certain at what time Vibhīṣaṇa acquired the position of a god. The Laṅkātilaka inscription of Bhuvanekabāhu IV records that among many gods, that came to guard the Buddha the image of Vibhīṣaṇa was installed in the lower storey of the image house.[170] The *Nikāyasaṅgrahaya,* written in the latter part of the fourteenth century, mentions Vibhīṣaṇa as one of the four gurdian deities of Sri Lanka.[171] These references to Vibhīṣaṇa in the Gampola period suggest that he had, by this time, risen to a position of eminence as one of the four guardian deities and must therefore have been included in the Sinhalese pantheon at some earlier stage. It is stated in the *Nikāyasaṅgrahaya* that Alakeśvara III, when he had built the fort of Jayavardhana Kōṭṭē, built four temples for the protection of the four quarters of the city and dedicated them to the gods Upulvan, Saman, Vibhīṣaṇa and Kārtikeya (Skanda) and ordained that daily services should be performed with music and drums of every sort.[172]

Vibhīṣaṇa's speciality among the other deities seems to have been the boon of granting offspring to supplicants. His reputation in this field stood very high in this period as the belief gained ground that the son of Queen Ratnāvalī, later Parākramabāhu I, was obtained by the favour of this god.[173] The story in the *Cūlavaṃsa* related to the birth of Parākramabāhu I says that his father, Mānābharaṇa, was granted a boon of son by a god designated as *devarāja* (The king of gods).[174] Geiger and Wijesinha are of the opinion that this god was Indra or Sakka, who was usually regarded as the king of the gods.[175] But a different identification of this god seems to have been adhered to in the medieval period. For, the *Sälaḷihiṇi-sandeśaya* of Śrī Rāhula definitely says that it was Vibhīṣaṇa who granted the boon of a son to Mānābharaṇa and Ratnāvalī.[176] This would suggest that Vibhīīṣaṇa came into prominence in medieval Sri

Lanka not only as guardian deity but also as a deity capable of granting offspring, who had enhanced his reputation on account of Parākramabāhu's fame. This would further suggest that Vibhīṣaṇa, like Saman, was a local deity worshipped particularly in the ancient Māyāraṭa, which included Kelaṇiya, his site of worship, and Jātigāma (mod. Dädigama), the birth place of Parākramabāhu I.

The best known centre of the cult of Vibhīṣaṇa during the Kōṭṭē period was at Kelaṇiya, which was supposed to have become his centre of power after the death of his brother Rāvaṇa. Our sources do not furnish evidence to ascertain the date of erection of the shrine of Vibhīṣaṇa at Kelaṇiya. However, there is little doubt that his presence at this important sacred place of the Buddhists, which gained reputation as one of the places visited by the Buddha, was as important factor in the growth of Vibhīṣaṇa into one of the prominent deities of Sri Lanka. He is referred to in the most of the *sandeśa* poems in this period.[177] A relatively long account of Vibhīṣaṇa is given in the *Haṃsa-sandeśaya*.[178] Here the author says that Vibhīṣaṇa was installed on the throne of Laṅka by Rāma of the *Rāmāyaṇa*, who overthrew the forces of Rākṣasas. The author adds that the god constantly granted requests and prayer of kings of ancient Laṅkā who worshipped and honoured him, and in return for the boons granted, these kings had made gifts of elephants, horses, fields and villages to the temple of the god at Kelaṇiya.[179] As has been mentioned earlier, Śrī Rāhula was a votary of Vibhīṣaṇa. In his *Säḷalihiṇi- sandeśaya*, this hierarch says that he was not only the brother of Rāvaṇa, but also belonged to the Palatisi (Pulasti) clan.[180] The object of this *sandeśaya* was to make a request to the god to grant the boon of a son to Ulakuḍayadevi, the younger daughter of Parākramabāhu VI, who could be a worthy successor to the king. Here Śrī Rāhula mentions the god having granted the boon of a son, i.e. Parākramabāhu I, the Mānābharaṇa and Ratnāvalī and urges him to ensure that the would be son of Ulakuḍayadevi could emulate his great namesake. Indeed a son was born to Ulakuḍayadevi, but though he succeeded to the throne of Parākramabāhu VI, he by no means emulated Parākramabāhu I; on the contrary, he was slain by Bhuvanekabāhu VI after two years of unsuccessful reign.

The *Haṃsa-sandeśaya* alludes to the recitation of *paritta* in the shrine of Vibhīṣaṇa by the monks headed by the *gaṇanāyaka*, Bhuvanekabāhu *thera*, of the Kelaṇiya monastery.[181] According to the *Kokila-sandeśaya*, among the ceremonies carried out in the temple of the god there was dancing performed by young, beautiful damsels.[182] They chanted hymns composed in praise of the god. Śrī Rāhula requests the messenger that he should, after having delivered the message, also worship his consort and son. This suggests that there were three images in the shrine room, one of the god, the other of his consort and the third one of his son. The consort and son are not named in the poem. It may be assumed that they were placed in the shrine room so as to continue the popular practice of representing a Trinity of gods.[183]

In modern popular religion the cult of the god of Kataragama, who has been identified with Skanda, plays an important part. Geiger traces the first reference to Skanda back to the Anurādhapura period, and maintains that Dappula of Rohaṇa (seventh century) made offerings to him.[184] Skanda is also mentioned with his old name Kumāra in the *Cūlavaṃsa* account of Mānavamma's incantation.[185] It is recorded in the Kapuruväḍū Oya inscription of Gajabāhu II (1132-1153) that the king made grant of lands to a person who made images of Kanta (Skanda).[186] On the basis of this reference Godakumbura suggests that the worship of Skanda would have been very popular with the Sinhalese during the Polonnaru period.[187]

According to a Sinhalese text called *Kañda Upata*, attributed to the late Kandyan period, Duṭṭhagāmaṇi would have rebuilt and richly endowed the forest shrines of Kataragama, offering it to god Skanda, whose favour enabled him to march against the Tamil king Eḷāra and to re-establish the Sinhalese monarchy at Anurādhapura.[188] Kataragama became a very important centre of the Sinhalese military preparations against the Coḷa empire in the eleventh century, but we have no reference to the god at this particular time.

The *Nikāyasaṅgrahaya* informs us that Alakeśvara III dedicated four shrines to four guardian deities at the four corners of the new Sinhalese stronghold, Kōṭṭē.[189] It is said that one of these was dedicated to Kārttikeya, another name for Skanda. The Laṅkātilaka inscription also mentions Kārttikeys as one of four guardian deities of Laṅkā.[190] The vast learning of the celebrated scholar Śri Rāhula was believed to have been due to a boon granted by Skanda-Kumāra. In his *Pañcikāpradīpaya* and the *Kāvya śekharaya,* this hierarch claims that he obtained a boon from Skanda (Kañda-kumariñdu) at the age of fifteen which enabled him to be a master of six languages and the Tripiṭaka.[191] We have seen earlier that a grandfather of Śrī Rāhula, in monastic succession, was also a devotee of Skanda.[192] The *Haṃsa-sandeśaya* refers to Skanda as the six-faced god, and mentions the sounds of beating drums emanating from his temple and the numerous offerings made to him by devotees in the shrine of Kōṭṭē.[193] The *Sälalihiṇi-sandeśaya* makes reference to the shrine of Mahasen (Skanda), at Kōṭṭē.[194] In the *Mayūra-sandeśaya* and the *Sävul-sandeśaya* passing references are made to this god in the descriptions of the two birds, which carried the messages. The peacock in the *Mayūra-sandeśaya* is described as being his vehicle while the cock in the latter is mentioned as being in one of the numerous hands of Skanda.[195]

In the literature of the period, there is, in connexion with this deity, no reference to Kataragama, which is now the principal centre of his cult, but the *Jinakālamālī*, written in Chieng Mai in 1516, names the god of Kaṭṭhagāma (obviously meant for Skanda at Kataragama) as one of the four guardian deities of Sri Lanka.[196] On the basis of this reference, Paranavitana has suggested that the shrine of Kataragama, dedicated to the cult of Skanda, had by the end of the fifteenth century acquired such a fame that it was known in countries as far away from Sri Lanka as Thailand.[197] However, it seems that Skanda emerged as a deity of outstanding eminence in the Kandyan period for, in the Äsaḷa festival in Kandy during the reign of Nāyakkar kings, the procession in which the image of Skanda was carried, played an important part.[198]

Among the many Hindu gods who had been accepted into the Sinhalese pantheon during the medieval period Gaṇeśa or Gaṇapati seems to have held a prominent place. Out of the many Hindu temples referred to in the *sandeśa* poems those of Gaṇeśa stand out. Two places of worship dedicated to the cult of Ganapati in the southern part of the country are mentioned in these poems. The *Tisara-sandeśaya* mentions the Gaṇeśa temple at Vällemaḍama close to Magulvälla in the precincts of Devinuvara.[199] The *Kokila-sandeśaya* says that the temple was so close to the sea that the waves struck against it.[200] The *Parevi-sandeśaya* also mentions this same temple of Gaṇeśa at Vällemaḍama and adds that it was built by a South Indian merchant-prince called Rāmacandra.[201] The author describes the rites and ceremonies carried out at the temple in memory of Rāmacandra. The beating of drums at dawn in the temple was followed by a chanting of hymns and stories by the Tamil chaplain of the temple. The *Kokila- sandeśaya* mentions another temple dedicated to the cult of Gaṇeśa situated near the Kalu-gañga.[202]

The cult of Gaṇeśa has also been traced back to the Anurādhapura period on the evidence of the figure of this deity found in the frienzes of the *vāhalkaḍas* of the Kanṭhaka-cetiya at Mihintale.[203] Godakumbure identifies one of the *kovil* foundations near the Śiva Dēvālaya No. 5 of Polonnaruva with that of Gaṇapati.[204] His image was installed in the image house of Laṅkātilaka along with other gods.[205] It may be surmised that the cult of Gaṇeśa was popular in this period among the Tamils rather than among the Sinhalese.

The most important of the cults of Hindu gods who had some influence on the Sinhalese popular religion was that of Śiva, who had many *dēvālayas* and *kovils,* dedicated to his various forms such a Sudarśaan and Bhairava in various parts of the country. The *sandeśa* poems have numerous references to the cult of this god prevailing in this period. Certain archaeological discoveries and ruins point to the prevalence of this cult during the Polonnaru *Uttaratantra* period.[206] Most of these are attributed to the period of Coḷa occupation of the northern parts of the country in the eleventh century. A twelfth-century Sinhalese poem, *Sasadāvata,* names Śiva among the gods who came to pay homage to the Buddha.[207] In the painting in the relic-chamber of Mahiyaṅgaṇa-*cetiya,* Śiva is represented in the company of divinities who came to laud the Buddha after the defeat of Māra.[208] These instances may indicate that even before the Kōṭṭē period there were attempts to include Śiva in the Buddhist pantheon, as elsewhere in the Buddhist world.

However, until the Gampola period no attempt seems to have been made to install the images of Śiva in Buddhist shrines. It was in the Laṅkātilaka temple at Gampola that Śiva found a place in a Buddhist shrine for the first time.[209]

A temple dedicated to the Bhairava form of Śiva was situated at Sītāvaka, and is mentioned in the *Sävul-sandeśaya.*[210] Alagiyavanna describes the ceremony of dancing conducted at the temple in honour of the god. The temple was decorated with numerous paintings depicting the wars of Rāma and Rāvaṇa, the stories of *Mahābhārata,* the achievements of Skanda and the wars of Śiva.[211] The Bhairava temple, now known as Bäräṇḍi Kovila, and Alagiyavanna's enthusiasm in describing its flourishing conditions in the reign of Rājasiṁha I are generally in keeping with the accounts in the *Cūlavaṃsa* and *Mandārampura-puvata* concerning the Śiva sympathies of this king.[212] Another temple dedicated to Śiva at Munneśvarama, near Halāvata, is mentioned in the *Kokila-sandeśaya.*[213] It is stated in the work that the *dēvālaya* was dedicated to Isvara, another form of Śiva. The *Munneśvaram Dēvālaya Sannasa* of Parākramabāhu VI gives a long account of repairs carried out by the king in the temple and the appointment of various officials and attendants to maintain the services of the institutions.[214] In this respect, the *sannasa* resembles the *Maha Saman Dēvālaya Sannasa* of the same king at Sabaragamuva.[215] It is stated in the document that the reconstruction of the temple was carried out by a *brahmin* called Bārāṇsi Nīlakanṭha on behalf of the king. After the reconstuction of the temple, the king ordered the reorganization of the *dēvālaya* administration. The appointed chief of the new administrative body was Bārāṇasi Nīlakanṭha, who was honoured with the title 'Modanmoi'., which in case of the Maha Saman Dēvālaya was Banḍāranāyaka.[216] The document further enumerates sixteen newly appointed attendants to the institution. The head of this body was Kapuvā, who was given the title 'Kapuvā Deva', and was entrusted with the daily services of the institution. As in the case of the Maha Saman Dēvālaya, the Munneśvaram Dēvālaya also had a Buddhist temple attached to it, but the document gives no details regarding the administration of that institution. In view of the information given in the document, it can be assumed that the Munneśvaram Dēvālaya was in a flourishing condition in the fifteenth century.

These outstanding Śiva temples in the Sinhalese areas of the country by no means suggest that the faith had a Sinhalese following, except for a few converts like Rājasiṅha I. The fact that almost all the epigraphic sources found at these places are in Tamil and the prayers and hymns were said to have been in Tamil shows that these temples were mainly meant for the Tamil population in various parts of the Island. However, this may not imply that the cult had no influence at all on the Sinhalese Buddhists. A close examination of the sources of the period shows that the cult had devotees even among the community of monks.[217] This growing popularity of the cult of Śiva nevertheless seems to have aroused bitter feelings of at least some members of the Sangha. Dharmasena, the author of the *Saddharmaratnāvalī* of the thirteenth century, admonishes the people to give up faith in Viṣṇu and Maheśvara and to take refuge in the Triple Gems.[218] The *Pūjāvaliya* and the *Saddharmalaṅkāraya* also make references to the prevalence of the cult of Śiva, but only to point out the uselessness of it and to uphold the cause of Buddhism.[219] The most vehement attack of the worship of Śiva came from Vīdāgama Maitreya in the fifteenth century. There is no doubt that the latter was surprised and angered by the interest in the cult shown by even some prominent monks like Śrī Rāhula and the principal of the Tilaka Pirivena at Devinuvara.[220] Vīdāgama's attacks are directed at all the gods of popular religion in general and Śiva and Viṣṇu in particular. He attacked even those who held these deities in great reverence. Why call them gods, he asks, if they hang about at the doors of people waiting to receive their gifts like beggars?[221] Vīdāgama ridicules *brahmins* who regard the fire as a god by relating an amusing story about a *brahmin.*[222] The Elder's strong opposition to Śiva is reflected in his following description of the god:-

With trident in hand, the black colour conspicuous on his throat, wearing a gown of thin air and bearing on his body half the body of Umā,

The cresent moon on his turban, and a dreadful serpent round his neck, dancing everyday and going about on a descrepit old ox,

Raised to the supreme position with his head washed by the heavenly river, this god who burned the body of Anaṅga, verily is he meet to be adored?[223]

The worship of Viṣṇu is also severely attacked by Vīdāgama. We have seen earlier that owing to the growing influence of Vaiṣnavism in Sri Lanka, there were attempts to identify Upulvan with Viṣṇu in the latter part of the fifteenth century, and such attempts proved successful in the succeeding centuries.[224] Vīdāgama questions the greatness of Viṣṇu in an arguement refuting the supremacy of this god:-

That Viṣṇu is everywhere, that Sītā was separated from her lover, that therefore, there was a war, why speak such balderdash?

A stretch of water across which a monkey swam, Rāmā was unable to cross; he needed a bridge to go over it, they say, such is the might of these gods.[225]

After this denunciation of popular gods, the Elder admonishes all people to give themselves up to the Buddha in the fullest devotion of their hearts, and to worship his relics, his image and the sacred Bodhi tree to the exclusion of all gods, constantly thinking of the virtues of the Buddha and hoping for the sight of the next Buddha Maitreya, who will appear in future.[226]

Among the popular cults of the period, Nāga cult is mentioned in the *Parevi-sandeśaya* and the *Kokila-sandeśaya.*[227] The temple of this cult was at a place beyond Mātara. This was probably a survival of ancient Nāga worship, which is considered to have been introducted to Sri Lanka at a very early time. The temple is said to have been built in the likeness of a large cobra with its numerous coils and hood.[228]

The cult of Pattini also appears to have gained some popularity in Sri Lanka during this period. Some literary works, attributed to the Kandyan period, describe how Gajabāhu I invaded South India and brought a large number of war captives with the anklet of Pattini.[229] Although the historicity of this story is extremely doubtful, there is no doubt that with the growing influence of Tamil culture throughout the medieval period the cult of Pattini gained a strong foothold in the minds of the people. Parākramabāhu VI is said to have erected a temple for this goddess in his capital, Kōṭṭē.[230] Pattini became one of the most important and popular deities in the Kandyan period. One of the four *dēvālayas* situated near the temple of the Tooth Relic is consecrated to Pattini.[231] The famous Äsaḷa festival of Kandy also has a section devoted to this goddess.

Ayyanār, a South Indian village god, appears to have entered the Sinhalese pantheon in this time. The *Kokila-sandeśaya* describes the Ayyanāyaka (the Sinhalese form of Ayyanār) *kovila* as situated just beyond Mannārama, and the author requests the bird to enter it and pay homage to the deity inside.[232] The author refers to the deity as Ayyanāyaka Banḍāra suggesting that the god had been fully 'Sinhalized' by his devotees by this time. The *Vannipuvata,* a Sinhalese poem attributed to the Kandyan period, says that Ayyanāyaka came to Sri Lanka with the 'Āryans' who migrated to the country during the reign of Bhuvanekabāhu IV (1335-1341) of Gampola.[233] We are not certain whether the deity had some connexions with the Āryacakravartis who ruled some parts of the Sinhalese areas about this time. The work adds that the deity was Dravidian. This identification of the god may suggest that the South Indians who migrated to Sri Lanka on the eve of Muslim invasions in South India brought their local deities with them and subsequently introduced them into the Sinhalese pantheon. This supposition is further strengthened by the fact that the *Ayyanāyaka Devi Kavi,* another Sinhalese poem attributed to the Kandyan period, states that this god was born through the right side of his mother by the virtue of Upulvan, and came to Sri Lanka with the permission of the latter.[234] Thus the poet justifies the right of Ayyanāyaka to being a Sinhalese god, for Upulvan was supposed to be the chief of the four guardian deities and the protector of Buddhism in Sri Lanka. In addition, the poet says that Ayyanāyaka was entrusted by the Buddha with the protection of the world when he visited the Sāla grove of the Mallas.[235] This shows the enthusiasm with which Ayyanāyaka was included into the Buddhist pantheon. According to the *Ayyanāyaka Devi Kavi*, the deity embarked from the city of Madurai, landed at Jaffna and protected the sea coast from Jaffna to Kalutara, travelling on the back of an elephant.[236]

The most striking feature of the worship conducted at the *dēvālayas* of various gods at this time was the dance performed by nautch girls in the evening, of which poetic descriptions are found in the *sandeśas*. The *Sälaḷihiṇi-sandeśaya* of Śrī Rāhula gives a vivid description of the dancing performed by young damsels at the temple of Vibhīṣaṇa at Kelaṇiya.[237] The inauguration of the dancing ceremony at the temple of Upulvan at Devinuvara is picturesquely described in the *Parevi-sandeśaya* and the *Kokila-sandeśaya*.[238] Alagiyavanna also gives a vivid description of the dancing ceremony at the Maha Saman Dēvālaya of Ratnapura.[239] The Devinuvara temple, according to Ibn Baṭūta, had, 'five hundred or so of Hindu girls who sing and dance the whole night in the front of the idol'.[240]

Another noteworthy aspect of this side of popular religion during this period was the important part played by *brahmins*, the majority of whom were from South India, at the centres of these cults. It appears that most of the *dēvālayas* and *kovils* had *brahmin* priests entrusted with rituals conducted in honour of these deities. Ibn Baṭūta informs us that there were thousands of *brahmins* and *yogis* at Devinuvara in the fourteenth century.[241] The Devinuvara slab inscription of Parākramabāhu II testifies to the existence, in the thirteenth century, of a freehold of *brahmins (agrahāra)*.[242] The author of the *Sarajotimālai*, a Tamil astrological work in verse, presented to Parākramabāhu VI, claims to be a resident of this *agrahāra*.[243] Several inscriptions recording grants made by kings of Kōṭṭē also indicate that there was a *brahmin* village at Devinuvara, and most of the residents of that place were Tamil-speaking.[244] The Nāimana inscription and the Trilingual inscription at Galle afford further evidence of the dominating influence exerted by Tamil *brahmins* on the form of religious worship at Devinuvara.[245] We have seen earlier that it was a *brahmin* who initiated the establishment of the Maha Saman Dēvālaya at Ratnapura.[246] The part played by *brahmins* in the administration of this institution and that of Munneśvarama in the fifteenth century has already been considered.[247]

The influence which *brahmins* exerted on the popular religion was reflected not only in the administration of these institutions but also in their attempts to transform the Sinhalese gods into those of Purāṇic Hinduism as well. It has been discussed earlier that the metamorphosis of Upulvan into Viṣṇu has taken place some time after the reign of Parākramabāhu VI, and before the arrival of the Portuguese.[248] Similar attempts seem to have been made to transform Saman into Lakṣmaṇa, but this had little success.[249] The *Ayyanāyaka Devi Kavi* testifies to the manner in which a South Indian local deity was transformed into a Sinhalese deity with the help of Upulvan.[250]

Despite their influence on the religious life of the people, some ardent Buddhists of the time appear to have considered *brahmins* a menace to their own religion. This opposition to *brahmins* was most fervently expressed by Vīdāgama Maitreya, who made a scathing denunciation of the pretensions of *brahmins* and their religious beliefs in his *Buduguṇālaṃkāraya*. In fact, Vīdāgama's condemnation of *brahmins* is no less venomous than his contempt of their gods. He says of them :-

What good did ever come to this world from these *brahmins* of heretical faith, who ever deceive the world with false charms and concocted Vedas.[251]

The *Budguṇālaṃkāraya* refers to various non-Buddhist practices that had become incorporated into popular religion at this time, and the author expresses his strong disapproval by ridiculing them of the utmost.[252] In spite of his strong denunciation of Hindu practices, Vīdāgama does not seem to have succeeded in arresting the influence of *brahmins*. After Parākramabāhu VI, the influence of the Sangha on the kings and nobles of Kōṭṭē steadily waned, and that of *brahmins* gained ground until by the time of the arrival of the Portuguese, the upper strata of Sinhalese society were more or less becoming Hinduised.[253]

## References


1. *Samyutta Nikāya* (PTS), I, pp.212; *Sāratthappakāsinī*, (PTS), I.pp.316-337; See also, J.Mason, *La religion populaire dans le canon bouddhique pali, Louvain, 1942, pp.126-129.*
2. *Dāthāvamsa*, ed. M.Ananda, 1956, Gampaha, 5, vv.1-3; *Daladāsirita*, ed. W.Sorata, Colombo, 1961, p.35.
3. *UCHC.*, p.571 ff.
4. *CCMT.*, p.214.
5. *Cv.*, XI, 64.
6. *Dls.*, p.49 ff; *ASCM.*, III, pp.34-37.
7. *Sdhrt.*, p.297; *JCBRAS.*, No.65, p.312.
8. *Cv.*, 90.72.
9. *Sls.*, v.16; *Prs.*, vv.39-40; *Grs..*, vv.50-51; *Sdhrt.*, p.297.
10. *Grs.*, v.51.
11. Hugh Nevill, *Ethnology*, 'Sinhala Kavi', ed.P.E.P. Deraniyagala, Colombo, III, 155; *Saparagamuvl Pärani Liyavili*, ed. K.Nana- vimala, Ratnapura, p.36.
12. See above, Ch.III.
13. *Ethnology*, III, p.155; Queroz., *op.cit.* p.223.
14. *SPL.*, p.36.
15. *SPL.*, p.36.
16. *Mv.*, 5.77.
17. S. Paranavitana, *The God of Adam's Peak*, p.2 ff; *Manimekhalai*, II, pp.122-123.
18. *Cv.*, 60.14-67; *CJSG*, II, p.185 and 196; *EZ.*, pt.II, pp.202-208.
19. *CJSG.*, II, pp.20-21.
20. *Cv.*, 85.118-121.
21. *Cv.*, 88.48.
22. *Samantakūtavannanā*, ed.M.Nanissara, Colombo, 1910; *PS.* p.420 ff.
23. *Grs.*, v.21; *Sls.*, v.25; *Hms.*, v.76; *Svls.*, v.152.
24. *GAP.*, p. 21.
25. *SPL.*, p.36; Wachissara, *op.cit.*p.65.

26. Forneau, *Le Siam Ancien*, Paris, 1895, I, pp. 242-254; G. Coedés, *Receuil des inscriptions du Siam*, p.46 ff.
27. *IA*, XXII, (1895), p.44.
28. *EZ.*, III, pp.337-338; *GAP.*, p.17.
29. *The Book of Ser Marco Polo*, tr. and ed. by Sir. H.Yule, II, pp.316-322.
30. *Ribeiro*, pp.80-82; *Queroz.*, pp.37- 42.
31. E. Carpenter, *From Adam's Peak to Elephanta*, London, 1892, p.62.
32. *HBC.*, pp.316-322.
33. *AAGP.*, pp.46-54 and 63-70.
34. *Sls.*, v.60.
35. *Sls.*, v.61.
36. ibid.v.62.
37. ibid.v.66.
38. ibid.v.68.
39. ibid.v.69.
40. ibid.v.70.
41. *Mv.*,38.66; *HBC.*, p.283.
42. *Mv.*, 39.40.
43. *Sdhrt.*, p.561 f.
44. Rosa Centifolia, Rosa Damaseoene, sv.*ŚSS.*, p.1084.
45. *Shrt.*, p.562.
46. S. Paranavitana, 'Pre-Buddhist beliefs in Ceylon', *JCBRAS*, XXX, p.92; *HBC.*, p.34 ff.
47. *UCR.*, XVIII, Nos.I. and II, p.5 ff; *AAGP.*, p.64.
48. See above, Ch.III.
49. E. Lamotte, *Histoire du Bouddhisme Indien*, p.786 f.
50. See, eg., *EZ*, III, p.258, II, pp.7-13; Gunawardhana, *op.cit*. p.214.
51. *Cv.*, 37.242.
52. *Dīgha Nikāya*, (PTS), III, p.75 f.
53. *Anāgatavaṃsa*, in the *JPTS.*, 1886, v.57.
54. *Pjv.*, p.234; *Sdhlk.*, p.586; *Sdhrt.*, p.214.
55. *Kts.*, p.40.
56. *CJSc.*, G.II, p.60.
57. *CJSc.*, G.II, p.60 ff; N.Mudiyanse, *Mahāyāna Monuments in Ceylon*, p.14 ff; Gunawardhana, *op.cit*.217; Dhammavisuddhi, *op.cit*.p.352 ff.
58. *Kks.*,v.48.
59. *Tss.*, v.124 ff.
60. *Kss.*, v.239.

61. *Grs.*, vv.230,251.
62. *Grs.*, v.251.
63. ibid.
64. ibid.
65. See below, p. 195.
66. *Grs.*, v.11.
67. *Grs.*, v.230.
68. *Kks.*, v.50.
69. *Grs.*, vv.234-5.
70. *Trs.*, v.124 f.
71. *Prs.*, v.76.
72. *Kvsk.*, canto,xv,v.24.
73. See above, Ch.V,p. 150.
74. See for the name Avalokiteśvara, M.Therése de Mallmann, *Introduction A L'Etude D''Avalokitesvara*, Paris, 1948, pp.59-82.
75. *CJSc.*, G.II, p.56 ff.
76. ibid. pp.53-54.
77. *Trs.*, v.125.
78. *CJSc.*, G.II, p.54.
79. Hugh Nevill, *op.cit.* 'Nāthdevi-puvata', p.574 ff.
80. *Vadan Kavipota*, ed. J.G. Gunasekara, Colombo, 1908.
81. ibid.p.23 ff.
82. *EZ.*, IV, pp.93; *SHC.*, p.88.
83. *Prs.*, v.195.
84. *Mv.*, 7.5 ff; G.P.Malalasekara, *Dictionary of Pali Proper Names*, p.558.
85. *Sdhrlk.*, p.395.
86. *Myrs.*, v.156.
87. *Mv.*, 7.5 ff.
88. S.Paranavitana, *The Shrine of Upulvan at Devinuvara, MASC.*, Vol.VI, p.19.
89. *Cv.*, 83.49.
90. *Cv.*, 83.85.
91. *A.D.K.*, folio. *ki* ff.
92. *Cv.*,85.89; *pjv.*, p.57.
93. *Pärakumbāsirita*, ed. K.D.P. Wickramasingha, Colombo, 1954.
94. *Prs.*, v.142.
95. *SUD.*, p.22.
96. ibid.p.47 f.
97. *Prs.*, v.162.
98. ibid.v.161.

99. *Myrs.*, v.116.
100. *Kks.*, v.10 ff.
101. *CRJ.*, Vol.V, No.I.p.48.
102. *Prs.*, v.163; *Kks.*, v.24.
103. *EZ.*, III, 333 ff.
104. *Prs.*, v.140.
105. *Ibn Baṭuta, Travels in Asia and Africa,* (1354- 58), tr. and, ed.H.A.R.Gibb, London, p.260.
106. *Queroz.*, p.35.
107. *Queroz.*, p.35.
108. *Cv.*, 90.100-103.
109. *ADK.*, folio,*ka* ff.
110. *JCBRAS.*, X.No.34, pp.64-68; *UCR.*,XVIII, Nos.I and 2, 1960, pp.1-45.
111. *Kks.*, v.28.
112. W.F. Gunawardhana, in his tr. of *Kks.*, *CALR.*, IV, p.157, and his edition of *Myrs.*, p.5 f.
113. *CALR.*, IV, p.157.
114. *Tss.*,v.21.
115. ibid. v.23.
116. D.B. Jayatilake, in his edition of the *Tisara-sandeśaya*, Colombo, 1935, p.ix.
117. *SUD.*, p.21.
118. *Prs.*, v.158 f.
119. *ADK.*, folio.*ki.*
120. *SUD.*, p.43.
121. *Queroz.*, p.35.
122. Wachissara, *op.cit.*p.126.
123. *Mv.*, 7.5.
124. See above, p. 195.
125. *UCHC.*, p.663 f.
126. *Prs.*, vv. 196-198.
127. *Prs.*, v.198.
128. *Hms.*, v.197.
129. *Kks.*, v.287 ff.
130. *Kks.*, v.23; *Myrs.*, v.27.
131. *SUD.*, p.61 ff.
132. ibid. p.47.
133. *Kks.*, v.30.
134. Ananda Maitreya, *Savistara Buddhacaritaya,* Colombo, 1954, p.324.

135. *Prs.*,v.178 ff.
136. *Prs.*, vv.200-291.
137. *Mv.*, 1-7; *Vaṃsatthappakāsinī*, (PTS), ed.G.P.Malalasekara, p.114.
138. *Mv.*, 1-7.
139. *Samantakuṭa-vaṇṇana*, v.718 ff.
140. *GAP.*, p.21 ff.
141. *UCHC.*, p.578.
142. *Cv.*,86.21 ff; *Pjv.*, p.745.
143. *Cv.*,86.21 ff.
144. *Hms.*,v.198.
145. *Svls.*,v.202 ff.
146. *CALR*,II, part.I, pp.42-53.
147. See above, p. 198.
148. *Svls.*,v.188.
149. *Svls.*,v.202 ff.
150. *Samansirita*, Br.Mus.Ms. Or. 6679 (123).
151. *CALR.*,II,pt.I,p.42 f.
152. *Samansirita*, folio. *klu*.
153. ibid.
154. *CALR*,II, Part.I,p.42 f.
155. *Hms.*,v.53. See above, Chapter III,p.
156. Every temple had at least a *dāgäba, bodhi,* and an image house (*piḷima-ge*). The *dāgäbas* or *cetiyas* were the sanctuaries where the relics of the Buddha were deposited. The worship of the *bodhi* tree was as common and widespread as that of the *dāgäbas*. Almost every temple had to be equipped with an image house which is decorated with various paintings depicting *jātaka* stories or the life of the Buddha. These three important parts of a monastery are called together *tumbodhi* or tunbo.
157. *CALR.*, II, part.I, p.44; for *gaṇanāyaka*, see above ch.III, p. 75f.
158. ibid.
159. For *teraḅana*, see above, ch.V, p. 144f.
160. *CALR.*, II, pt.I, p.44.
161. See above, ch.IV, p. 121.
162. *CALR.*, II, pt.I, p.14.
163. v.204.
164 ibid.v.205.
165. Sls.,v.77 ff.
166. *GAP*, p.56 ff.
167. Svls., v.206.

168. *The Vālmikī Rāmāyana*, VI, (*Yuddhakaṇḍa*), ed. P.L. Vaidya, Baroda, 1971, v.22.
169. *UCR*, XVIII, Nos.1 and 2, p.7.
170. ibid.
171. Nks., p.92.
172. ibid.
173. *UCHC*., p.764.
174. *Cv*., 62.11.
175. CCMT., p.170; *Mahāvaṃsa*, 67.11-12. tr.Wijesingha; *Cv.* tr.I,pt.233,n.2.
176. *Sls*.,v.101 ff.
177. *Hms*., v.110 ff; *Sls*., v. 77 ff; *Kks*., v.165; *Tss*., v.100.
178. *Hms*., v.10 ff.
179. *Hms*., v.111.
180. *Sls*., v.92.
181. *Hms*., v.111.
182. *Kks*., v.165.
183. *Sls*., vv.106-107.
184. *Cv*.,45.55.n.4; *CCMT*.,p.172.
185. *Cv*.,57.7.
186. *EZ*., V,pt.III,p.398 ff.
187. ibid.
188. P. Arunachalam, 'The worship of Muruka or Skanda' (the Kataragama god), *JCBRAS*,XXIX,No.77,1924,p.234 ff; M.D. Raghavan, *India in Ceylon History and Culture*, London, 1964, p.65.
189. *Nks*., p.92.
190. *UCR*., XVIII, No. I, p.14.
191. *Pañcikāpradīpaya*, v.4; *Kvsk*., canto.I,v.24.
192. See above, ch.III, p. 67.
193. *Hms*.,v.197.
194. *Sls*., v.26.
195. *Myrs*., v.2; *Svls*., v.2.
196. *Jkm*., p.87.
197. *UCHC*., p.
198. Wachissara, *op.cit*.p.116 ff.
199. *Tss*., v.25.
200. *Kks*.., v.42.
201. *Prs*., v.129.
202. *Kks*., v. 101.

203. J. Smither, *Architectural Remains, Anuradhapura, Ceylon,* plate.XXXII; S.Paranavitana, *The Stupas in Ceylon,* Colombo, 1946, p.51 f.
204. C.E. Godakumbure, 'Bornzes from Polonnaruva', *JCBRAS.*, XXIV, No.68, p.76 ff.
205. *UCR.*, XVIII, Nos.1 and **2, pp.5 and**7.
206. P. Arunachalam, 'Polo**nnaruva** Bronzes and Śiva Worship', *JCBRAS.*, XXIV, No.68, p.76 ff.
207. *Sasadāvata,* ed. A. Dhammapala, Colombo, 1934, v.181.
208. *ASCAR.*, 1951, p.18; *UCHC.*, p.578.
209. *AAGP.*, p.82.
210. *Svls.*, v.93.
211. ibid.vv.94-97.
212. See above, ch.IV.
213. *Kks.*, v.v.205.
214. *Vidyodaya,* III, No.8, p.230 f, and No.9, p.269 f.
215. *CALR.*, II, pt.I,p.42 ff.
216. See above, p.210.
217. See above, p. 217.
218. *Sdhrtnl.*, p.516.
219. *Pjv.*, p.342; *Sdrlk.*, p.689.
220. *Sls.*, v.22; *Prs.*, vv.50-52; *Kkks.*, v.205.
221. Bdgnl., v.143.
222. ibid.v.134 ff.
223. ibid. vv. 159-161.
224. See above, p. 201 ff.
225. *Bdgnl.*, v.174-175.
226. ibid. v.184 ff.
227. *Prs.*, v.128; *Kks.*, v.44.
228. *Kks.*, v.44.
229. Hugh Nevill, *Sinhala Verse (Kavi), Ethnology,* III, 'Gajabā Puvata', p.114 f., 'Gajabā kavi', p.202 f.
230. *Kks.*, v.118.
231. Wachissara, *op.cit.*p.87.
232. *Kks.*, v.205.
233. Hugh Nevill, *op.cit.*, I, 'Vannipuvata', p.296; III, p.283.
234. ibid. III, p.303 f.
235. ibid.
236. ibid.
237. *Sls.*, vv.72-76.
238. *Prs.*, vv.162-177; *Kks.*, vv.12-29.

239. *Svls.*,
240. *The Rehla of Ibn Baṭuṭa*, tr. Mahdi Hussain, Baroda, 1953, (2), p.222.
241. ibid. p.223.
242. *ASCM.*, VI, p.70.
243. *JCBRAS.*, XXX, No.85, p.339.
244. *RKD.*, p.96.
245. *ASCM.*, VI, pp.70-74; *EZ*,III, pp.331-357.
246. See above, p. 219.
247. See abvoe, p. 216.
248. See above, p. 201 ff.
249. *CALR.*, II, pt.I, p.43.
250. Hugh Nevill, *op.cit.* III, p.303.
251. *Bdgnl.*, v.159.
252. ibid. v.160 ff.
253. *UCHC.*, p.767.

# Conclusion

The foregoing study of the period of about two centuries from the reign of Parākramabāhu VI of Kōṭṭē to that of Vimaladharmasūrya of Kandy reveals important developments in the history of Buddhism in Sri Lanka. As most of ancient Rajaraṭa and Rohaṇa had been abandoned, cultural activities of this period were confined to the areas known as Māyāraṭa and Malayaraṭa which comprised the south-western plains and central highlands of the country respectively. Kōṭṭē, a south-western seaboard city, became the centre of the political as well as religious activities of this period, and retained this position until the end of the sixteenth century.

The Sangha in this period underwent considerable changes in its organisation. The two fraternities, Vaṇavāsa and Gāmavāsa, which had become the main institutions of the Sangha after the disappearance of the *nikāyas* in the Polonnaru period, played an important role in the monastic life of this period. As both fraternities claimed to be the followers of the ancient Mahāvihāra, there was hardly any evidence for ideological conflicts. Although the basic ideal of the life of the Vanavāsi monk was to lead a life completely cut off from the centres of population, so that he could devote most of the time to meditation, this principle does not seem to have been rigidly adhered to in this period. Yet, the Vanavāsi monk led a more austere and disciplined life than his counterpart in the Gāmavāsa. The life of the Gāmavāsi monk was more susceptible to corruption owing to its close contact with the laity, and this demanded great efforts in purifying this fraternity at various times.

Both the fraternities suffered a general decline by the end of the fifteenth century. This led to complete disorganization of the Sangha, for there is no evidence of new institutions taking the place of the fraternities.

The institutions called *āyatanas,* which also played a prominent part in the organization of the Sangha during the early medieval period, had receded to the background by the beginning of our period. Yet, some of the hierarchs of this period perpetuated the memory of these institutions by using their names as titles. The institutions called *gaṇas*, the formation and functions of which are not known for certain, continued to appear in our period.

Teacher-pupil relationship within the Sangha held a significant place in the monastic life of this period. Some lineages, such as that of Dharmakīrti of Palābatgala, excelled in religious as well as literary activities. Class and caste seem to have had considerable influence on the monastic life of this period. This development, which had started in the later Polonnaru period, gradually gained ground in monastic institutions, so that the teacher-pupil relationship seems sometimes to have been based on this factor. One striking feature of this was the attention which was paid to the caste of new entrants to the order. However, this was not so apparent or rigid in this period as it would become later in the Kandyan period. Probably because of class and caste considerations, certain families seem to have enjoyed special privileges in religious affairs. This led to another development: the privilege which these families enjoyed with regard to the administration of monastic property. As a consequence, a new system of inheritance of monastic property emerged in the fourteenth century; it appears to have been applied also in the succeeding centuries.

The reign of Parākramabāhu VI of Kōṭṭē, which lasted more than half a century, witnessed a period of intense activity for the advancement of Buddhism. The relationship between the State and the Sangha during this period was remarkable. Parākramabāhu VI devoted much energy to the prevention of further decadence of the religion, which had suffered through neglect or otherwise in the troubled times that preceded his reign. Through the munificence of the king and chiefs as well as of ordinary people, a large number of religious institutions flourished in the Sinhalese areas, and the old ones were kept in good repair.

The peace and prosperity that existed under Parākrambāhu VI did not long survive his death. Political instability and internal dissension again became the order of the day. In spite of their political troubles, the kings of Kōṭṭē were able to extend some patronage towards the Sangha, but not to the same extent as under Parākramabāhu VI, nor in accordance with its real needs. The influence of *brahmins* became a significant factor in the court of Kōṭṭē, and this may to some extent have resulted in weakening of the relationship between the state and the Sangha.

In contrast to the situation in Kōṭṭē, the newly emerged kingdom of Kandy in the central highlands enjoyed a period of comparative peace and tranquility under Sēnāsammata Vikramabāhu. This king realized the grave situation that faced Buddhism, and turned his attention towards its advancement. His efforts did not produce lasting results; nor did they reach beyond the boundaries of his kingdom. The Sangha enjoyed liberal benefactions of Sītāvaka rulers for a limited period in the sixteenth century until the time when Rājasinha I turned against them.

Our period witnessed a number of hierarchs actively engaged in politics; this is manifested even in the literary works produced by some of them. After the death of Parākramabāhu VI, the political instability led to factionalism, in which some leading monks of the day actively participated. In the reign of Rājasiṅha I some senior members of the Sangha even took part in conspiracies against the king. The interest shown by the Sangha in politics did not always produce the expected results; for the factionalism which developed after the death of Parākramabāhu VI led to the decline of most of the religious institutions that had flourished in the reign of that king, and political activities by the Sangha in the reign of Rājasiṅha I brought disaster upon the Buddhist Order.

In the second part of the sixteenth century a new factor emerges in the religious life of the country. The Catholic missionaries started their activities with the conversion of Dharmapāla, and this was followed by the dedication to them of a large number of Buddhist monasteries and their property.

This deprivation of royal patronage was compensated for by the patronage extended by the Sītāvaka rulers for a limited time. This lasted till the time when Rājasiṁha I adopted Saivism and expelled Buddhist monks from his realm. Consequently, the Sangha had to face one of the darkest periods of its history.

The first half of the fifteenth century saw a large number of ecclesiastical educational establishments called Pirivenas in various parts of the country. They appear to have contributed to the disappearance of the *āyatanas* which played a significant role in the monastic education in the medieval period. Pirivenas catered for the educational needs of the clergy as well as the male population of the laity. Students from foreign countries came to some of the Pirivenas seeking instruction on Theravāda. The curriculum of the Pirivena assumed a religious outlook, but this did not exclude other subjects.

The traditional pattern was followed in the method of teaching in the Pirivenas. The teacher recited the texts and the student listened to him carefully and learnt the text from the mouth of the teacher. The monastic student was provided board and lodging in the premises of the Pirivena, and, on the whole, the education imparted by these institutions seems to have been free of charge.

As with other religious institutions, Pirivenas also relied upon the king for their maintenance. Parākramabāhu VI generously extended his hand to the maintenance of these religious establishments. After the reign of this king, Pirivenas also suffered a general decline. Political disunity in the country as well as the disorganization of the Sangha contributed to the decline of the Pirivenas.

The Sangha of this period maintained close contact with other Theravāda countries in South East Asia. For the Buddhists of these countries Kōṭṭē kingdom became the main source of inspiration, since it was regarded as the centre of pure Theravāda tradition. Pilgrims from these countries came to Sri Lanka with lavish offerings to the Sinhalese religious centres. They returned home with relics, images and the scriptures which were regarded in high veneration in their homelands.

One spectacular result of these contacts was the emergence and development of a fraternity called Sīhaḷa Sangha in some South East Asian countries. The Sīhaḷa Sangha originated from the monks who received their higher ordination under the Sinhalese Sangha. The activities of the Sīhaḷa Sangha largely contributed to the cultural development in parts of South East Asia.

Cults of relics, images and deities held an important place in popular religion of the period. Among the important relics that emerged in the early medieval period, the Tooth Relic retained its position throughout our period.

The political significance attached to this relic in the Polonnaru period remained undiminished. And this made the kings pay great attention to the protection of the Relic, and the maintenance of traditional rites and ceremonies attached to it. Samantakūṭa became a very important place of pilgrimage of this period. Ancient religious centres like Anurādhapura do not appear to have been accessible in this period, probably because the surrounding areas had become jungle after the end of the Polonnaru period.

Boddhisattva cult became a common feature of the popular religion of the time. The Mahāyāna *bodhisattva* Nātha was worshipped in several shrines in various parts of the country, and among these, the shrine at Toṭagamuva became the main centre of this cult. The belief in four guardian deities became increasingly important in popular religion from the fourteenth century. A noteworthy aspect of the cult of these deities was the important position held by *brahmins* at the centres of these cults. The influence which *brahmins* exerted on popular religion was reflected not only in the administration of the centres connected with these cults but also in their attempts to transform the Sinhalese gods into those of Puranic Hinduism. The influence of *brahmins* on the religious life of the people did not go without opposition. This opposition to *brahmins* was most fervently expressed in the literary works of some prominent monks of the period, but this does not seem to have succeeded in arresting the growing influence of *brahmins*.

# Bibliography

## 1. Literary Sources

### Pali and Sanskrit Sources


*Anāgatavaṃsa*, in the *JPTS*, 1886. ed. T.W. Rhys Davids

——— ed. W. Medhananda, Colombo, 1934.

*Aṅguttara Nikāya*, ed. R. Morris, PTS, London, 1885.

*Bhaktiśataka*, ed. A.D. de S. Batuvantudave, Colombo, 1914.

*Bodhicaryāvatāra*, ed. W. Medhananda, Colombo, 1953.

*Cūlavaṃsa*, ed. W. Geiger, 2 vols, PTS, London, 1925, 1927.

*Cullavagga*, ed.H. Oldenberg, London, 1880.

*Dāṭhāvaṃsa*, ed. M. Ananda, Gampaha, 1956.

*Dhammapadaṭṭhakathā*, ed. H.C. Norman, 2 vols, London, 1906

*Dīgha Nikāya*. ed. J.E. Carpenter and T.W. Rhys Davids, PTS, London, 1947.

*Hatthavanagalla Vihāravaṃsa*, ed. Sri Silakkhanda, Colombo, 1909.

*Jinakālamālī*, ed. A.P. Buddhadatta, PTS, London, 1962.

*Kalyāṇipakaraṇa*, ed. G. Medhankara, Colombo, 1924.

*Mahāvagga*, ed. H. Oldenberg, London, 1879.

*Mahāvaṃsa*, ed. W. Geiger, PTS, London, 1908.

*Majjhima Nikāya*, ed. R. Chalmers, London, 1876.

*Majjhimanikāyaṭṭhakathā*, ed. Sri Dharmarama, Colombo, 1913.

*Pācittiyapāli*, ed. Sri Ariyavamsa, Colombo, 1929.

*Padasādhana-ṭīka*, ed. Dhammanda and Wachissara, Colombo, 1908.

*Paramatthajotikā*, ed. H. Smith, PTS, London, 1916.

*Pāramīmahāsataka*, ed. W. Dipankara, Devinuvara, 1921.

*Rāmāyaṇa* ed. ed. P.L. Vaidya, Vol. VI, Baroda, 1971.

*Samantakūṭa-vaṇṇanā*, ed. M. Nanisara, Colombo, 1910.

*Saṃyutta Nikāya*, ed. L. Feer, I, PTS, London. 1884.

*Sāratthadīpanī*, ed. B. Devaraksita, Colombo, 1914.

*Sāratthappakāsinī*, ed. F.L. Woodward, I, PTS, London, 1929.
*Sāsanavaṃsa*, ed. M.H. Bode, PTS, London, 1897.
*Sāsanavaṃsa- dīpikā*, ed. K. Saddhammavamsa, Colombo, 2474 B.E.
*Sumaṅgalavilāsinī*, ed. W. Stede, III, PTS, London, 1932.
*Vaṃsatthappakāsinī*, ed. G.P. Malalasekara, PTS, London, 1935.
*Vṛttaratnākara-pañjikā*, ed. M.Dipankara, Panadura, 1924.
*Vuttamālā-sandesa-Sataka*, ed. R. Batuvantudave, Clombo, 1923.
*Vṛttamālā*, ed. M. Dipankara, Panadura, 1918.

## SINHALESE SOURCES

*Alakeśvarayuddhaya*, ed. A.V. Suravira, Colombo, 1965.
*Buduguṇālaṃkāraya*, ed. D.B. Jayatilaka, Kelaniya, 1948.
*Dahamsoṅḍadā-kava*, ed. M. Kumaratunga, Colombo, 1947.
*Dharmapradīpikā*, ed B. Vimalavamsa, Colombo, 1955.
*Daḷadāsirita*, ed. W. Soraṭa, Colombo, 1954.
*Girā-sandeśaya*, ed. M. Kumaratunga, Colombo, 1955.
*Guttila-kāvyaya*, ed. D. Sumanajoti, Kelaniya, 1956.
*Haṃsa-sandeśaya* ed. C.E. Godakumbura, Colombo, 1953.
*Kavlakuṇu-ṁiṇimala*, ed. S. de. Alwis, Colombo, 1914.
*Kāvyaśekharaya*, ed. Sri Dharmarama, Kelaniya, 1935.
*Kokila-sandeśaya*, ed. M.Pannatissa, Colombo, 1945.
————W.F. Gunawardhana, Colombo, 1934.
————K.T.W. Sumanasuriya, Colombo, 1956.
*Kusajātaka-kāvyaya*, ed. M. Fernando, Colombo, 1931.
*Kuveṇi-asna*, ed. K. Nanawimala, Ratnapura, 1950.
*Mandārampura-puvata*, ed. L.Lankananda, Panadura, 1956.
*Mayūra-sandeśaya*, ed. W.F. Gunawardhana, Colombo, 1938.
*Nikāya- saṅgrahaya*, ed. D.P.R. Samaranayaka, Colombo, 1960.
*Pañcikā-pradīpaya*, ed. Sri Dharmarama, Kelaniya, 1936.
*Pansiyapaṇas-jātakapota*, ed. C.de. Silva, Kandy, 1957.
*Parevi-sandeśaya*, ed. M. Kumaratunga, Colombo, 1943.
*Pūjāvaliya*, ed. K.Nanawimala, Ratnapura, 1960.
*Rājaratnākaraya*, ed. S. de. Silva, Colombo, 1930.
*Rājāvaliya*, ed. B. Gunasekara, Colombo, 1953.
————W. Pemananda, Colombo, 1945.

*Saddharmālaṃkāraya*, ed. Sri Nanesvara, Colombo, 1914.
*Saddarmaratnākaraya*, ed. K. Nanawimala, Panadura, 1931.
*Saddharmaratnāvalī*, ed. D.B. Jayatilaka, Kelaniya, 1946.
*Säḷalihiṇi-sadeśaya*, ed. K.D.P. Wickramasinha, Colombo, 1960.
*Sävul-sandeśaya*, ed. U. Dharmasiri and S. Gamage, Delgoda,
*Sulu Rājāvaliya*, ed. 1968. C.P.K.S. Jayawardhana, Colombo, 1914.
*Tisara-sandeśaya*, ed. p.Wimaladhamma, Colombo, 1936.
————D.B. Jayatilaka, Kelaniya, 1935.
*Vimuktisaṅgrahava*, ed. H. Silaratana, Homagama, 1925.

***Manuscripts***

*Alutnuvara Dēvalē Karavīma*, British Museum Manuscript, or, 6608, (123).
*Moratoṭa Dinapota*, Sri Lanka Government Archives, Or. Ms. 125 (N).
*Nikāya- saṅgrahaya* British Museum Manuscript, Or. 6079, (128).
*Samansirita*, British Museum Manuscript, Or. 6679 (123).
*Seṅkhaṇḍa-saila-śasanavaṃsa*, British Museum Manuscript, Or. 6606 (128).
*Vṛttamālākhyā*, British Museum Manuscript, Or. 6611 (180).

**EPIGRAPHIC SOURCES**

*Archaeological Survey of Ceylon, Progress Reports and Annual.* Reports, Colombo, 1890 - (in progress).
Codrington, H.W. 'Päpiliyāna Pilibañda Lipi Samaharak' *Vidyodaya*, Vol. I, Nos. 8, 10, 11, (1926).
Coedēs, G. *Receuil des inscriptions du Siam*, Bangkok, 1924-29.
————'Documents sur la dynastie de Sukhodaya' *BEFEO*, XVII, No.2, p.4 ff.
————'Documents sur I'Histoire politique et religiouse du Laos Occidental' *DEFEO*, XXV, 1925.
*Epigraphia Birmanica*, Rangoon, 1949, -(in progress).
*Epigraphia Zeylanica*, London and Colombo, 1904, - (in progress).
Müller, Eduard, Ancient Inscriptions in Ceylon, 2 Vols, London, 1883.

Soin Ko, Taw, *'A Preliminary Study of the Kalyānī inscriptions of Dhammaceti', Indian Antiquary,* XXII, 1893, pp.11- 17, 29-53, 150-159, 206-213, 236-243, 274-275.

Ratanasara, N. *'Śrī Munneśvaram Dēvālē Gal Sannasa', Vidyodaya, III, No. 8, 1928, pp. 238-9; No. 9, pp. 269- 70.*

**III. Foreign Accounts and Translations**

*Annals du Siam,* II Volume, *Chronique de La:p'un, Histoice de la Dyndastie Chamat'evi:*

———III Volume, *Chronique de Xieng Mai,* Tr. and ed. N. Camille Notton, Paris, 1923, 1930.

*Cūlavaṃsa,* tr. W. Geiger, translated from the German into English by C. Mabel Rickmons, 2 pts, Colombo, 1953.

*Ibn Batuta, travels in Asia and Africa,* (1334-54), tr. H.A.R. Gibb, London, 1929.

*L'Abbidharmakoṣa de Vasubandhu,* tr. Louis de la Vallee Poussin Paris, 1923.

*Nikāyasaṅgrahaya,* tr. C.M. Fernando, revised edition by W.F. Gunawardhana, Colombo, 1908.

*Rājavaliya,* tr. B. Gunasekara, Colombo, 1954.

*Rebeiro's History of Ceilaō,* tr. P.E. Peiris, Colombo, 1905.

*The Book of Ser Marco Polo,* tr. H.Yule, London, 1903.

*The Glass Palace Chronicles of the Kings of Burma,* tr. P.M. Tin and G.H. Luce, Oxford, 1923.

*The History of the Buddha's Religion (Sāsanavaṃsa),* tr. B.C. Law, London, 3952.

*The History of Ceylon, as related by Josāo de Barros and Deogo de Couto,* tr. D. Ferguson, *JCBRAS,* XX, NO. 60, 1908.

*The Mahāvansī, the Rājaratnākarī, and the Rājāvalī,* Original texts edited by E. Upham, tr. Y.B.Fox, 3 Vols, London, 1833.

*The Sheaf of Garlands of the Epochs of the Conqueror (Jinakālamālī),* tr. N.A. Jayawickrama, PTS, London, 1968.

*The Temporal and Spiritual Conquest of Ceylon, (Conquista Temporal, e. Espiritual de Ceylaō, by Fernao de Queyroz)* tr. S.G. Perera, Colombo, 1930.

**IV. Modern Works**

Abeyasinha, T.B.M. *Portuguese Rule in Ceylon*, Colombo, 1968.

Adikaram, E.W. *Early History of Buddhism in Ceylon*, Colombo, 1946.

Altekar, A.S. *Education in Ancient India*, Benares, 1934.

Anonymous, 'Alagakkonara Family and its connection with Royalty', *JCBRAS*, XXXII, No. 86, pp. 296-303.

————*Toṭagamuve Vihāraya Pilibañda Ithihāsa Kathāva, Colombo, 1889.*

Ariyapala, *M.B. Society in Medieval Ceylon*, Colombo, 1956.

Arunachalam, P. *'Polonnaruva Bronzes and Śiva Worship and Symbolism'*, *JCBRAS*, XXIV, No.G8: 1915, pp.189-222.

———'The Worship of Muruka or Sankara' (the Kataragama god), *JCBRAS*, No.77, 1924, pp. 234-261.

Baily, S.D. *Ceylon*, London, 1952.

Beal, S. *Buddhist Records of the Western World*, II, London, n.d.

Bell, H.C.P. *Report on the Kāgalla District of the Province of Sabaragamuva*, Sessional Papers, Colombo, 1892.

Bode, M.H. *A Burmese Historian of Buddhism*, London, 1898.

———*The Pali Literature of Burma*, London, 1909.

Boudens, R. *The Catholic Church in Ceylon under Dutch Rule*, Rome, 1957.

Buddhadatta, A.P. *Pali Sāhityaya*, Ambalangoda, 1960.

———*Thervādī Bauddhācāryayo*, Colombo, 1960.

Cady, J.F. *South East Asia,; its Historical Development*, New York,1964.

Casparis, J.G.de, 'A New evidence on cultural relations between Java and Ceylon; *Artibus Asiae*, XXIV, 1961, pp. 241-248.

Carpenter, E. *From Adam's Peak to Elephanta*, London, 1892.

Codrington, H.W. *Ceylon Coins and Currency*, Colombo, 1924.

———*'Some Documents of Vikramabāhu of Kandy'*, *JCBRAS*, XXXII, No.84, 1931, pp.64-75.

———'The Gampola Period of Ceylon History', *JCBRAS*,XXXII, No.56, 1933, pp. 260-309.

————A Short History of Ceylon, Colombo, 1947.

*Angkor, An Introduction*,tr.E.F. Gardiner, Oxford, 1963.

———*The Indianized States of Southeast Asia*, Honalulu, p.1968.

Dutt, N. *Aspects of Mahāyāna Buddhism and its relation to Hīnayāna*, London, 1930.

Dupont, Pierre. 'Les Buddha dits d' Amaravati en Asie du Sud-Est', *BEFEO*, XLIX, 1959, PP.632-636.

Ellawala, H. *Social Institutions in Ceylon from the 5th B.C. to the 4th Century A.D. Colombo, 1971.*

Ferguson, S.C. *History of Indian and Eastern Architecture* Rome, London.

Fernando; P.E.E. 'Development of the Sihalese Script from the 8th Century A.D. to the 18th Century A.D. '*UCR*, III, pp.222-242.

Fornosu, Le Siam Ancient, Paris, 1895.

Geiger, V. 'The Trustworthiness of the Mahāvaṃsa', *Indian Historical Quarterly*, VI, 1930 pp. 228.

——*Culture of Ceylon in Medieval Times*, ed. H. Bechert, Wiesbaden, 1960.

Godakumbure, C.E. 'Historical Writtings in Sinhalese'
*Historians of India, Pakistan and Ceylon* ed. H.C. Phillips, London, 1962.

————'Bronzes from Polonnaruva' *JCBRAS*, (KS), VII,
1906, pt.2, pp-240-250.

————*Sinhalese Literature* , Colombo, 1955.

Gosh. D. 'Two Boddhisattva Images from Ceylon and Śrī Vijaya', *Jnl. of the Greater India* Society, IV, 1937,pp.125-127.

Gunawardhana, R.A.L.H, *Robe and Plough*, University of Arisona Press, 19

Hall, D.G.E. *A History of South-East Asia*, New York, 1970.

Hardy, R.S. *Mannual of Buddhism*, London, 1880.

Harvey, G.E. *History of Burma*, London, 1925.

Husain, Mahdi. *The Rehla of Ibn Batuta*, Baroda, 1953.

Jayatilaka, D.B. *Sinhala Sāhitya Lipi*, Kelaniya, 1954.

————*Katikāvat Sañgarā*, Kelaniya, 1955.

Jayavardhana, A. *'Kāli Kovila' JCBRAS*, XVIII, No. 29, pp.439-49.

Lamotte, Etienne. *Histoire du bouddhisme inden, Louvain, 1958.*

Lawri , A.C. *Gazetteer of the Central Province of Ceylon*, Colombo, 1896.

Le May, R. *A Concise History of Buddhist Art in Siam*, Cambridge, 1938.

Levi D' Ancona, Mirella, '*Amarāvatī*, Ceylon, and the Three 'Imported' Bronzes', *Art Bulletin*, XXXIV, pp.1-17.

Levi, M. Sylvain. 'Chinese References to Ceylon: *JCBRAS*,XXIV, No. 68, 1915-16, pp. 75-105.

Liyanagamage, A. *The Decline of Polonnaruva and the Rise of Dambadeniya*, Colombo, 1968.

Luce, G.H. *Old Burma, Early Pagan, 3 Vols, New York, 1969.*

———-'Mons of the Pagan Dynasty' *JCBRAS*, XXXVI, 1933, pp.1-19.

Majumdar, R.C. *An Advanced History of India*, London, 1948.

Malalasekara, G.P. *Pali Literature of Ceylon*, London, 1925.

Mallaman, T. Therese. d. *Introduction a L' Etude- D'Avalokitecvara*, Paris, 1948.

Mallert, L. *L'Archaeologie du Delta du Mekong*, Paris, 1962.

Masson, J. *La religion populaire dans le canon bouddhique Pali*, Louvain, 1942.

Mendis, G.C. *Early History of Ceylon*, Colombo 1954.

Mookerji, R.K. *Ancient Indian Education*, London, 1947.

Mudiyanse, N. *Mahāyāna Monuments in Ceylon*, Colombo, 1967.

————*The Art and Architecture of the Gampola Period*, Colombo, n.d.

Nanawimala, K. *Saparagamuvē Pärani Liyavili*, Ratnapura, 1952.

Nevill, Hugh. *Ethnology*, ed. P.E. P. Deraniyagala, Colombo, 1956.

Nicholas, C.W. and *A Concise History of Ceylon*, Colombo, 1962. Paranavitana, S.

Pandita, V. '*Kōṭṭē Yugayē Bauddha Tatvaya, Sāhityaya*, I, 1957.

Pannasara, K, *Pali Sinhala Pirit Pota*, Kelaniya, 1963.

Paranavitana, S. 'Pre-Buddhist Beliefs in Ceylon', *JCBRAS*, XXXI, No. 82, 1929, pp. 302-328.

———-'Religious Intercourse between Ceylon and Siam in the 13th-15th Centuries', *JCBRAS*,XXXII, No.85, 190- 213.

———'Mahayanism in Ceylon', *CJSc.* G. II, 1928, pp. 35-72.

———*The Shrine of Upulvan at Devundara, ASCM, Colombo, 1955.*

———'Ceylon and Malasia in Medieval Times', *JCBRAS* NS. VII, 1960, pp. 86-111.

———'The Emperor of Ceylon at the time of the Arrival of the Portuguese',*UCR*, XIX, 1961, p. 167 ff.

———*The Stupa in Ceylon*, Colombo, 1946.

———'*Laṅkātilaka* Inscriptions', *UCR*, XVIII, 1960, pp.1-45.

*The God of Adam's Peak, Ascone*, 1958.

———*Ceylon and Malasia*, Colombo, 1966.

Paulasz, J.H.C. 'Some Sinhalese Royal Families', *JCBRAS*, XX, 1952, pp. 21-30.

Peiris, P.E. and Eitzeler, M.A. *Ceylon and Portugal*, Leipzig, 1927.

———*Ceylon: The Portuguese Era*, Colombo, 1914.

Perera, B.J. 'The Foreign Trade and Commerce of Ancient Ceylon', *CHJ*, I, 1952, No. 3, pp. 92-204.

Perera, E.W. '*Age of Śrī Parākramabāhu VI*', *JCBRAS*, XXII, No. 63, 1912, pp. 6-45.

Perera, S.G. *The Date of King Bhuvanekabāhu VII'*, JCBRAS, XXII, No. 55, pp. 267-302.

———*A History of Ceylon* (*The Portuguese and the Dutch Periods*), Colombo, 1951.

Philatethes, A.M. *History of Ceylon*, London, 1817.

Poussin, Louis de la Vallee. '*The Two Nirvāṇadhātus according to the Vibhāṣa*', *IHQ*, VI, 1930, pp.39-45.

Raghavan. MD. *India in Ceylon History, Society and Culture*, London, 1964.

Rahula, W. *History of Buddhism in Ceylon*, Colombo, 1956.

Rammandala, M.*Śrī* '*Daṁbadeni Katikāvat a hā Sāsana Tatvaya*', *Sāhityaya, (Daṁbadeni Kalāpaya)*, 1958, pp. 90-96.

Ray, H.C. *University of Ceylon History of Ceylon*, I, 2 pts, Colombo, 1959, 1960.

Ray, N.R. *Theravāda Buddhism in Burma*, Calcutta, 1946.

Sannasala, P.B. *Siṅhala Sandeśa Sāhityaya*, Colombo, 1955.

———*Siṅhala Sāhitya Vaṃsaya*, Colombo, 1961.

Sasanaratana, M. *Lakdiva Mahāyāna Adahas*, Colombo, 1962.

Silva, C.M.A. *'Alakeśvara, the Founder of Jayavardhana Kōṭṭē'*, *CHJ*, I, No.I, 1951, pp. 42-45.

Silva, Colvin, R.de, *Ceylon under the British Occupation*, Colombo, 1945.

Silva, M. *Rāhula Saṅghrājatumā*, Colombo, 1930.

Silva, S.dc, *'Vijayabāhu VI'*, *JCBRAS*, XXII, No.65, 1912, pp. 316-326.

Silva, S.F.de. 'The Historical Geography of Some of the Capital Cities of Ceylon', *CHJ*, No, I, 1951, pp.13- 22.

Smither. J. *Architectural Remains, Anuradhapura, Ceylon*, London, n.d.

Somadasa, K.D. *Catalogue of Manuscripts in the Temple Libraries In Ceylon*, Colombo, 1959.

Sumanajoti, D. *Daṁbadeni Yugaya*, 3 pts, Vakkunuvala, 1958, 1960.

Tennent, J.E. *Christianity in Ceylon*, London, 1856.

———*Ceylon*, London, 1859.

Turnour, G. *Epitome of History of Ceylon*, London, 1896

Varasambodhi, G. *Gampola Ithihāsaya*, Colombo, 1948.

Vimalakirti, M. *'Daṁbadeni Samayē Pañdivarun hā Piriven'*, *Sāhityaya*, 1958, *(Daṁbadeni Kalāpaya)*, pp. 35-39.

————*Sinhala Ānḍuva*, Colombo, 1958.

———*Sāsanavaṃsa Pradīpaya, Matara*, 2498 B.E.

Wachissara, K. *Saranaṅkara Saṅghrāja Samaya*, Colombo, 1963.

Wales H.G. Quartch, *Dvāravatī* (The Earliest Kingdom of Siam), London, 1969.

Weerasuriya, P.D.S. *Devundara Itibhāsaya*, Matra, 1953.

Wickramsinha, D.M.de.Z. *Catalogue of the Sinahlese Manuscripts and Printed Books in the British Museum*, London, 1901.

Wickramasinha, K.D.P. *Kōṭṭē Yugayē Siṅhala Sāhityaya*, Colombo, 1960.

————*Siṅhala Lekhaka Parapura*, Colombo, 1964.

Wickramasinha, M. *Siṅhala Sahityayē Nägīma*, Colombo, 1954.

Wijesekara, O.H.de.A. 'Sanskrit Civilization among the Ancient Sinhalese', *CHJ*, I, pp. 23-29.

**V. Theses**

Dharmmavisuddhi, Y. *The Buddhist Saṅgha in Ceylon,* (circa.1200-1400), London, 1970, 1970.

Gunawardhana, R.A.L.H. *History of the Buddhist Saṅgha in Ceylon from the time of Sena I to the Invasion Māgha,* 800- 1215, London, 1965.

Mirando, A.H. *Buddhism in Ceylon in the Seventeenth and Eighteenth Centuries with Special Reference to Sinhalese Literary Sources,* London, 1968.

Panabokke, G. *The Evolution and the History of the Buddhist Monastic Order, with Special Reference to the Saṅgha in Ceylon,* Lancaster, 1969.

Pathmanathan, S. *Kingdom of Jaffna,* London, 1969.

Somaratna, G.P.V. *Political History of the Kingdom of Kōṭṭē,* London, 1969.

Wachissara, K. *Väliviṭa Saranaṅkara and the Revival of Buddhism in Ceylon,* London, 1961.

Wickramasinha, S. *The Age of Parākramabāhu* I, London, 1958.

VI. Reference Works

Childers, R.C. *A Dictionary of the Pali Language,* London, 1875.

Davids, T.W.Rhys and Stede, W. *Pali-English Dictionary,* PTS, London, 1925.

Macdonnell, A.A. *A Sanskrit-English Dictionary,* London, 1893.

Malalasekara, G.P. *Dictionary of Pali Proper Names,* London, 1937.

Sorata, W. *Śrī Sumaṅgala Śabdakoṣaya,* 2 Vols. Colombo, 1952. 1956.

Williams, Monier. *Sanskrit English Dictionary,* Oxford, 1892.

# Index (1)

## Personal Names

### d. deity; k. king; m. monk.

# Index (II)
## Religious and Educational Establishments and Institutions

# Index (III)
## Geographical Names

# Index (IV)
## Families, Offices and Titles

f. family; o. office; t. title.

# Index (V)
## Pali, Sanskrit and Sinhalese Terms